NOLS
Wilderness
First Aid

Tod Schimelpfenig
and
Linda Lindsey

Illustrated by
Joan Safford

second edition

NOLS

A Publication of the
National Outdoor Leadership School
and
Stackpole Books

Printed in the United States of America.

For ordering information contact NOLS Publications,
288 Main Street, Lander, Wyoming 82520, (307) 332-6973.

Library of Congress Cataloging-in-Publication Data

Schimelpfenig, Tod, 1954-
    NOLS wilderness first aid / Tod Schimelpfenig and
    Linda Lindsey : illustrated by Joan Safford. — 2nd ed.
       p.   cm.
    Includes index.
    ISBN 0-8117-3084-0
    1. First aid in illness and injury.   2. Outdoor life
    Accidents and injuries. I. Lindsey, Linda, 1952-   .
    II. Title.
    RC88.9.095S35   1992   92-19090
                                                                    CIP

*The pronouns "he" and "him" are used in this text to include
both males and females. This is for grammatical purposes
only. No gender discrimination is intended.*

To the students at NOLS. We hope this text helps you to be better outdoor leaders.

To all NOLS instructors, who on a daily basis teach and practice first aid and safety in the wilderness and are the source of the practical experience that is the foundation of this text.

To our families: Betsy, Sam, Dave and Mark, and Michael, Laura and Hannah for their support and patience during the time we devoted to this project.

—Tod and Linda

To the St. Michael's Rescue Squad, where I first learned quality patient care.   —Tod

About NOLS

The National Outdoor Leadership School (NOLS) is a private, non-profit school based in Lander, Wyoming. NOLS branch schools are located in the Rocky Mountains (Wyoming), the Pacific Northwest (Washington), the Southwest (Arizona), Alaska, Kenya, Mexico and Patagonia (Chile). Since our founding in 1965, we have graduated over 30,000 students.

The mission of the National Outdoor Leadership School is to be the best source and teacher of leadership and wilderness skills that protect the user and the environment.

Correspondence and catalog requests may be addressed to:

> The National Outdoor Leadership School
> 288 Main Street
> Lander, Wyoming 82520
>
> Telephone: (307) 332-6973

Other NOLS Publications
NOLS Cookery (Stackpole Books, 1991)
Soft Paths (Stackpole Books, 1988)
The NOLS Wilderness Guide (Simon & Schuster, 1983)

THE AUTHORS

Tod Schimelpfenig is the safety and training director at NOLS. An EMT for 18 years, he has gained extensive experience in search and rescue and ambulance work. In 1990, he was named Wyoming EMT Instructor of the Year. Tod has been a NOLS instructor for 19 years and has been associated with the school for 21. He teaches NOLS' Wilderness EMT and Wilderness First Responder courses and serves as a critical stress debriefer. He has been compiling the school's injury and illness statistics since 1984 and is in the process of publishing the first definitive paper on the epidemiology of wilderness injuries and illness.

Linda Lindsey, RN, BSN, EMT, is NOLS' safety and training coordinator and a senior staff instructor. She is responsible for NOLS' extensive staff training program and is an instructor for the school's Wilderness EMT and Wilderness First Responder courses. She is the former coordinator of the Colorado Outward Bound first aid program and has five years' experience as a staff nurse in obstetrics and neonatal intensive care.

Acknowledgments

THANKS go to NOLS instructors Joe Austin, Rich Brame, Mark Cole, Phil Powers, Mike Riley, Lori Rose and Craig Stebbins, whose editing reflected their years of experience in wilderness settings.

To Dr. Kathryn Collins, former NOLS medical advisor, and Dr. Herbie Ogden, NOLS instructor and medical advisor, who carefully reviewed the medical aspects of the manuscript.

To Buck Tilton, wilderness medicine educator and director of the Wilderness Medicine Institute, for his review of the text.

To Dr. Steve Jarrard, Lander, Wyoming, emergency physician, for his ongoing support.

To Joe Costello, NOLS instructor and sports medicine specialist, who reviewed the chapter on athletic injuries.

A very special thanks to Dr. Bruce Paton, board member of the Wilderness Medical Society and Outward Bound, who not only reviewed the medical aspects of the text but gave us valuable editing suggestions.

To Jim Ratz, executive director of NOLS, for his support of this project.

To Kathy Bogan, who edited the first draft, which was no small task.

To Chavawn Woodall, NOLS publications manager, for creating a text from our manuscript and for representating the perspective of the novice in editing and formatting this book.

To Joan Safford, who brought wit, imagination and experience as a NOLS graduate and EMT to the process of creating the illustrations.

CONTENTS

PREFACE

On my student course in 1970, NOLS founder Paul Petzoldt began his first aid class with the observation that we would be better off spending our time learning how to avoid accidents. The rest of the class was short on detail–wilderness medicine had hardly begun–and long on common sense. Paul had his priorities in order: good judgment, prior planning, and an appreciation for accident prevention will dramatically decrease your odds of an accident. Nevertheless, as Petzoldt so often stated, you will never reduce those odds to zero, and acquiring the basic skills of wilderness first aid is a requirement for all outdoor leaders.

It is important to note that the accident and illness statistics we have assembled over the years representing thousands of students tell us that the probability is certain that there will be at least one injury or illness per month-long course. Fortunately, the vast majority of accidents we see would not be considered serious back in civilization; I worked for years as an instructor before I had to deal with an accident more troubling than a cut finger.

An experienced outdoor leader knows that in the backcountry a simple sprain or a persistent cough can have dramatic implications if not recognized and treated correctly. It is almost inevitable that if you travel and teach in the wilderness long enough you will have to attend to a serious medical situation. This text will give you a sound foundation upon which to build your wilderness first aid education, help you prevent accidents and illness and enable you to become a more confident outdoor leader.

The great strides the school has made in safety awareness and education are due largely to the efforts of the authors of this text, Tod Schimelpfenig, NOLS safety and training director, and Linda Lindsey, safety and training coordinator. Both are experienced NOLS instructors and highly trained emergency care providers. They are two of the best in their field and possess a thorough understanding of the unique problems confronted by the care giver in the wilderness and the need for practical solutions. They have produced a text based on their extensive experience and, most important, on the cumulative experience of our instructors.

Petzoldt's first aid class was an eye-opener for me; his was the first class that I had ever heard that placed good judgment before the rote learning of technical skills. Having recently finished school, I wasn't accustomed to such down-to-earth statements. I realize now, however, that Paul wasn't simply teaching a class, he was setting the direction that has made NOLS a leader in the field of wilderness education and safety. This book is one more step in a great tradition.

Jim Ratz
NOLS Executive Director

INTRODUCTION

Wilderness has no handrails, no telephones and no simple solutions for complex emergency situations. Yet it does have dangers. Some are obvious: rockfall, moving water, stormy weather, avalanches, crevasses and wild animals. Others are less obvious: boulder fields, deadfall, impure water, dehydration and altitude illness.

Although these risks can be minimized with skill, experience and judgment, outdoor leaders know that despite their best efforts, accidents and illnesses will happen. They prepare for the challenge of providing emergency medical care in remote and hostile environments.

This book is designed as a course text to accompany the wilderness first aid curriculum presented on NOLS semester courses. This curriculum is designed to train the student to 1) prevent, recognize and treat common wilderness medical problems and 2) to stabilize a severely ill or injured patient for evacuation. *NOLS Wilderness First Aid* may also be used as a basic text for wilderness first aid courses, as an information source for outdoor enthusiasts or as a resource to tuck into your pack or kayak.

Chapters one through eight cover fundamental topics in first aid—patient assessment, shock, soft tissue injury, burns, fractures and dislocations, and chest, head and abdominal injury. They prepare us to assess and treat seriously ill or injured persons. Chapters nine though fifteen present medical problems associated with heat, cold, water, altitude and poisonous plants and animals.

The final six chapters discuss a variety of topics—athletic injuries, hygiene, hydration, gender-specific medical concerns, dental emergencies and stress in the rescuer. These concerns may not threaten life or limb, but our safety history has shown them to be common in the everyday medical experience of the wilderness leader. Hydration and hygiene are especially important to ensuring that backcountry trips are safe and healthy. Finally, summaries at the end of each chapter provide snapshot views of assessment, treatment and key points. These may also serve as quick emergency reference.

Wilderness first aid is patient care in which communication with a physician and rapid transport are rarely possible. It is first aid with limited equipment, often requiring improvisation. It involves caring for the patient for long periods and protecting him from the weather.

The first step in safety and first aid is prevention. Wilderness first aid training, in addition to preparing us to deal with serious illness and injury and environmental emergencies, should also discuss prevention and treatment of common wilderness medical problems such as infected wounds, hygiene-associated illness and treatment of athletic injuries. You will find prevention to be a recurring theme in this text.

An essential but often neglected component of wilderness first aid is the ability to care for and lead others under adverse conditions. Developing the skills and experience to be safe and comfortable in the outdoors is what the NOLS core curriculum is all about.

Simply reading the text or successfully completing a NOLS course does not qualify a person to perform any procedure. The text is not a substitute for thorough, practical training, experience in emergency medicine and the outdoors, critical analysis of the needs of specific situations or the continued education and training necessary to keep skills sharp.

This text does not discuss the details of cardiopulmonary resuscitation (CPR). The American Heart Association and American Red Cross are sources for CPR training and certification.

Advanced programs in wilderness medicine include the First Responder and Emergency Medical Technician programs. The First Responder program, usually presented over 80 hours of classroom and practical instruction, currently represents the minimum standard for first aid training for outdoor leaders. Many leaders choose the more in-depth training available through Emergency Medical Technician programs. Both are available from NOLS, the Wilderness Medicine Institute, SOLO, the National Association for Search and Rescue and the National Ski Patrol, to name a few.

Professionals who experience daily emergencies still train routinely. There is no substitute for knowing how to respond to a medical emergency, for the group knowing what needs to be done in an emergency and for having the basics wired so you can make a sound decision on how best to treat a patient. Plan ahead for emergencies. Research emergency procedures prior to your wilderness trip. Carry a well-stocked first aid kit and consider your inventory of available splinting and litter equipment. Practice first aid and emergency skills with your group.

Paul Petzoldt asked students at the beginning of NOLS courses to look at the person sitting next to them. There is a chance, Paul said, that that person will not finish the course due to illness or injury. There is also a chance he or she will end up providing first aid for you in the wilderness.

At NOLS, we routinely use the term "expedition behavior" to refer to how we interact and care for one another. Being prepared for emergencies is an essential component of good outdoor leadership. It is also good expedition behavior. First aid classes, when compared to opportunities to climb, hike, paddle or fish, may not be as fun, but by dedicating only a portion of the time spent working on technical skills to emergency preparedness, you will enhance the health and safety of your expedition.

CHAPTER 1
PATIENT ASSESSMENT

Introduction

Assessing Scene Safety

Providing Emotional Care for the Patient

The Primary Survey

Establishing Responsiveness

The ABCs

The Secondary Survey

Head-to-Toe Examination

Vital Signs

Medical History

The Critical Assessment

Extended Patient Care

Final Thoughts

Summary: Patient Assessment

Introduction

Imagine yourself kneeling beside a fallen hiker, deep in the wilderness. As you begin to examine the victim, thoughts of your remoteness, the continued safety of the group, the incoming weather, evacuation, communication and shelter possibilities swirl through your brain. You are about to make decisions and initiate a series of events that will greatly affect the safety and well-being of the patient, your group and outside rescuers.

In the city, the patient could be quickly transported to a hospital. In the wilderness, patient care may be your responsibility for hours or days. You cope with improvised gear and inclement weather and take care of yourself, the other members of your group and the patient. The rescue or evacuation may be strenuous and can jeopardize the safety of the group and the rescuers.

You need information to help you determine how to best care for and transport the patient. You will gather that information during the patient assessment, the foundation of your care.

Patient assessment—analyzing what happened in an accident or illness and what you should do about it—begins immediately upon encountering the first aid situation. Your observations of weather, terrain, bystanders and the position of the patient are your first clues to how an injury occurred, the patient's condition and possible scene hazards. Cold temperatures, wind, rain or snow, steep terrain, rockfall, avalanche or the presence of lightning contribute to the seriousness of an accident. All directly affect patient treatment and emergency procedures.

Assessing Scene Safety

As a first-aider, your top priority should be maintaining your own well-being and the well-being of any fellow first-aiders. A patient can only be served by healthy rescuers, not by other patients. Protect your patient by protecting yourself.

Inclement weather may make constructing on-the-spot shelter

an immediate priority to avoid hypothermia or other threats to the patient and first-aiders. For example, rockfall or an avalanche may dictate a move out of the path of danger.

Providing Emotional Care for the Patient

The ill or injured patient will experience a variety of emotions, including fear about the quality of care and the outcome of the injury or illness, the length of evacuation, loss of control and independence, loss of self-esteem and embarrassment. To help the patient cope with such roller-coaster feelings, maintain your calm, respond promptly and clearly to questions, and treat the patient with respect and sensitivity.

Respecting your patient means using manners as you would in an average social situation. Introduce yourself, call the patient by name and ask permission to give treatment. In doing so, you show respect for the patient and begin to involve him in his own care. As you examine and treat the patient, explain your actions. Warn the patient if you might cause pain. Involve the patient in evacuation decisions.

Reassurance, concern and sympathy are appropriate. It's healthy to allow the patient to discuss the incident. Talking about an accident begins the process of emotional healing. Do not critique the incident or lay blame on any party involved. This will only increase the patient's anxiety and agitation.

Anticipate a lull in your enthusiasm and energy as the initial excitement wears off, fatigue sets in and you realize the amount of work still to do to care for and evacuate the patient. These emotions are a reality of rescue. They should not be communicated to the patient as a lack of concern. See Chapter 21 (Stress And The Rescuer) for more on rescue stress.

The Primary Survey

The primary survey is a rapid check of the respiratory and circulatory systems and should be a ritual performed on every patient. The purpose of the primary survey is to find and treat life-threatening medical problems. Besides attending immediately to vital functions, it provides order during the first frantic minutes of an emergency.

The Primary Survey

Assess scene safety

Assess for responsiveness

    Attempt to arouse the patient with a shake or shout

Assess for airway

    Open the airway

    Look, Listen, Feel

Assess for breathing

    Look for chest movement

    Listen for air movement

    Feel air movement on your cheek

Assess for circulation

    Check pulse at the neck

Assess for bleeding

    Look for severe bleeding

    Feel patient's clothing for hidden bleeding

Observe cervical spine precautions

    Avoid moving the patient

    Consider the jaw thrust to open the airway

Treat for shock

    Protect the patient from cold and wet

    Maintain the airway

    Elevate the legs

Establishing Responsiveness

As you approach the patient, introduce yourself and ask if you may help. Attempt to arouse the patient by gently shaking his shoulder. If he responds verbally, his airway is not obstructed; he is breathing and has a pulse. If he cannot respond verbally, check the airway and if necessary assist in opening it and maintaining breathing and circulation as learned in cardiopulmonary resuscitation (CPR).

The ABCs

The primary survey checks the airway, breathing, circulation, plus possible serious bleeding and shock. The airways are the mouth, nose and throat, and the trachea. The trachea brings oxygen to the lungs and is also known as the windpipe. Oxygen is exchanged between the air and the blood in the lungs. Circulation is composed of the heart, the blood vessels and the blood. It transports nutrients and waste products throughout the body. We use the acronym "ABC" (airway-breathing-circulation) as a memory aid for the sequence. ABC is the initial phase of cardiopulmonary resuscitation (CPR).

Airway
The airway is the path air travels from the atmosphere into the lungs. An obstructed airway is a medical emergency because oxygen cannot reach the lungs. Assess the state of the airway by opening it with the chin-lift head-tilt method or the jaw thrust and by looking, listening and feeling for air movement. The airway opening technique for an unconscious victim or an accident victim is the jaw thrust because it does not require shifting the neck or spine. See Chapter 6 (Head and Spinal Cord Injuries).

If you can see, hear or feel air moving from the lungs to the outside, the airway is open. A patient making sounds is able to move air from the lungs to the outside and past the vocal cords. This indicates the airway is at least partially open.

Signs of an obstructed airway are lack of air movement, labored breathing, use of neck and upper chest muscles to breathe and cyanosis. If you discover an airway obstruction, attempt to clear the airway before proceeding to assessment of breathing. The appropriate techniques are those used in CPR for treating a foreign-body-obstructed airway.

Breathing
Assess breathing using the "look, listen and feel" format taught in CPR. Look for the rise and fall of the chest as air enters and

leaves the lungs. Listen for the sound of air passing through the upper airway. Feel the movement of air from the patient's mouth and nose on your cheek. If the patient is not breathing, give two slow, even breaths, then proceed with a check for a pulse.

Circulation

Check for the presence or absence of a pulse. Place the tips of your middle and index fingers over the carotid artery for at least ten seconds. The carotid is a large central artery, accessible at the neck. Other possible sites are the femoral artery in the groin and the radial artery in the wrist. (See illustration, p. 23.)

It may be difficult to feel a pulse if the patient has weak pulses from shock, is cold, is wearing bulky clothing or if the accident scene is confused by wind and water noise, blowing snow or alarmed bystanders. Finding a pulse is not always easy. If you are unsure about location or presence of the carotid pulse, try the femoral or the radial pulse.

If the patient is conscious or moaning, he must have a pulse. If there is no pulse, start CPR. If there is a pulse but no breathing, start rescue breathing.

Bleeding

Now that the ABC survey is complete, look for bleeding. Severe bleeding can be fatal within minutes. Look for obvious bleeding or wet places on the patient's clothing. Run your hands quickly over and under the patient's clothing, especially bulky sweaters or parkas, to find moist areas that may be caused by serious bleeding. Most external bleeding can be controlled with direct pressure and elevation of the wound. Chapter 3 (Soft Tissue Injuries) addresses bleeding control in detail.

Cervical Spine

The "C" in ABC can stand for "cervical spine" as well as for circulation. You should initially assume a spinal injury on any accident victim. And since moving a spine-injured patient can cause permanent paralysis, move the patient only if necessary and as little as possible.

The PRIMARY SURVEY:

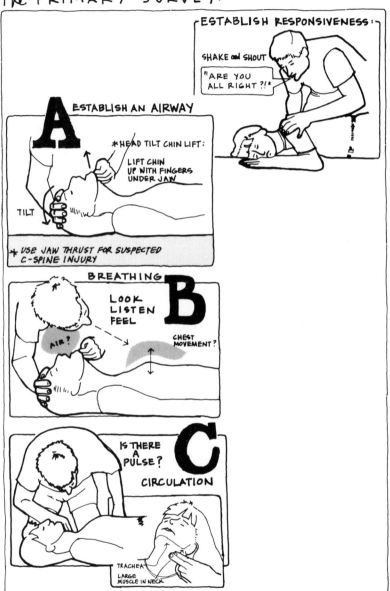

Shock
Shock is a subtle and dangerous syndrome discussed in depth in Chapter 2 (Shock). Treat every patient for shock. Protect the patient from cold and wet, maintain the airway and elevate the legs.

The Secondary Survey

Now pause a moment to look over the scene. The primary survey is complete. Immediate threats to life have been addressed. Consider the patient's and rescuers' needs. If the location of the incident is unstable—such as on or near rockfall, unstable scree or a potential avalanche slope—move to a safer position. Provide insulation, adjust clothing, rig a shelter. Assign tasks: boil water for hot drinks, build a litter, set up camp, write down vital signs. Establishing clear delegation of tasks helps the rescuers by giving everyone something to do and helps the patient by creating an atmosphere of order and leadership. See Appendix C (Emergency Procedures for Outdoor Groups).

The secondary survey is a complete assessment of the patient done after life-threatening conditions have been stabilized. It consists of a complete physical exam, vital signs and a thorough medical history.

Secondary Survey
Complete this assessment after life-threatening problems have been treated.

Head-to-Toe	*Vital Signs*	*Medical History*
Look	LOC	Chief complaint
Listen	Pupils	(PQRST)
Feel	Pulse	AMPLE
Smell	Skin	AEIOUTIPS
	Temperature	
	Respiration	
	Capillary refill	
	Blood pressure	

The SECONDARY SURVEY:

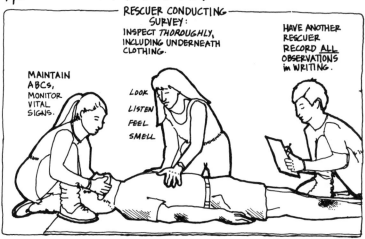

RESCUER CONDUCTING SURVEY: INSPECT *THOROUGHLY*, INCLUDING UNDERNEATH CLOTHING.

HAVE ANOTHER RESCUER RECORD ALL OBSERVATIONS in WRITING.

MAINTAIN ABCs, MONITOR VITAL SIGNS.

LOOK
LISTEN
FEEL
SMELL

Head-to-Toe Examination

The head-to-toe exam is a comprehensive physical examination. Begin the head-to-toe examination by first making the patient comfortable. Except in cases of imminent danger, avoid moving an injured patient until after the exam. Your hands should be clean and warm. The examiner should be of the same gender as the patient; otherwise an observer of the same gender should be present during all phases of the exam. Designate a note taker to record the results of the secondary survey.

As you examine the patient, explain what you are doing and why. Besides being a simple courtesy, this helps involve the patient in his or her care. This survey starts with the head and systematically checks the entire body down to the toes. One person should perform the survey in order to avoid confusion, provide consistent results and minimize discomfort to the patient. Also, with a single examiner the patient will be able to respond to one inquiry at a time.

The examination technique consists of looking, listening, feeling and smelling. If you are uncertain of what is abnormal, compare the injured extremity or the condition with the other side of the body or with a healthy person.

NOLS FIELD EVACUATION REPORT

Name of Evacuee_T. Smith_____Evacuation Date_8/9/92_
Course/Section_WRW 8/2____ Course Leader_L. Black_
Evac team Leader_N/A_____
Location of Evacuee (latitude/longitude, common name, TRS)
Latitude 44 05' 30" Longitude 110 18' 45"
Fox Creek Meadow T 10PN R 34 W 55
Accident Location_as above_

Patient Report

Age_18_ Sex_F_
Chief Complaint (PQRST)_Pt. states " I just cut my_
hand." Pain is throbbing/burning, 5 on scale of
1-10. Does not radiate.
Date & Time of Incident_8/8/92 18:00_
History of Present Illness/MOI_Terri was cutting cheese,_
knife slipped and lacerated (L) hand.

Vital Signs (quantity and quality)

Time	LOC	Pulse	RR	BP	T°	CRT	SCTM	Pupils
18:05	AAOx4	82	24	✓	✓	3 sec.	Pale, cool Clammy	PERRL
18:20	AAOx4	68	16	✓	✓	1 sec.	Pink, warm dry	PERRL

Physical Findings/Appearance_Pt. sitting up holding (L) hand_
c̄/o dizzyness + nausea. 1 in + 1/2 - 1/4" deep laceration just
proximal to (L) index finger. Finger pink + warm "feels
like it's asleep." Unable to flex (L) index finger.

Past History_no surgeries_

Allergies_none_
Medications_20:00 Percocet 1 tablet_
Emergency Care Rendered/Changes in Patient's Condition___
Applied direct pressure to laceration, laid pt. on foam
pad. Cleaned laceration with 1:3000 Zephiran. Direct
pressure reapplied for 5 mins. Dressed + bandaged hand in
position of function. No change in CSM. 19:00 Dime size area
of blood on dressing - will watch 20:30 ↓ in pain, no other
changes in assessment. Pt going to bed 8/9 0:900 Pain 4 on
scale of 1-10. No other changes.
Details of Evac Plan (timetable, backup, pickup point)___
Will evac. at Fox Creek. reration. 8/9/92 10:00

Course Leader Signature_L Black_
Date_8/9/92_   Time_10:00_

The Secondary Survey
Head-to-Toe Examination

Look for wounds, bleeding, unusual movements or shapes, deformities, penetrations, excretions, vomit.
Listen for abnormal sounds, such as crepitus and airway noises.
Feel for wounds, rigidity, hardness, softness, tenderness, deformity.
Smell for unusual odors.

Be alert for:
Head—airway, ears and nose for fluid or blood
Neck—airway, cervical spine
  Shoulders—deformity
  Arms—deformity, pulse, movement and sensation
  Chest—deformity, painful or difficult breathing
Abdomen—tenderness, rigidity, distention, bruising
  Back—pain, possible spine injury
  Pelvis—pain, instability
  Legs and feet—deformity, pulse, movement and sensation at feet.

Head
Check the ears and nose for fluid, and the mouth for injuries that may affect the airway. Check the face for symmetry; all features should be symmetrical down the midline from forehead to chin. The cheekbones are usually accurate references for facial symmetry. Feel the entire skull for depressions, tenderness and irregularity. Run your fingers along the scalp to detect bleeding or cuts. Check the eyes for injuries, pupil abnormalities and vision disturbances.

Neck

The trachea, or windpipe, should be in the middle of the neck. Feel the entire cervical spine from the base of the skull to the top of the shoulders for pain, tenderness, muscle rigidity and deformity.

Shoulders

Examine the shoulders and the collarbone for deformity, tenderness and pain.

Arms

Feel the arms from the armpit to the wrist. Check the pulse in each wrist; it should be equal on both sides. Ask the patient to move his fingers. Check for sensation by gently pinching the fingers or scratching the palm of the hand and fingers. If no injury is apparent, ask the patient to move each arm through its full range of motion.

Chest

Feel the entire chest for deformity or tenderness. Push down from the top and in from the sides. Ask the patient to breathe deeply as you compress the chest. Observe the rise and fall of the chest for symmetry.

Abdomen

Feel the abdomen for tenderness or muscle rigidity with light pressure. If there is tenderness, localize it into a quadrant. Look for distension, discoloration and bruising.

Back

Feel the spine. Feel each vertebra from the shoulders to the pelvis. It may be difficult to accomplish this without moving the patient, but it is important to slide your hand as far as possible under the patient. There may be a hidden injury.

Pelvis

Press down on the front of the pelvis and in from the sides. Is there deformity or instability? Does the pressure cause pain?

Legs and Feet
Check the legs from the groin to the ankle. Check the pulse in each of the feet; they should be equal. Check for sensation and motor function in the feet by touching the patient's feet and by asking him to move his toes for you.

Vital Signs

Vital signs are objective indicators of respiration, circulation, heart function, blood volume and body temperature. Checking the vital signs is analogous to the ABC steps of the primary survey. Airway and breathing are checked by noting skin color, respiratory rate and depth, and level of consciousness. Circulation is evaluated from pulse, skin color, skin temperature, capillary refill time and level of consciousness.

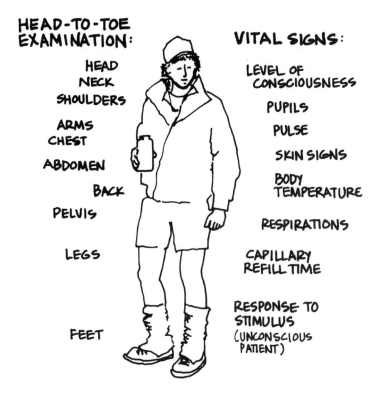

HEAD-TO-TOE EXAMINATION:

HEAD
NECK
SHOULDERS

ARMS
CHEST

ABDOMEN

BACK

PELVIS

LEGS

FEET

VITAL SIGNS:

LEVEL OF CONSCIOUSNESS

PUPILS

PULSE

SKIN SIGNS

BODY TEMPERATURE

RESPIRATIONS

CAPILLARY REFILL TIME

RESPONSE TO STIMULUS (UNCONSCIOUS PATIENT)

Measure and record vital signs every fifteen minutes. Keeping a flow sheet with time on the vertical scale and the vitals on the horizontal scale is helpful for tracking vital signs. The initial set of vitals–pulse, respiration rate, temperature, level of consciousness–provides baseline data on the patient's condition. The changes that occur thereafter provide information on the progress of the patient.

The Secondary Survey
Vital Signs

Level of Consciousness–Assess with AVPU

Pupils–Assess reactivity to light

Pulse–Assess rate, rhythm, force

Skin Signs–Assess skin color, temperature and moisture

Temperature–Assess oral temperature with a thermometer

Respiration–Assess rate, rhythm, force

Capillary Refill Time–Assess circulation in fingers and toes

Blood Pressure–Unlikely to be recorded in the backcountry

Level of Consciousness

Level of consciousness (LOC) reflects brain function. This may be affected by the ability of circulation and respiratory systems to deliver oxygen to the brain, by head injury, metabolic disturbances such as low blood sugar, or diseases of the brain such as a stroke.

A memory aid for assessing
Level of Consciousness is AVPU:

Alert
Verbal
Pain
Unconscious

Alert
Normally we're awake, alert and know who we are, where we are and the date and time.

Verbal
The patient is not fully awake but responds to verbal stimuli by opening eyes, moving or waking up. Higher levels of brain function respond to verbal input, lower levels to pain. Test for responsiveness to verbal stimuli first, painful stimuli second.

Pain
The patient is not awake, does not respond to verbal stimuli but does respond to painful stimuli by moving, opening eyes or groaning. To stimulate for pain, pinch the muscle at the back of the shoulder or rub the sternum.

Unconscious
A patient who does not respond to voice or painful stimuli is unconscious.

Pupils
Pupils are clues to brain function. They can indicate head injury, stroke, drug abuse or lack of oxygen to the brain. Both pupils should be round and equal in size. They should contract symmetrically when exposed to light and dilate when the light dims. Evaluate pupils by noting size, equality and reaction to light.

PUPIL SIZE:

NORMAL SIZE
BOTH SIDES SAME SIZE — IRIS / PUPIL

BOTH PINPOINT

UNEQUAL IN SIZE

BOTH DIALATED

In the absence of a portable light source, such as a flashlight or headlamp, shield the patient's eyes for 15 seconds, then expose to ambient light. Both pupils should contract equally. When in doubt, compare the patient's reactions to those of a healthy individual in the same light conditions.

The patient whose brain cells are deficient of oxygen may have equal but slow-to-react pupils. A wide, non-reactive pupil on one side and a small, reactive pupil on the other side indicates damage or disease on the side with the larger pupil. Very small, equal pupils may indicate drug intoxication.

Pulse

A pulse pressure wave generated every time the heart beats is transmitted through the arteries. The pulse rate indicates the number of heartbeats over a period of time. For an adult, the normal range is 60 to 90 beats per minute. An athlete may have a normal pulse rate of 50. Shock, exercise, altitude, illness, emotional stress or fever will increase the heart rate.

The pulse rate can be measured at the radial artery on the thumb side of the wrist, the carotid artery in the neck or the femoral artery in the groin. Place the tips of the middle and index fingers over the artery. Count the number of beats for 10 seconds and multiply by six or count the number of beats for 15 seconds and multiply by four.

In addition to rate, note the rhythm and strength of the pulse. The normal rhythm is regular. Irregular rhythms can be associated with heart disease and are frequently rapid. The strength of the pulse is the amount of pressure you feel against your finger tips. It may be weak or strong.

A standard pulse reading includes the rate, rhythm and strength of the pulse; for example, "The pulse is 110, irregular and weak," or "The pulse is 60, regular and strong."

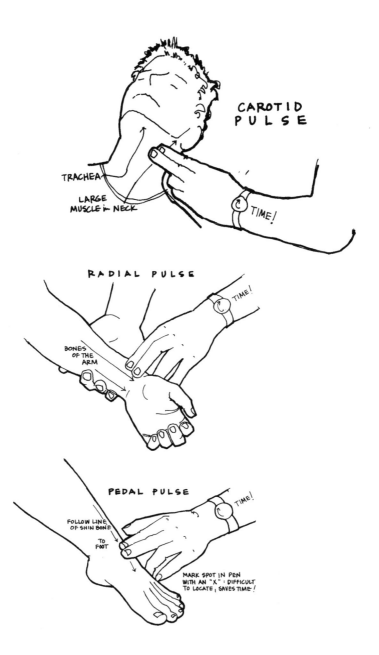

CAROTID PULSE

TRACHEA

LARGE MUSCLE in NECK

TIME!

RADIAL PULSE

BONES OF THE ARM

TIME!

PEDAL PULSE

FOLLOW LINE OF SHIN BONE

TO FOOT

TIME!

MARK SPOT IN PEN WITH AN "X" : DIFFICULT TO LOCATE ; SAVES TIME!

Skin Signs

Skin signs indicate the condition of the respiratory and cardiovascular systems. These include skin color, temperature and moisture.

Pink

In a lightly colored person normal skin color is pink. In darker skinned individuals skin color can be assessed at the nail beds, palms of the hands, soles of the feet or at the lips.

Redness

Redness indicates that the skin is unusually flushed with blood. It is a possible sign of heat stroke, carbon monoxide poisoning, fever or allergic reactions.

Paleness

Pale skin indicates blood has withdrawn from the skin. Paleness may be due to fright, shock, fainting or cooling of the skin.

Cyanosis

Blue skin, or cyanosis, appears when circulation to the skin is reduced or the level of oxygen in the blood falls. Well-oxygenated blood is brighter red than poorly oxygenated blood. Cyanosis indicates that oxygen levels have fallen significantly.

Jaundice

Yellow skin combined with yellow whites of the eyes—jaundice—is a sign of liver or gallbladder disease. The condition results from excess bile pigments in the blood.

Temperature and Moisture

Quickly assess the temperature and moisture of the skin at several sites including forehead, hands and trunk. In a healthy person the skin is warm and relatively dry. Skin temperature rises when the body attempts to rid itself of excess heat, as in fevers or environmental heat problems. Hot, dry skin is a sign of fever and heat stroke. Hot, sweaty skin occurs when the body attempts to eliminate excess heat and can also be a sign of fever or heat illness.

Skin temperature falls when the body attempts to conserve heat by constricting blood flow to the skin; for example, during exposure to cold. Cool, moist (clammy) skin is an indicator of extreme stress and a sign of shock.

A report on skin condition should include color, temperature and moisture; for example, "The patient's skin is pale, cool and clammy."

Body Temperature
Temperature measurement is an important component of a thorough patient assessment, but it is the vital sign that is least often recorded in the field. It can tell us of underlying infection or of abnormally high or low body temperatures. While a normal temperature is 98.6°F (37°C.), daily variation of body temperature is also normal, usually rising a degree during the day and subsiding through the night.

Temperature can be measured orally or rectally. Axillary readings—taken under the armpit–are the least reliable. Rectal temperatures are the most accurate indication of the core temperature available to first-aiders. Rectal temperature is sometimes considered necessary for suspected hypothermia but is rarely measured due to patient embarrassment and cold exposure. Diagnosis of hypothermia in the outdoors, discussed in Chapter 9 (Cold Injuries), is often based on other factors, such as behavior, history, appearance and LOC.

SHAKE THERMOMETER BULB END DOWN
TO PUSH MERCURY DOWN BELOW TEMPERATURE MARKINGS :

MERCURY
(SILVERY IN COLOR)

DEGREE MARKINGS
LINES SHOW .2° INCREMENTS

PLACE UNDER PATIENT'S TONGUE FOR 3 MINUTES.
REMOVE, ROTATE THERMOMETER UNTIL MERCURY CAN BE SEEN ;
READ TEMPERATURE BY NOTING WHERE MERCURY STOPS: NORMAL TEMP. READING below :

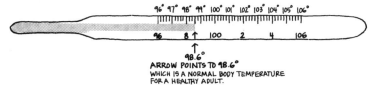

98.6°
ARROW POINTS TO 98.6°
WHICH IS A NORMAL BODY TEMPERATURE
FOR A HEALTHY ADULT.

Before taking a temperature, shake down the thermometer to push the mercury below the degree markings. This is essential for an accurate reading. Place the thermometer under the patient's tongue for at least three minutes. The patient should refrain from talking or drinking during this time. A report on temperature should include the method, such as "100°F oral," or "98°F rectal."

Respiration
Respiratory rate is counted in the same manner as the pulse: each rise of the chest is counted over fifteen seconds and multiplied by four, or thirty seconds and multiplied by two. Normal respiration range is 12 to 20 breaths per minute.

The patient's depth and effort of breathing enable you to gauge his need for air and the presence or absence of chest injury. In a healthy individual breathing is relatively effortless and unconscious.

A patient experiencing breathing difficulty may exhibit air hunger with deep, labored inhaling efforts. A patient with a chest injury may have shallow, rapid respirations accompanied by pain. Irregular respirations are a sign of a brain disorder. Noisy respirations indicate some type of airway obstruction. Assess and if necessary clear the airway.

Smell the breath. Fruity, acetone breath is a sign of diabetic coma. Foul, fecal-smelling breath may indicate a bowel obstruction.

Report respirations by their rate, rhythm, effort, depth, noises and odors. For example, the patient in diabetic ketoacidosis may have respirations described as "20 per minute, regular, labored, deep. There is an odor of acetone on his breath."

Capillary Refill Time
Capillary refill time measures the ability of the cardiovascular system to bathe the skin with blood. It is a tool for checking circulation.

To check capillary refill time, press the patient's forehead or nail beds to blanch a spot. In a healthy individual the blood returns and the white skin at the blanch site becomes pink within two seconds (the time it takes to say "capillary refill time"). Delayed capillary refill time tells us the heart and blood vessels are not delivering oxygen-rich blood to the skin. You should measure and report the capillary refill time.

Blood Pressure
The concept of blood pressure is discussed in Chapter 2 (Shock). Although blood pressure is always measured when professional medical care is being administered, accurate measurement requires a stethoscope and a sphygmomanometer—equipment rarely carried on wilderness trips. Because evacuation decisions can be made without measuring blood pressure, this vital sign is not presented.

Medical History
The patient's medical history provides background often relevant to the present problem. Preparing the history is an ongoing process that you typically carry out while measuring vital signs and performing the head-to-toe exam. Obtaining an accurate history depends greatly on the quality of communication between you and the patient. This rapport begins as soon as you approach the scene. Communicating clearly, acting orderly and appearing in control will make it easier to obtain an accurate history.

The Secondary Survey
Medical History

The Chief Complaint
(PQRST)
AMPLE
AEIOUTIPS

Chief Complaint (PQRST)
Obtain the patient's chief complaint—the problem that caused him to solicit help. Pain is a common complaint; for example, pain in the back after a fall, abdominal pain or simple nausea.

A memory aid for pursuing
questions about pain is PQRST:

Provokes
Quality
Radiates
Severity
Time

Provokes
What provoked the injury? If the problem is an illness, under what circumstances did it occur? What makes the problem worse and what makes it better?

Quality
What qualities describe the pain? Adjectives may include stabbing, cramping, burning, sharp, dull or aching.

Radiates
Where is the pain? Does it move or radiate? What causes it to move? Chest pain from a heart attack can radiate from the chest into the neck and jaw. Pain from a spleen injury can be felt in the left shoulder.

Severity
On a scale of one to ten (with one being no pain or discomfort, and ten being the worst pain or discomfort the patient has ever experienced), how does the patient rate this pain? This question can reveal the level of discomfort the patient is experiencing.

Time
When did the pain start? How frequently does it occur? How long does it last? Correlate the patient's complaints with the history of his vital signs.

AMPLE

The second step in taking the medical history can be remembered as AMPLE. Using AMPLE, you create an important "history within the history."

> A memory aid for taking the
> "history within the history" is AMPLE:
> **A**llergies
> **M**edications
> **P**ast history
> **L**ast meal
> Recent **E**vents

Allergies, Medications and Last Meal
Ask the patient questions about allergies, medications and his last meal. The information on allergies and medications may help prevent negative drug interactions during treatment. The "last meal" information is crucial should the patient require surgery.

Recent Events
Recent events are unusual circumstances which have occurred within the past few days that may be relevant to the patient's present situation. Recent events might include symptoms of mountain sickness preceding pulmonary edema or changes in diet preceding stomach upset.

Past History
The past history consists of a series of questions you ask the patient in order to discover any previous medical problems. First ask these general questions: Has the patient ever been in a hospital? Has the patient been treated by a physician? Is he seeing a physician now?

Next, ask about specific body systems. Avoid medical jargon and leading questions. For example, asking the patient if he has ever had problems with his heart is less confusing than asking, "Do you have a cardiac history?"

Review all body systems
for the past history:
Cardiovascular (heart, blood pressure)
Respiratory (breathing, lungs, asthma)
Neurological (seizures, nerves, head injury)
Digestive (stomach, bowel function)
Urinary (kidney and bladder, infection, stones)
Skin
Reproductive (menstrual, pregnancy)
Skeletal (accidents, broken bones)

Additional sources of information may include a medical alert tag or a medical information questionnaire. A medical alert tag is a necklace, bracelet or wallet card that identifies the patient's medical concern or concerns. It will report a history of diabetes, hemophilia, epilepsy or other disorder, allergies to medication, and other pertinent information. Medical forms are common to many outdoor schools, camps and guide services. The NOLS student medical history form is filled out by the student prior to the trip and is available for review by field staff.

AEIOUTIPS

The final step in taking the medical history can be remembered as AEIOUTIPS. Particularly useful for investigating causes of unconsciousness, this list of reasons why a person might become unconscious is also useful in assessing a conscious patient. Investigate each possibility and look for clues that will either rule out or confirm its presence. Since obtaining a history on an unconscious patient is impossible, carefully question bystanders for any background information they may be able to provide.

A memory aid for common reasons why a person
might become unconscious is AEIOUTIPS:

Alcohol

Epilepsy

Insulin (diabetes)

Overdose

Underdose

Trauma

Infection

Psychological/**P**oison

Stroke

The Critical Assessment

The critical assessment is a review of the information gathered during the patient assessment. Examine the records of the head-to-toe examination, the vital signs and the medical history. Think through the ABCs, the PQRST, AMPLE and AEIOUTIPS.

Rule out possibilities as you assess. Many diagnoses are made by physicians on the basis of what a condition is not, rather than what it could be. Is chest pain a muscle pull or a heart attack? Does the patient have the flu, mountain sickness or early cerebral edema?

After thinking through all the available information, prioritize the patient's medical problems and begin to treat them.

The initial exam provides a baseline. Periodically repeat the exam to judge the patient's response to treatment and any changes for better or worse. If there is any change or deterioration in the patient, return to the beginning and repeat the ABCs and the primary survey.

> **The Critical Assessment**
>
> Review available information
> Rule out possibilities
> Develop a diagnosis
> Decide on treatment
> Prioritize and treat
> Review and repeat exam

Extended Patient Care

Emergency medical care in the wilderness may be prolonged over hours or days in isolated locations. Splints, shelter and litters may need to be improvised. In addition to first aid, basic nursing care is necessary to manage the physical and emotional needs of the patient.

Keep the patient warm, clean and comfortable. Remove soiled and wet clothing, and wash the patient at intervals. An individual immobilized on a litter may need extra insulation to keep warm. Hot water bottles, fires or other expedition members may be needed as sources of warmth.

Drinking and eating are not appropriate in patients with an abnormal level of consciousness or abdominal or head injuries. Do not give food and fluids to a patient likely to undergo surgery within six hours.

If the patient can drink, give water or clear soups and juices. Avoid hot chocolate, coffee, tea or beverages with high concentrations of sugar or caffeine. Excess sugar can delay fluid absorption; excess caffeine increases fluid loss.

Over a period of a few days, fluid intake will be more important than solid food, as dehydration can complicate any existing medical condition. Dehydration is discussed in Chapter 19 (Hydration).

Arrange for the patient to urinate and defecate as comfortably as possible. These basic body functions are essential to overall well-being, despite embarrassment or temporary discomfort. The first-aider's sensitivity to and support for the patient is essential here.

For male patients, a water bottle usually works well as a urine receptacle. For female patients, a bedpan can be fashioned from a frying pan or an article of clothing can be used as a diaper. Bowel movements can be managed by assisting the patient with an improvised bedpan.

Final Thoughts

An incomplete patient assessment—failure to measure vital signs or review history and physical findings—has been the source of unnecessary and needlessly rushed evacuations. Helicopters have flown into wilderness areas for simple knee sprains and for hyperventilation misdiagnosed as head injury. Rescue teams have hiked through the night expecting to treat serious injuries, only to find a walking patient with minor injuries. Resources are wasted. The patient, rescuers and expedition members are needlessly put at risk.

Likewise, the same mistake has delayed the evacuation of patients to a physician. Life-threatening fevers have been overlooked because a temperature was not measured. Diabetic complications have been missed because no one asked about the patient's medical history.

There are also many stories of outdoor leaders who, although they lacked medical experience, performed a simple and methodical assessment, checked the ABCs for life-threatening problems, then followed the secondary survey protocols. They used a checklist, took their time and made a written record of their findings. The information gathered was the foundation for quality first aid.

Summary: Patient Assessment

Safety of the rescuer is a priority

Primary Survey. Assess for immediate threats to life: unresponsiveness, airway, breathing, circulation and bleeding. Observe cervical spine precautions. Begin treatment for shock.

> **R**esponsiveness: shake and shout
> **A**irway: open airway
> **B**reathing: look, listen, feel
> **C**irculation: check pulse
> **C**-spine: jaw thrust
> **B**leeding: control serious bleeding
> **S**hock: protect from cold, maintain the airway, elevate the legs

Secondary Survey. Complete this assessment after life-threatening problems have been treated.

Head-to-Toe	*Vital Signs*	*Medical History*
Look	LOC	Chief Complaint
Listen	Pupils	(PQRST)
Feel	Pulse	AMPLE
Smell	Skin Signs	AEIOUTIPS
	Temperature	
	Respiration	
	Capillary Refill	
	Blood Pressure	

The Critical Assessment
> Review available information
> Develop a diagnosis
> Decide on treatment
> > Rule out other possibilities
> > Review and repeat exam
> > Prioritize and treat

CHAPTER 2
SHOCK

Introduction

Shock is a simple name for a complex disorder of the circulatory system. Mid-nineteenth century descriptions of shock as "a deadly downward spiral" and "a rude unhinging of the machinery of life" accurately portray a condition in which the circulatory system collapses in apparent disproportion to the initial injury. Shock is often the lethal component of burns, serious illness, fractures, injuries to the chest and abdomen and of severe bleeding and catastrophic injury. A first-aider must anticipate, recognize and treat shock.

The Circulatory System

The circulatory system is composed of the heart, the blood vessels and the blood. Its primary function is to deliver a constant supply of oxygen to the tissues, and an interruption will cause cells and tissues to malfunction and eventually die. The circulatory system also transports carbon dioxide from the cells to the lungs, keeps the electrolyte environment stable, delivers hormones from their source to their place of action and mobilizes body defenses.

The heart is a two-sided pump that propels blood through a system of pipes (arteries, veins and capillaries). The right side receives blood from the veins and pumps it through the lungs for oxygen replenishment. The left side pumps the oxygen-rich blood from the lungs to the rest of the body. Blood leaves the heart through arteries, which narrow into smaller vessels called arterioles and eventually become a vast network of microscopic vessels called capillaries.

Capillaries are woven throughout the tissues. The exchange of nutrients and waste products from the blood to the cells takes place across capillary walls only one cell thick. Blood vessels leaving the capillary beds widen into veins, conduits for blood returning to the heart. The venous blood returns to the right side of the heart and then to the lungs to be replenished with oxygen. The circuit is complete.

The circulatory system adjusts automatically to our energy demands, activity level, position and temperature. The rate and force of pumping, the diameter of the vessels and the amount of fluid in the system vary to meet the requirements of exercise, stress, sleep and relaxation.

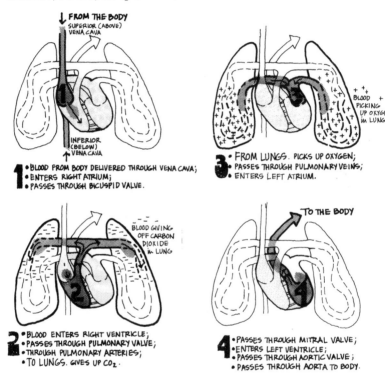

1 • BLOOD FROM BODY DELIVERED THROUGH VENA CAVA;
• ENTERS RIGHT ATRIUM;
• PASSES THROUGH BICUSPID VALVE.

2 • BLOOD ENTERS RIGHT VENTRICLE;
• PASSES THROUGH PULMONARY VALVE;
• THROUGH PULMONARY ARTERIES;
• TO LUNGS. GIVES UP CO_2.

3 • FROM LUNGS. PICKS UP OXYGEN;
• PASSES THROUGH PULMONARY VEINS;
• ENTERS LEFT ATRIUM.

4 • PASSES THROUGH MITRAL VALVE;
• ENTERS LEFT VENTRICLE;
• PASSES THROUGH AORTIC VALVE;
• PASSES THROUGH AORTA TO BODY.

Shock

Cardiologist and wilderness medicine specialist Dr. Bruce Paton suggests the following analogy for shock: Imagine the body as a healthy wetland with a river running through lush vegetation. The vegetation depends on the river's flow of pure, unpolluted water and the nutrients it carries. If the river dries up or the water becomes poisoned, the plants shrivel and die. The maintenance of a healthy, well-oxygenated flow of blood through the tissues is called good perfusion.

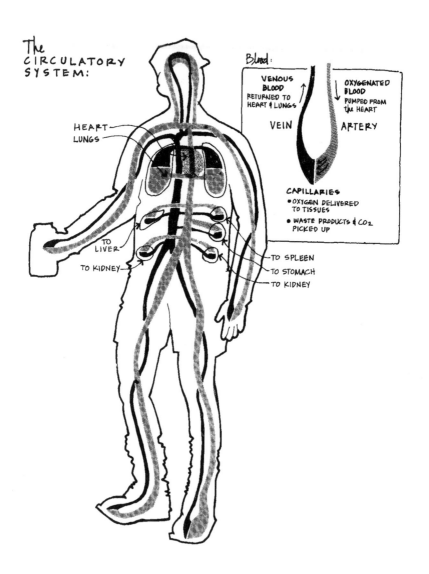

The
CIRCULATORY
SYSTEM:

HEART
LUNGS

TO
LIVER

TO KIDNEY

Blood:

VENOUS
BLOOD
RETURNED TO
HEART & LUNGS

OXYGENATED
BLOOD
PUMPED FROM
the HEART

VEIN   ARTERY

CAPILLARIES
• OXYGEN DELIVERED
  TO TISSUES

• WASTE PRODUCTS & CO_2
  PICKED UP

TO SPLEEN
TO STOMACH
TO KIDNEY

Shock is the inadequate perfusion of tissue with oxygenated blood. It is a failure of any or all of the three basic components of the circulatory system—heart, blood vessels, or blood—to deliver oxygenated blood to the tissues. Insufficient blood flow to the tissues causes inadequate oxygen and nutrient delivery and waste product removal. Shock is a state in which poor perfusion leads first to reversible then irreversible tissue damage. Bodily processes slow, and tissues begin to die.

Causes of Shock

Adequate blood pressure, like a healthy river flowing at proper level into the wetland, is essential to maintaining perfusion of vital organs. Three factors influence blood pressure, and changes in any of them can cause a serious fall in blood pressure. The three critical factors are blood volume, cardiac output (the volume of blood pumped per minute by the heart) and the state of constriction or dilation of the blood vessels (peripheral resistance).

Causes of Shock

Blood Volume Loss   *Decreased Cardiac Output*
Bleeding   Heart attack
Severe infection   Heart injury
Burns
Serious diarrhea

Blood Vessel Dilation
Severe infection
Spinal cord injury
Fainting

Blood Volume Loss

Fluid loss is a major cause of shock. The primary causes of fluid loss are bleeding, infections, extensive burns and metabolic disorders. Massive bleeding results in a reduced blood volume; blood vessels are inadequately filled and blood pressure falls.

Shock can also develop from fluid loss during watery diarrhea, from illness such as diabetes or from hidden bleeding into fractures of the femur and pelvis.

The average adult has six liters of blood. A 10 percent loss (one-half liter) is enough to affect blood pressure. A 25 percent blood volume loss (1.5 liters) can cause moderate shock. And a 30 percent loss (2 liters) is considered serious shock.

Decreased Cardiac Output
The heart muscle may become so damaged by a heart attack that it cannot maintain adequate output (pump failure). Shock secondary to a heart attack is referred to as cardiogenic shock.

Blood Vessel Dilation
Spinal cord injury can damage nerves controlling vessel diameter, allowing them to widen. Changes in blood vessel diameter, however, are not an important cause of shock except in overwhelming infection in which there is widespread dilation of small vessels. The expanded vessels cause blood pressure and perfusion to decrease despite the extra pumping of the heart in response to the shock.

Fainting results when momentary dilation of blood vessels occurs in a person's body as a response to a strong emotional stimulus. As the volume of blood returning to the heart diminishes, blood pressure falls and fainting occurs.

Assessment
The patient in shock will have a rapid pulse rate that may feel weak, irregular and "thready." A progressively increasing pulse rate is a bad sign, indicating continuing blood loss or increasing shock.

The skin is pale, cool and clammy. The patient may exhibit shallow, rapid breathing and be restless, anxious, irritable and thirsty. Level of consciousness is variable. If shock prevents the brain from being perfused with oxygen-rich blood, the level of consciousness will deteriorate.

Assessment For Shock
Rapid and/or weak pulse
Rapid and/or shallow respirations
Dilated pupils
Pale, cool, clammy skin
Anxiety or restlessness
Nausea
Thirst
Changes in level of consciousness

These signs and symptoms are due to our "fight or flight" response—our body's response to danger, wherein release of adrenaline increases heart rate, causes the skin to pale and sweat and causes nausea and restlessness. Blood is routed away from the digestive tract and concentrates around the muscles and essential organs.

These changes pump the blood faster, reduce the size of the blood vessels and route the blood to essential organs, possibly enabling the body to compensate for the shock. If the circulatory system is unable to adjust, a downward spiral of deterioration may begin in which first tissues, then organs and finally entire systems fail from lack of oxygen.

Treatment

Although shock is more likely with multiple injuries, serious illness, severe bleeding, dehydration or a major fracture, we initially treat every patient for shock. If the mechanism of injury is not serious and signs and symptoms stabilize or do not deteriorate, the patient is probably only experiencing a stress reaction.

If the mechanism of injury is serious and signs and symptoms deteriorate, our critical assessment indicates shock. Our basic treatments of bandages, splints, physical and emotional support reinforced by temperature maintenance, position and fluids are all assets in the wilderness management of shock. However, the definitive treatment for shock in the backcountry is evacuation.

Always assume that shock may occur, and begin treatment before signs and symptoms are manifested. Treatment begins with the triad of basic life support: airway, breathing and circulation (ABC) as well as control of bleeding and stabilization of fractures and other injuries. Thereafter, shock treatment moves to a second triad: temperature maintenance, position and fluids.

Treatment for Shock

Airway

Breathing

Circulation

Control bleeding, stabilize fractures

Maintain temperature

Elevate legs

Consider fluids

Maintain Temperature

Protect the patient from excess heat and cold. Your goal is to maintain body temperature within normal limits. Insulate the patient from cold ground, provide protection from wind and weather, and remove wet clothes and replace them with dry.

Elevate Legs

Unless injury to the legs or pelvis prevents it, position the patient with legs elevated eight to ten inches to enhance blood return to the chest and head. Even with minor injuries, this position is appropriate until you have assessed the problem.

Consider Fluids

Although fluid replacement is likely to be necessary, do not administer fluids at first, since surgery may be a possibility. If surgery will be necessary within six hours, withhold fluids.

Fluids may be given if surgery does not seem likely, the patient does not have an altered mental status, there is no abdominal injury and if you are more than six hours from the hospital.

When giving fluids by mouth, plain water is adequate. Using one teaspoon of salt per liter is acceptable, as are dilute bouillon drinks. Beware of strongly salty or sweet drinks. Sugar can interfere with the body's absorption of liquid; salt can be nauseating.

Some experts advise the use of electrolyte drinks. If available, these may be used at half strength. Most electrolyte drinks, however, have a lot of sugar, which can delay absorption of the needed water. The goal is to give the patient fluids, not cause nausea and vomiting.

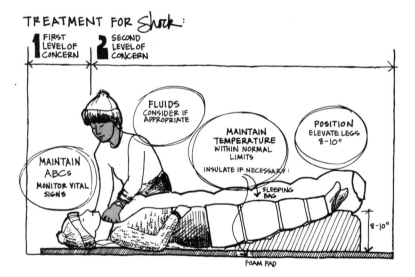

TREATMENT FOR Shock:

1 FIRST LEVEL OF CONCERN   2 SECOND LEVEL OF CONCERN

MAINTAIN ABCs
MONITOR VITAL SIGNS

FLUIDS
CONSIDER IF APPROPRIATE

MAINTAIN TEMPERATURE
WITHIN NORMAL LIMITS
INSULATE IF NECESSARY:
SLEEPING BAG

POSITION
ELEVATE LEGS 8–10"

8–10"

FOAM PAD

Final Thoughts

Shock, an insidious and complicated disturbance in the circulatory system, is difficult to treat in the backcountry. Paramedics, nurses and physicians in urban medical systems are trained to quickly assess, transport and use technical medical procedures to fight shock. None of this is available in the wilderness. The definitive treatment for shock in the backcountry is evacuation.

Summary: Shock
The main purpose of the circulatory system, which comprises the heart, blood vessels and blood, is to supply oxygen to the cells. Shock is the failure of this system to perfuse tissue with oxygen-rich blood.

Causes of Shock

Blood Volume Loss
Bleeding
Severe infection
Burns
Serious diarrhea

Decreased Cardiac Output
Heart attack
Heart injury

Blood Vessel Dilation
Severe infection
Spinal cord injury
Fainting

Signs and Symptoms of Shock
Rapid and/or weak pulse
Rapid and/or shallow respirations
Dilated pupils
Pale, cool, clammy skin
Anxiety/restlessness
Nausea
Thirst
Changes in level of consciousness

Treatment for Shock
ABCs: Open and maintain airway, perform CPR if necessary
Control bleeding, stabilize fractures
Maintain temperature: insulate, dry, protect from wind
Elevate legs 8-10 inches to aid blood return to upper body
Consider fluids: plain water if no imminent surgery

Introduction

Outside the wilderness we give little thought to the consequences of soft tissue injuries. Our lives are not disrupted by small wounds, and infection is an unusual aftermath. On NOLS courses, however, backcountry travelers take falls while carrying packs and experience lacerations while preparing meals or walking or swimming barefoot. On an expedition, even relatively minor injuries can have serious consequences. Cut or blistered feet can result in litter evacuations and hand wounds can end climbing trips. Infection is a real and ever-present risk.

Responding with the proper first aid is essential to expedition members' health and safety. In addition to controlling bleeding, first aid for soft tissue injuries in the wilderness includes cleaning the wounds, monitoring for signs of infection and making decisions about when to evacuate.

Skin Anatomy

The skin is the largest organ of the body. It protects the internal organs by providing a watertight shell that keeps fluids in and bacteria out. The skin helps regulate body temperature by providing a means of heat dissipation. Sweat glands produce sweat, which evaporates, cooling the body. Nerves near the skin's surface send messages to the brain about heat, cold, pressure, pain and body position.

The skin is composed of three layers. The innermost layer is subcutaneous tissue, which consists mostly of fat. This layer is an insulator for the body and a reservoir for energy. Beneath the subcutaneous tissue lies muscle.

The second layer is the dermis, which contains sweat glands, sebaceous glands, hair follicles, nerves and blood vessels. Sweat glands are found on all body surfaces, with most on the palms of the hands and soles of the feet. Sweat glands secrete one half to one liter of sweat per day and can produce up to a liter per hour during strenuous exercise.

The sebaceous glands produce sebum (oil) and lie next to the hair follicles. Sebum waterproofs the skin and keeps the hair supple. Blood vessels in the dermis provide nutrients and oxygen to each cell and remove waste products such as carbon dioxide.

The outermost layer of the skin is the epidermis. The epidermis is made up primarily of dead cells held together by sebum. These dead cells continually slough off and are replaced by more dead cells.

LAYERS OF THE SKIN:

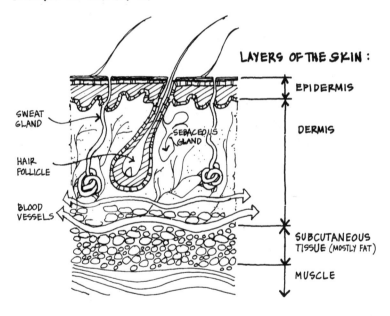

LAYERS OF THE SKIN:

EPIDERMIS

DERMIS

SWEAT GLAND

SEBACEOUS GLAND

HAIR FOLLICLE

BLOOD VESSELS

SUBCUTANEOUS TISSUE (MOSTLY FAT)

MUSCLE

Closed Injuries

Soft tissue injuries are classified as open or closed. With closed injuries the skin remains intact, while open injuries involve a break in the skin's surface.

Closed injuries include contusions (bruises) and hematomas. With both, the tissue and blood vessels beneath the epidermis are damaged. Swelling and discoloration occur because blood and plasma leak out of the damaged blood vessels. With contusions, blood is dispersed within the tissues. Hematomas contain a pool of blood—as much as a pint surrounding a major bone fracture. Depending on the amount of blood dispersed, re-absorption can take from 12 hours to several days. In some cases the blood may have to be drained by a physician to enhance healing.

Treatment for Closed Injuries

A memory aid for treating closed injuries is RICE: rest, ice, compression and elevation.

Treatment For Closed Injuries: RICE
Rest to allow clots to form
Ice 20 to 40 minutes every two to four hours
Compression to reduce swelling and bleeding
Elevate above heart level

Rest
Rest decreases bleeding by allowing clots to form. Extremities may be splinted to decrease motion that may cause newly formed clots to break away and bleeding to continue. See Chapter 5 (Fractures and Dislocations).

Ice
Ice causes the blood vessels to constrict, decreasing bleeding. Never apply ice directly to bare skin, as this can cause frostbite. Instead, wrap the ice in fabric of a towel-like thickness before

applying to the skin. Ice the wound for 20 to 40 minutes every two to four hours for the first 24 to 48 hours.

Compression
Apply manual pressure or a pressure dressing. When applying a pressure dressing, apply it snugly enough to stop bleeding but not so tightly that the blood supply is shut off. Check by feeling for a pulse distal to the injured site. Check pressure dressings every 20 to 30 minutes for the first two hours then every two hours thereafter to ensure that swelling has not turned the pressure dressing into a virtual tourniquet.

Elevate
Elevate the injury above the level of the heart. Elevation reduces bleeding by decreasing the blood flow to the affected area and causing a decrease in pressure in the veins.

Open Injuries
Open injuries include abrasions, lacerations, puncture wounds and major traumatic injuries—avulsions, amputations and crushing wounds.

Abrasions
Abrasions occur when the epidermis and part of the dermis are rubbed off. These injuries are commonly called "road rash" or "rug burns." They usually bleed very little but are painful and may be contaminated with debris.

Abrasions heal more quickly if treated with ointment and covered with a semi-occlusive or occlusive dressing. (See page 61.)

Lacerations
Lacerations are cuts produced by sharp objects. The cut may penetrate all the layers of the skin, and the edges may be straight or jagged. If long and deep enough to cause the skin to gap, lacerations may require sutures. Sutures are also indicated if the cut is on the face or hands or over a joint, or if it severs a tendon, ligament or blood vessel. Tendons and ligaments must be sutured together to heal properly. Lacerations

OPEN INJURIES

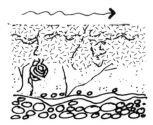

ABRASION
EPIDERMIS / DERMIS
RUBBED OFF.

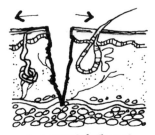

LACERATION
CUTS PRODUCED BY
SHARP OBJECTS.
EDGES CAN BE CLEAN
OR RAGGED.

AVULSION
THE TEARING OFF OF A
FLAP OF SKIN OR ENTIRE
LIMB.

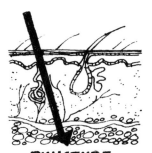

PUNCTURE
POINTED OBJECT
PENETRATES SKIN AND
POSSIBLY AN UNDERLYING
ORGAN OR ARTERY.

on the hands or over a joint may be sutured to prevent the wound from being continually pulled apart by movement. Lacerations on the face are usually sutured to decrease scarring.

The first step in treating a laceration is to clean the wound. Then dress the wound and apply a bandage to help protect the laceration from contamination from debris. A butterfly bandage will help keep the edges together.

Puncture Wounds

Puncture wounds are caused by pointed objects. Although the skin around a puncture wound remains closed and there is little external bleeding, the object may have penetrated an artery or organ, causing internal bleeding.

Unless the impaled object is causing an airway obstruction, leave it in place. Removing the object can increase bleeding by releasing pressure on compressed blood vessels. If the impaled object is causing an airway obstruction, however, it must be removed to allow the patient to breathe.

Puncture wounds are difficult, sometimes impossible to clean. Depending on the size of the wound, high pressure irrigation with a syringe of povidone-iodine or zephiran chloride may clean some of the debris. Tetanus is a rare but serious complication.

> Although Tetanus is more likely to occur in a farm or ranch environment than on a "clean" mountainside, it is a good idea to make sure your tetanus booster is up to date before you take off into the backcountry. Tetanus boosters should be given at least every ten years.

Major Traumatic Injuries

Major traumatic injuries include avulsions, amputations and crushing injuries.

Avulsion

An avulsion is a "tearing off" that can range in severity from a small skin flap to the near amputation of an entire limb. Skin tends to separate along anatomical planes, such as between subcutaneous tissue and muscle.

To treat a small-to-moderate-sized avulsion, clean the skin flap and reposition it over the wound. Apply small strips of tape or butterfly bandages to the edges, leaving a space between each strip so the wound can drain. If the area avulsed is larger than two inches in diameter, a skin graft may be required for the wound to heal properly.

Amputation

Amputation is the complete severance of a part or extremity. Bleeding may be profuse or relatively light. If blood vessels are partially torn, they cannot constrict, and bleeding may be massive. In contrast, the stump of a cleanly severed extremity may not bleed profusely because the cleanly severed blood vessels respond by retracting and constricting.

After treating the patient, rinse the amputated body part with clean water, wrap it in dry sterile gauze and place it in a plastic bag. Then place the bag in cold water or on ice. Do not bury the part in ice as this may cause cold injury. Make certain that the wrapped part accompanies the patient to the hospital. If elevation and direct pressure do not stop the stump from bleeding, a tourniquet may be necessary.

Crushing Injuries

Crushing injuries can cause extensive damage to underlying tissue and bones, and large areas may be lacerated and avulsed. Always consider what underlying body parts may be damaged, and always conduct a secondary survey to find out if any bones have been fractured or if an internal organ has been crushed.

Treatment for Open Injuries

To protect against any disease that an injured person may be carrying, the Centers for Disease Control (CDC) recommends using rubber or latex gloves when touching blood, body fluid, mucous membranes or any non-intact skin or when you are handling any items or surfaces that are soiled by blood or body fluid.

Controlling Bleeding

Controlling bleeding is the first priority when treating open wounds. Death can come quickly to a patient with a tear in a major blood vessel. There are four methods for controlling bleeding. The most effective—direct pressure and elevation—will stop most bleeding when used in combination. Also used are pressure points and tourniquets.

Controlling Bleeding
Direct Pressure
Elevation
Pressure Points
Tourniquets

Direct Pressure

The best method for controlling bleeding is to apply pressure over the wound site. Using your hand and a piece of wadded fabric—preferably sterile gauze—apply direct pressure to the wound. Be sure to wear rubber or latex gloves or place your hand in a plastic bag. If the wound is large, you may need to pack the open area with gauze before applying pressure. Maintain pressure for five minutes, then slowly release. If the bleeding resumes, apply pressure for 15 minutes.

Elevation

As with closed injuries, the combination of splinting, a pressure dressing and elevation will help decrease the bleeding. Direct pressure and elevation control almost all bleeding. In fact, it is unusual for a wound to require the first-aider to utilize pressure points or a tourniquet.

Pressure Points

Pressure points are areas on the body where arteries lie close to the skin and over bones. Pressure applied to the artery at one of these points can slow or stop the flow of blood in that artery, thereby reducing bleeding at the site of the injury. Pressure on these points is rarely effective by itself and is usually applied in conjunction with other techniques.

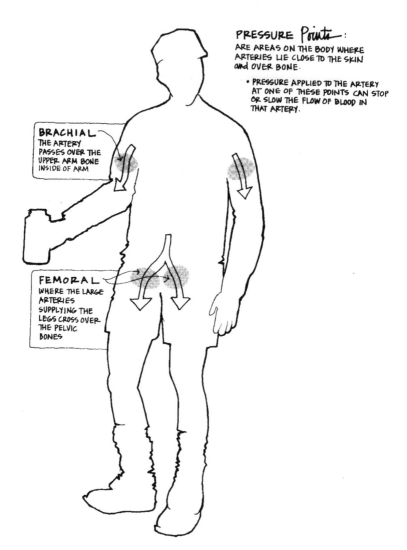

PRESSURE Points:
ARE AREAS ON THE BODY WHERE
ARTERIES LIE CLOSE TO THE SKIN
and OVER BONE.

• PRESSURE APPLIED TO THE ARTERY
AT ONE OF THESE POINTS CAN STOP
OR SLOW THE FLOW OF BLOOD IN
THAT ARTERY.

BRACHIAL
THE ARTERY
PASSES OVER THE
UPPER ARM BONE
INSIDE OF ARM

FEMORAL
WHERE THE LARGE
ARTERIES
SUPPLYING THE
LEGS CROSS OVER
THE PELVIC
BONES

Tourniquets

Apply a tourniquet only as a last resort when no other method
will stop the bleeding. Tourniquets completely stop the blood
flow, and if the tourniquet is left on for more than a few hours,
tissue distal to the tourniquet will die and the extremity may
require amputation.

How To Apply A Tourniquet

1. Once you've determined that a tourniquet is necessary, apply it as close to the injury as possible, between the wound and the heart. Use a bandage that is three to four inches wide and six to eight layers thick. Never use wire, rope or any material that will cut the skin.

2. Wrap the bandage snugly around the extremity several times, then tie an overhand knot.

3. Place a small stick or similar object on the knot and tie another overhand knot over the stick.

4. Twist the stick until the bandage becomes tight enough to stop the bleeding. Tie the ends of the bandage around the extremity to keep the twists from unraveling.

5. Using a pen, write "TK" on the patient's forehead and the time the tourniquet was applied. Once in place, do not remove the tourniquet! It should remain in place until the patient arrives at the emergency room.

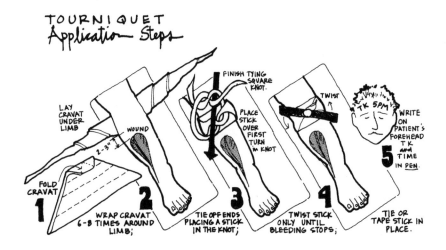

TOURNIQUET Application Steps

Cleaning Wounds

When you clean a wound, you eliminate as much potentially infectious bacteria and debris as possible without further damaging the skin. At NOLS we use zephiran chloride 1:3000 dilution or 10 percent povidone-iodine.

Cleaning Wounds

Wash your hands with soap and water

Put on rubber or latex gloves

Check circulation, sensation and movement

Scrub and irrigate the wound

    Scrub the area around the wound

    Use sterilized tweezers to remove debris

    Use pressure irrigation

Rinse thoroughly with disinfected water

Dress and bandage the wound

Wash Your Hands and Put on Gloves

Wash your hands. Use soap and water to prevent contamination of the wound. Put on rubber or latex gloves.

Scrub and Irrigate the Wound

Scrub or irrigate an open wound for least three minutes with either zephiran chloride or povidone-iodine. At NOLS we carry 35cc syringes in the first aid kit for pressure irrigating wounds. Try to remove all debris even if this requires some painful scrubbing. Remove large pieces of debris with tweezers that have been cleaned with one of the above cleaning solutions.

Rinse with Disinfected Water

After cleaning the wound, rinse off the solution with liberal amounts of disinfected water. See Chapter 17 (Hygiene and Water Disinfection). Check underneath the patient to make sure he is not lying in a pool of solution, as prolonged exposure to the solution can cause burning. Also check for further bleeding— you may need to apply direct pressure again if blood clots were broken loose during the cleaning process.

Dressings and Bandages

Dressings are sterile gauzes placed directly over the wound; bandages hold the dressing in place. Both come in many shapes and sizes. Semi-occlusive (Telfa) or occlusive (Second Skin) dressings promote healing by keeping the area moist. Ointments (such as Polysporin or Bacitracin) serve the same purpose. Dry dressings that adhere to the wound impede the healing process.

Next, apply an antibiotic ointment. The ointment should be applied to the dressing rather than directly to the wound. This will avoid contaminating the remaining antibiotic in the tube or bottle. Apply the bandage neatly and in such a way that blood flow distal to the injured area is not impaired. After applying the bandage check the pulse distal to the injury.

Do not close wound edges until the wound has been thoroughly cleaned. If the skin is stretched apart, butterfly bandages can hold the edges together. If the injury is over a joint, the extremity may require splinting—also to prevent the edges from pulling apart.

After The Bandage is Applied
Check circulation, sensation and movement of the body part distal to the injury. Can the patient tell you where you are touching? Can he flex and extend the extremity? Is the area distal to the injury pink and warm, indicating good blood perfusion? Any negative answers to these questions may indicate nerve, artery or tendon damage that will require evacuating the patient.

If a dressing becomes soaked with blood, leave it in place and apply additional dressings. Removing the dressing disturbs the blood clots that are forming. After bleeding has been controlled, dressings should be changed daily and the injured area checked for signs of infection.

Infections

Redness, swelling, pus, heat and pain at the site, faint red streaks radiating from the site, fever, chills or swollen lymph nodes are all signs of infection. Drawing a circle around the red area with a pen will help you determine if the infection is spreading or resolving.

An infection that is localized to the site of the injury can be treated in the field. If the edges of the wound are closed, pull them apart and soak the area in warm antiseptic solution or warm salt water for 20 to 30 minutes three to four times a day. If the infection starts to spread—as evidenced by fever, chills, swollen lymph nodes or faint red streaks radiating from the site—or if the wound cannot be opened to drain, evacuate the patient.

Signs of Infection
Redness and swelling
Pus, heat and pain
Red streaks radiating from the wound
Fever and chills
Swollen lymph nodes

**Treatment for
Infected Wounds**
Pull wound edges apart and clean wound
Soak in warm antiseptic solution

Indications for Evacuation
Fever, chills and swollen lymph nodes
Red streaks radiating away from wound
Wound cannot be opened to drain

Treating Blisters

Blisters—a common backcountry occurrence—can be debilitating. Blisters are caused by friction and occur in areas where the epidermis is thick and tough enough to resist abrasion. At first there will be a red, sore area called a "hot spot." If the friction continues, the epidermis separates and fluid enters the space, causing a blister.

The First Step: Prevention
Prevent blisters by making sure boots fit properly, wearing two pairs of socks to decrease friction on the skin, checking feet frequently at rest breaks, and stopping at the first sign of rubbing. Apply a solid piece of moleskin or athletic tape to areas that you suspect may cause problems.

Hot Spots
Cut a doughnut-shaped piece of moleskin and center it over the hot spot as a buffer against further rubbing.

Small Blisters
If a small blister has already developed, cut a doughnut-shaped piece of molefoam and center it over the blister. The doughnut "hole" prevents the adhesive from sticking to the tender blister and ripping it away when the molefoam is changed.

Larger Blisters
If the blister is nickel-sized or larger, drain it. Begin by carefully cleaning your hands and putting on rubber or latex gloves. Clean the area around the blister to decrease the risk of infection. Use a needle that has been soaked in an antiseptic solution such as povidone-iodine or zephiran chloride for three minutes or has been heated until it glows red, then cooled. Insert the needle at the base of the blister, allowing the fluid to drain from the pinprick. After draining the blister, apply an antibiotic ointment and cover the area with gauze. As with an intact blister, center a doughnut-shaped piece of molefoam over the drained blister and gauze. Follow up by checking the blister every day for signs of infection.

Final Thoughts
Most bleeding can be stopped by using pressure and elevation. Wounds should be aggressively cleaned with zephiran chloride or povidone-iodine and irrigated with copious amounts of disinfected water. Monitor wounds for signs and symptoms of infection.

Summary: Soft Tissue Injuries

Controlling Bleeding
Direct Pressure
Elevation
Pressure Points
Tourniquets

Treatment for Soft Tissue Injuries

Closed Injuries (RICE)
Rest to allow clots to form
Ice, 20-40 minutes, every 2-4 hrs
Compression to reduce swelling and bleeding
Elevate above heart level

Open Injuries
Stop bleeding
Assess damage
Clean the wound
Dress and bandage
Monitor for signs of infection

Cleaning Wounds
Wash your hands with soap and water
Put on rubber or latex gloves
Check circulation, sensation and movement
Scrub and irrigate the wound
    Scrub the area around the wound
    Use sterilized tweezers to remove debris
    Use pressure irrigation
Rinse thoroughly with disinfected water
Cover with antibiotic ointment
Dress and bandage the wound

Signs of Infection
Redness and swelling
Pus, heat and pain
Red streaks radiating from the wound
Fever and chills
Swollen lymph nodes

Treatment for Infected Wounds
Pull wound edges apart and clean wound
Soak in warm antiseptic solution
Indications for evacuation
    Fever, chills and swollen lymph nodes
    Red streaks radiating from wound
    Wound cannot be opened to drain

CHAPTER 4
BURNS AND LIGHTNING INJURIES

Introduction

Burns are an infrequent injury on NOLS courses, but the potential for serious burns from the sun, fires, stoves and lanterns is great. Improper stove use has caused stoves to flare or pressure caps to release and flame, burning unwary cooks. People have tripped and fallen into fires. The most serious burns experienced on NOLS courses have been been caused by spilled hot water. Chemical burns may occur from spilled gas or carbide from carbide lamps.

Minor burns may be no more than a trivial nuisance, yet they represent a potential site of infection. Burns of joints, feet, hands, face and genitalia, however, can impair these complex structures. A large burn causes significant loss of fluid and may rapidly cause shock. Severe burns of an entire limb are potentially lethal.

Types of Burns

There are four types of burns: thermal, inhalation, chemical and electrical. Electrical burns in the wilderness are caused by lightning.

Thermal Burns

Thermal burns are caused by flames, flashes of heat (as in explosions), hot liquids or contact with hot objects. The degree of associated tissue death depends on the intensity of the heat and the length of exposure. Water at 140°F will burn skin in five seconds, water at 120°F in five minutes.

Inhalation Burns

Inhalation burns are caused by breathing hot air or gases and/or particles; for example, from being caught inside a burning structure. The cilia (hair-like structures lining the upper airways) and mucous membranes lining the respiratory tract may be destroyed instantly. The mucous membranes swell and fluid leaks into the lungs. The body is unable to expel mucus because the cilia are damaged. Mucus collects in the upper airway, decreasing carbon dioxide and oxygen exchange. Oxygenation is impaired when carbon monoxide from burning material competes with oxygen for binding sites on red blood cells.

Chemical Burns

Chemical burns are caused by contact with alkalis, acids or corrosive material. Backcountry chemical burns are rare, but burns from leaking batteries or spilled gas are a possibility.

Assessing Burns

Depth of the Burn

Burns are classified as "partial thickness," as in first and second degree burns, and "full thickness," as in third degree.

First Degree Burns

First degree burns injure only the epidermis. A first degree burn is red and painful and blanches white with pressure. The area heals in four or five days with the epidermis peeling.

Second Degree Burns

Second degree burns injure both the epidermis and dermis and are extremely painful. The skin appears red, mottled, wet and blistered and blanches white with pressure. Blisters may take as long as 24 hours to form. The burn takes from five to 25 days to heal and longer if it becomes infected.

Third Degree Burns

Third degree burns injure the epidermis, dermis and subcutaneous tissue. The skin appears leathery, charred, pearl gray and dry. The area is sunken and has a burned odor. The skin does not blanch and is not painful because blood vessels and nerve endings are destroyed. Painful first or second degree burns may surround the third degree area. Third degree burns destroy the dermis and, if large, require skin grafts to heal.

Extent of the Burn: The Rule of Palms

The extent of burns can be determined by the Rule of Palms. The patient's palm represents one percent of his body surface area. Using the palm as a size indicator, estimate the percentage of body area involved.

ASSESSMENT of BURNS:

FIRST DEGREE
EPIDERMIS ONLY BURNED
- SKIN RED, PAINFUL

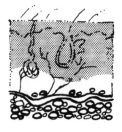

SECOND DEGREE
EPIDERMIS AND DERMIS BURNED
- SKIN BLISTERED (MAY TAKE 24 HOURS +)
- RED, MOTTLED, WET, PAINFUL

THIRD DEGREE
EPIDERMIS, DERMIS AND
SUBCUTANEOUS TISSUE BURNED
- LEATHERY, DRY, CHARRED
- PEARLY GRAY in COLOR

The "RULE OF PALMS"

A PERSON'S PALM REPRESENTS
ROUGHLY 1% OF HIS BODY SURFACE.
USE THIS ESTIMATE TO DETERMINE
THE EXTENT AND SEVERITY OF BURNS.

Treating Burns

Thermal, inhalation and chemical burns are all treated essentially the same. The source of the burn must be eliminated. If indicated, the airway should be checked. Then the burn itself is cooled, assessed, cleaned and dressed. The guidelines presented in this chapter under "Final Thoughts" will help you determine if the depth and extent of the burn calls for evacuation and if so, with how much urgency.

Treatment for Burns

Remove the source of the burn:

For thermal burns, stop, drop, roll

For dry chemical burns, brush off dry chemicals

For wet chemical burns, flush with water for 20 minutes

Remove clothing and jewelry

Assess the airway

For inhalation burns, consider carbon monoxide poisoning

Cool the burn

Assess the depth and extent of the burn

Clean the burn

Apply a cool, moist dressing

Thermal Burns
Put Out the Fire!

"Stop, drop and roll" is the sequence to follow if someone catches on fire. Stop him from running (which provides oxygen that keeps the fire burning). Make him drop to the ground and roll or roll him in a sleeping bag or jacket to put out the flames.

Quickly remove the patient's clothing and any jewelry. It retains heat and causes continued burning. Hot water spilled on legs clothed in polyproplyene or wool has caused serious burns, as has water spilled into boots, where the boot and sock retained and concentrated the heat on the ankle.

Check the Airway

If the patient is not breathing, begin artificial respiration. Check the pulse. If there is no pulse, start CPR.

Cool the Burn

After removing clothing, pour cool water (not ice cold) or apply cool, wet cloths on the burned site. No more than 10 percent of the body should be cooled at one time, as cooling introduces the risk of hypothermia. Never put ice directly on the site as it may cause frostbite. Ice also causes blood vessels to constrict, which deprives the burn area of blood and thus, oxygen and nutrients.

Assess the Depth and Extent of the Burn

Most burns are combinations of first, second and third degree. Assess the surface area of each burn type using the Rule of Palms.

Clean and Dress the Burn

Clean the burn with cool, clean water and apply antibiotic ointment. Dress it with a moist dressing. Keep the dressing moist with disinfected water, change the dressing once a day and monitor the site for signs of infection.

Inhalation and Chemical Burns

Inhalation Burns

If you suspect an inhalation burn, check the mouth, nose and throat for signs of soot, redness or swelling. Are the facial hairs or nasal hairs singed? Check for signs of respiratory distress, such as coughing or noisy, rapid breaths.

Other symptoms of inhalation burns include headache, weakness, nausea, vomiting, loss of manual dexterity, confusion, and lethargy. Carbon monoxide poisoning must be suspected in a patient with inhalation burns. A cherry red coloring to the skin is a very late sign of carbon monoxide poisoning and may not occur until after the person has died. Using stoves in tents or snow caves can cause carbon monoxide poisoning.

Inhalation burns always require that the patient be evacuated to a medical facility. Signs and symptoms of respiratory distress may not become apparent for 24 to 48 hours.

Chemical Burns

Flush chemical burns with any available water for a minimum of 20 minutes. Brush off any dry chemical before rinsing the burn. Remove clothing, jewelry and contact lenses, as these may retain the chemical and continue to burn the victim.

Speed is important. The longer a chemical stays on the body the more damage it causes. Looking for specific antidotes wastes time. Use plain water to flush, then wash the burn with mild soap and water.

Rinse a chemically burned eye with water for at least 20 minutes. After flushing the affected eye, cover it with a moist dressing. After 20 to 30 minutes, remove the dressing. If the patient complains of changes in vision, reapply the dressing and evacuate the patient.

Lightning Injuries

Lightning is the only significant cause of backcountry electrical burns. Lightning injures 1,000 people in the United States every year. Of those, approximately 30 percent die.

Types Of Injuries

Injuries can occur from the high voltage (200 to 300 million volts), secondary heat production or the explosive force of the lightning.

A person can be injured by lightning in five ways:

1. Direct hit: Actually being struck by lightning.

2. Lightning "splash:" Lightning hits another object and splashes onto objects or people standing nearby.

3. Direct transmission: Being in contact with an object that has been hit directly.

4. Ground current: Receiving the ground current as it dissipates from the object that has been hit.

5. Blunt trauma from the explosive force of the shock wave.

Most victims are splashed by lightning or hit by ground current. Very few people actually sustain a direct hit. While a direct hit can deliver 200 to 300 million volts, the duration is short (1 to 100 milliseconds) and severe burns are uncommon. More likely, a person will suffer internal injuries (cardiac arrest, damage to the brain and spinal cord) and fractures from shock waves.

Lightning burns form distinctive patterns. Linear burns follow areas of heavy sweat concentration. A linear burn may begin beneath the breasts, travel from the sternum to the abdomen, then split down both legs, or it may follow the midaxillary line (an imaginary line drawn through the middle of the armpit to the waist).

Lightning-caused punctate burns are circular, ranging in size from a few millimeters to a centimeter in diameter. Also, feather-like patterns may be caused by electron showers that leave imprints on the skin. Most lightning burns are first or second degree, with some of the punctate burns being third degree.

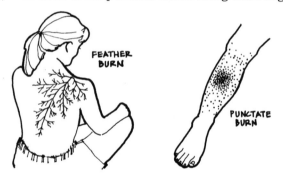

Most lightning burns are superficial, but lightning strikes may throw victims a considerable distance, causing head and spinal injuries, dislocations, fractures and blunt chest and abdominal trauma. The respiratory center in the brain may also be injured, causing respiratory and cardiac arrest.

Lightning knocks 72 percent of its victims unconscious. Of those, 66 percent suffer temporary lower extremity paralysis, 33 percent suffer upper extremity paralysis, and 50 percent have one or both eardrums ruptured. Other signs and symptoms are confusion, amnesia, temporary deafness or blindness and mottling of the skin. Pulses may decrease or disappear in the lower extremities due to injury-induced spasms of the blood vessels.

Treat cardiac arrest with CPR. The heart may restart beating before respirations begin. Artificial respiration may need to be continued due to paralysis of the respiratory center in the brain.

How To Prevent Lightning Injuries
Remember: Lightning usually hits the tallest object in the area, and water conducts electricity, therefore:

DON'T stand under the only tall object in the area. It is better to be in a large group of trees than under the only tree out in the open.

DON'T stay at or near the top of peaks or ridges. Head down as quickly as possible.

DON'T hide in shallow caves or stand at the entrance of a cave as you may be in the path of the electrical current.

AVOID being the tallest object near a body of water.

GET OUT of water and off of wet ground. Don't swim!

GET AWAY from objects that conduct electricity (ice axes, tent poles).

WATCH for hair standing on end and a blue ring around objects (St. Elmo's Fire). Listen for high pitched "zing-ing" sounds. These indicate a strike is imminent. Leave the area immediately.

STAY at lower elevations.

SQUAT down with your feet facing downhill, keep your hands off the ground (to avoid ground current going through you) or sit on something dry and non-conducting (foamlite pad, rope, day pack).

STAY alert to local weather patterns and cloud build-up. In the Rocky Mountains, the afternoons are generally more dangerous than the mornings.

FREQUENT STRIKES
EXTREMELY HAZARDOUS

OCCASIONAL STRIKES
HAZARDOUS

RELATIVELY SAFE

<u>LARGE</u> CAVE (<u>NOT</u> SHALLOW) SAFE ONLY IF WALLS / ENTRANCE AVOIDED.

SIT ON SOMETHING DRY and NON-CONDUCTING (FOAM PAD, ROPE, DAY PACK.)

SQUAT WITH FEET FACING DOWNHILL. TRY TO KEEP HANDS OFF the GROUND!

LIGHTNING *Safety*

DANGER FROM GROUND CURRENTS

HAZARDOUS
GRAY SHADING & ARROWS SHOW
PROBABLE FLOW.

RELATIVELY
SAFE

Final Thoughts

The American Burn Association and the American College of Surgeons classify burns by depth and extent. Burns are divided into three categories: minor, moderate and major.

These guidelines provide a useful reference for deciding if a patient can be treated in the field or if he should be evacuated. Moderate and major burns should be quickly evacuated to a physician for further evaluation. Minor burns should also be seen by a physician, but unless they are complicated by shock or infection, the evacuation need not be hurried. Infection is a risk when treating minor burns in the field. Burns, like other soft tissue wounds, must be kept clean to reduce the risk of infection.

A patient with burns of the face may also have inhalation burns. Second and third degree burns of the hands and feet may require special treatment to preserve function, and burns of the groin may produce enough swelling to prevent urination.

Burns are serious injuries, more easily prevented than treated. Keep safety in mind at all times, especially when around fires and stoves and when lightning develops.

Severity of Burns

Minor burns:

Second degree burns less than 15% of the body
Third degree burns less than 2% of the body and
   not involving the face, hands, feet or groin

Moderate burns:

Second degree burns of 15 to 25% of the body
Third degree burns less than 10% of the body and
   not involving the face, hands, feet or groin

Major burns:

Second degree burns more than 25% of the body
Third degree burns more then 10% of the body
Second or third degree burns involving critical
   areas: face, hands, feet or groin
Inhalation burns
Electrical burns
Burns with associated trauma
Burns with serious underlying medical problems

Summary: Burns

Types of Burns
Thermal: flames, flashes of heat, hot liquids
Inhalation: breathing hot air or gases
Chemical: alkalis, acids, corrosives
Electrical: lightning

Assessment of Burns
Assess Depth
First degree burns: affect only the epidermis. The skin
is red, painful and blanches white with pressure.

Second degree burns: injure the epidermis and dermis.
The skin is red, mottled, wet, blistered and painful.
It blanches white with pressure.

Third degree burns: affect the epidermis, dermis and
subcutaneous tissue. The skin is leathery, charred,
pearl gray and dry. The area is sunken and has a
burned odor. The skin does not blanch, is not painful.

Assess Extent
Rule of Palms

Treatment for Burns
Remove the source of the burn:
For thermal burns, stop, drop, roll
For dry chemical burns, brush off chemicals
For wet chemical burns, flush with water for 20 minutes
Remove clothing and jewelry

Assess the airway
  For inhalation burns, consider carbon monoxide poisoning
Cool the burn
Assess the depth and extent of the burn
Clean the burn
Inhalation
  Assess the airway

Lightning
  Assess using ABCs
  CPR if necessary
  Assess for injury

Chapter 5
FRACTURES AND DISLOCATIONS

Introduction

The Skeletal System

Fractures and Dislocations

> Signs and Symptoms
>
> Assessment
>
> Treatment
>
> Relocation and Realignment

Splinting

> Basic Splinting Techniques
>
> Specific Splinting Techniques

Final Thoughts

Summary: Fractures and Dislocations

Introduction

As recently as ninety years ago a fractured femur was a deadly injury. First aid was non-existent and broken bone ends often did not heal. Open fractures frequently became infected and amputation was a common unpleasant consequence. Modern emergency medicine, especially assessment and splinting in the field, has reduced these complications.

Fractures and dislocations are infrequent at NOLS, making up less than 3 percent of our field safety incidents. Among the general public, however, fractures and dislocations make up as much as 20 percent of reported wilderness injuries. NOLS instructors have cared for femur fractures in the remote backcountry of Yellowstone Park in the winter and at 16,000 feet on Denali. They've expertly splinted uncomplicated wrist fractures and walked patients as far as 20 miles out of the wilderness. They've accurately diagnosed a complicated elbow fracture requiring a helicopter evacuation.

The Skeletal System

A bony skeleton shapes the body. From this scaffolding hang the soft tissues: the vital organs, blood vessels, muscles, fat and skin. The skeleton is strong for support and protection of internal organs, flexible to withstand stress, and jointed to allow for movement.

Bone is living tissue combined with non-living intracellular components. The non-living components contain calcium and make bone rigid. Bones are connected by ligaments and connective tissue. An adult has 206 bones ranging in size from the femur or thigh bone—the largest—to the tiny ossicle of the inner ear.

The skeleton has axial and appendicular components. The axial bones are the pelvis, spinal column, ribs and skull. Injuries to these structures—except pelvic fractures—are discussed in the chest and head injury chapters. This chapter covers injuries to the appendicular skeleton, which is the appendages or arms and legs.

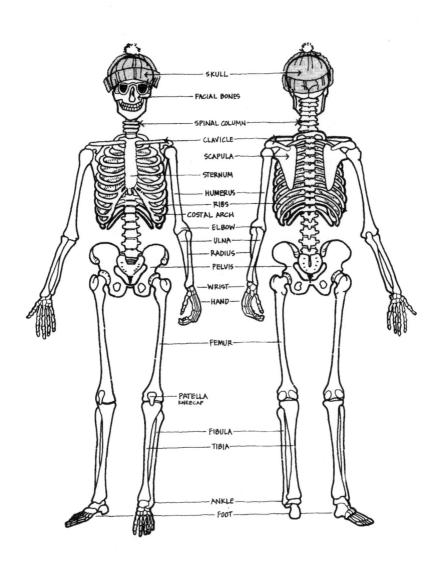

SKULL

FACIAL BONES

SPINAL COLUMN

CLAVICLE

SCAPULA

STERNUM

HUMERUS

RIBS

COSTAL ARCH

ELBOW

ULNA

RADIUS

PELVIS

WRIST

HAND

FEMUR

PATELLA
KNEECAP

FIBULA

TIBIA

ANKLE

FOOT

The upper extremity consists of the scapula or shoulder blade, the clavicle or collarbone, the upper arm bone or humerus, two bones in the forearm—the radius on the thumb side and the ulna on the little finger side—and 22 bones in the wrist and fingers.

The lower extremity consists of the pelvis, the thigh bone or femur, a small bone in front of the knee—the patella—two bones in the lower leg—the tibia and the fibula—and 26 bones in the ankle and foot.

Bones connect at joints. Some joints are fixed, others allow movement. Joints are held together by ligaments, connective tissue and muscle. Joint surfaces are covered with cartilage to reduce friction, while joint fluid lubricates them for smooth movement.

Fractures and Dislocations

A fracture is a break in a bone. Fractures can be open or closed. With open fractures the skin is broken, exposing the bone to contamination. Closed fractures are covered with intact muscle and skin.

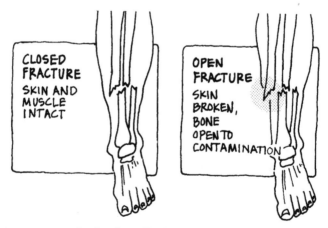

Fractures can also be described as transverse, spiral, oblique or crushed, referring to the type of fracture. This information is usually obtained from an X-ray and has little effect on first aid.

Fractures, in addition to causing pain, loss of function and swelling, can be complicated by infection and damage to blood vessels and nerves. Fractured bone ends can pinch or sever blood vessels, blocking circulation or causing bleeding. Fractures of large long bones such as the femur, the humerus or the pelvis are often accompanied by blood loss that can cause life-threatening shock. Infection is a potentially severe complication of an open fracture.

A dislocation is the displacement of a bone end from its normal position at a joint. Dislocations damage the supporting structures at the joint. Blood vessels and nerves can be disrupted. The ball and socket joint of the shoulder is a common site for dislocation. Elbow, finger and ankle dislocations are also possible. Less common are dislocations to the wrist, hip and knee. Fractures and dislocations can occur together.

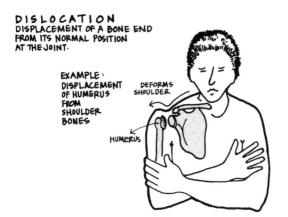

DISLOCATION
DISPLACEMENT OF A BONE END
FROM ITS NORMAL POSITION
AT THE JOINT.

EXAMPLE:
DISPLACEMENT
OF HUMERUS
FROM
SHOULDER
BONES

DEFORMS
SHOULDER

HUMERUS

Signs and Symptoms

Signs and symptoms of fractures or dislocations include pain and tenderness, crepitus—a grating sound produced by bone ends rubbing together, also a sign of instability and unnatural movement at the fracture site—swelling and discoloration (indicating fluids are pooling in the damaged tissue), deformity to a limb or joint and loss of function. Dislocations cause loss of function at a joint; fractures may cause loss of function to a limb.

**Signs and Symptoms
of Fractures and Dislocations**

Pain and tenderness

Crepitus

Swelling and discoloration

Deformity

Loss of function at a joint (dislocation)

Loss of function at a bone (fracture)

Consider the mechanism of injury

Assessment

Humans are bilaterally symmetrical animals, meaning one side is the mirror image of the other. Comparing an injured with an uninjured limb can reveal a subtle angulation or deformity. The mechanism of injury also provides a clue to the extent and location of the injury. Particularly violent incidents—including falls from height or direct blows to joints—are common fracture mechanisms in the outdoors.

Assess an extremity for bone or joint injury and circulatory and nerve function. To assess for bone or joint injury, remove clothing if possible and visualize the injury. Look at the limb for deformity, swelling or discoloration. Feel the limb for localized tenderness, abnormal bumps or protrusions and swelling.

Assess circulation by feeling the radial pulse at the wrist or the pedal pulse in the foot. Impaired circulation may also be evidenced by cold, gray or cyanotic extremities.

Assess nerve function by asking the patient to move fingers or toes. Test for reaction to touch or pain. A blocked artery with loss of distal circulation is an emergency. After six to eight hours, serious damage may result. Damage to a nerve is not as urgent, as the damage usually occurs immediately and may be irreparable.

**Assessment
of Fractures and Dislocations**
Assess the bone or joint
    Remove clothing, visualize the injury
    Look for deformity, swelling, discoloration
    Feel for tenderness, deformity, swelling
Assess circulation
    Check distal pulse in wrist or foot
    Check temperature and color in the hand or foot
Assess nerve
    Ask the patient to move fingers or toes
    Test for sensation to touch or pain

Treatment

Treat fractures and dislocations by immobilizing the injury. Immobilization prevents movement of bones, reduces pain, swelling and the possibility of further injury, prevents a closed fracture from becoming an open fracture and helps reduce disability.

Treatment for Fractures and Dislocations
    Immobilize the injury
        Bones above and below dislocations
        Joints above and below fractures
    Splint before moving
    Clean and dress wounds
    Remove jewelry, watches and tight clothing
    Elevate to reduce swelling
    Assess circulation, temperature and sensation before
        and after splinting
    Assess for other injuries
    Treat for shock

Immobilize the Injury

Any time there is loss of function to a limb or joint, the injury should be immobilized in a splint. It is better to immobilize a sprain than to fail to immobilize a fracture.

Splint Before Moving

Splint before moving the patient. A quick splint fashioned from a foamlite sleeping pad can stabilize the injury if you must move the patient off dangerous terrain or to drier, warmer conditions. Strap an injured arm to the body. Tie injured legs together. Immobilize the bones above and below a dislocated joint, and immobilize the joints above and below a fractured bone.

Clean and Dress Wounds

Clean and dress all wounds before splinting. Treat open fractures as contaminated soft tissue injuries and clean thoroughly. Clean exposed bone ends. Keep the bone end moist with a dressing soaked in disinfected water. An infected fracture is an extremely serious problem that can result in long-term complications.

Remove Jewelry, Watches and Tight Clothing

Remove jewelry and watches and loosen clothing that might compromise circulation should swelling occur. If you are managing a splint in cold weather, hot water bottles or chemical heat packs tucked into the splint can provide warmth.

Elevate to Reduce Swelling

Elevate the affected limb six to ten inches to reduce swelling. In warm environments where hypothermia and frostbite are not of concern, cold packs and ice or snow encased in a plastic bag and wrapped with a sock will help to reduce pain and swelling.

Assess Circulation, Temperature and Sensation

Before and after the splint is applied, assess circulation, warmth and movement to fingers or toes. Repeat this assessment periodically during transport as well.

Assess for Other Injuries

A fracture or dislocation warrants a full patient assessment for other injuries as well.

Treat for Shock

A fracture in and of itself will not cause shock. Damage to nearby tissues, organs and blood vessels are the life-threatening problems. Splinting is a basic treatment for shock because it reduces pain and continued injury. Be especially alert for shock with femur and pelvic fractures, multiple fractures and open fractures.

Relocation and Realignment

The relocation of an angulated fracture or a dislocation has been a controversial subject in wilderness emergency care for years. Blood vessels travel through joints, generally lie close to bones and can be cut or pinched during manipulation. When rapid transport to a hospital is available, dislocations are immobilized and relocation takes places in the emergency room after evaluation by a physician.

Medical opinion now favors relocation in remote settings by trained individuals. The dominant thought is that the danger of injury to nerves or blood vessels is less than the danger of damage to a dislocated joint or a fracture left angulated for long periods. We recommend that you contact a physician for advice and for training on specific relocation techniques.

The accepted exceptions are a fractured femur, which is splinted with traction, fractures that are unsplintable or untransportable in their current position and any fracture or dislocation in which there is no pulse distal to the injury.

A limb left without blood flow for several hours faces morbidity. In this instance, applying gentle traction and realigning the bone ends is acceptable in order to restore circulation. To do this, grasp the limb below the fracture site while another person supports the limb. Align with gentle traction applied on the long axis of the bone. If resistance or pain occurs, stop the realignment and splint in the deformed position.

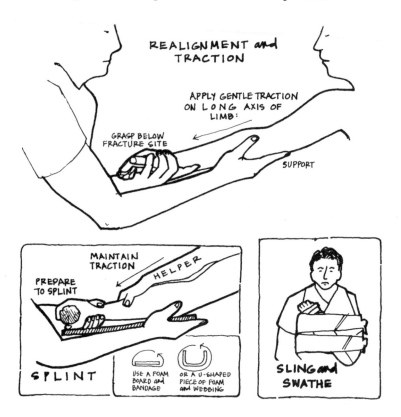

Splinting

In the wilderness, improvised splints are the rule, and they may remain in place for days. Splints should be rigid and should pad and support the limb and insulate the extremity from cold. They should be lightweight to make transporting the patient easier and allow access to feet or hands to check circulation. There are many commercial splints on the market, but in the backcountry two commonly available items easily meet these specifications. They are the foamlite pad used for insulation under sleeping bags and the triangular bandage.

> **Qualities of a Good Splint**
> Rigid; supports the injury
> Lightweight
> Pads the injury
> Insulates from cold
> Offers access to distal circulation

Basic Splinting Techniques

Two basic splinting techniques will cover most first aid situations. One is to make a foamlite tube to splint an arm or leg. The other is to fashion a sling and swathe to immobilize injuries to the upper extremities. The one exception is the case of a fractured femur, which should be immobilized using a traction splint.

The Foamlite Tube

To make a foamlite tube, roll the foam sleeping pad into a U-shaped tube and trim to fit the limb. Secure with cravats (triangular bandages), sling webbing or tape. For extra stability, fasten items such as tent poles, pack stays or tree branches to the outside of the splint.

The Sling and Swathe

The sling and swathe immobilizes arm, shoulder and collarbone injuries using two triangular bandages or cravats.

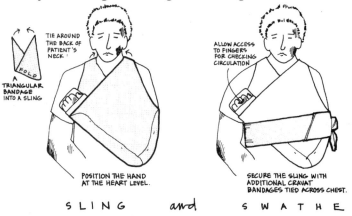

TIE AROUND THE BACK OF PATIENT'S NECK

A TRIANGULAR BANDAGE INTO A SLING

POSITION THE HAND AT THE HEART LEVEL.

ALLOW ACCESS TO FINGERS FOR CHECKING CIRCULATION

SECURE THE SLING WITH ADDITIONAL CRAVAT BANDAGES TIED ACROSS CHEST.

SLING and SWATHE

Specific Splinting Techniques

The Hand

The hand and fingers should be splinted in the "position of function," the position of the hand when holding a glass of water. If the injury is confined to the fingers, the wrist need not be splinted. If the injury involves the bones at the base of the fingers, splint the wrist as well.

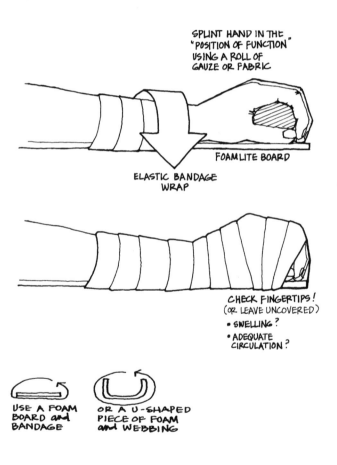

SPLINT HAND IN THE "POSITION OF FUNCTION" USING A ROLL OF GAUZE OR FABRIC

FOAMLITE BOARD

ELASTIC BANDAGE WRAP

CHECK FINGERTIPS!
(OR LEAVE UNCOVERED)
• SWELLING?
• ADEQUATE CIRCULATION?

USE A FOAM BOARD and BANDAGE

OR A U-SHAPED PIECE OF FOAM and WEBBING

The Wrist and Forearm

Splint injuries to the wrist and forearm with a foamlite stabilizer or a sling and swathe. Elevating the hand above the level of the heart will help reduce swelling and pain. The two bones of the forearm, the radius and ulna, are connected by a strong band of connective tissue. Forces applied to one bone can be transmitted to the other, and simultaneous fractures of both bones are common.

The Elbow

An elbow dislocation is a serious injury, which calls for rapid evacuation. Several nerves and arteries pass around the complex elbow joint and may be damaged by displaced bone ends. The simplest splint for the elbow is the sling and swathe. Splint this injury in the position in which you find it. If the elbow is at an awkward angle, a sling and swathe will not work well. Try a foamlite pad stabilized with a tent pole or the stay from a soft pack bent to the angle of the joint. If possible, bandage the whole arm to the trunk for greater stability.

The Upper Arm

The radial nerve and brachial artery lie close to the humerus and can be injured by a fracture. Damage to the artery is most common with elbow dislocations. Damage to the nerve is most common with mid-shaft fractures. Check the pulse at the wrist. The ability to bend back the hand tests the radial nerve. The humerus can be splinted with a combination of a foamlite splint and sling and swathe. Wrap foamlite on the inside of the arm, over the elbow and up the outside of the arm for added stability.

The Shoulder

The humerus fits into a shallow socket in the scapula, forming the shoulder joint and allowing for a wide range of motion. This range of motion makes the joint susceptible to injury. Most dislocations are anterior with the head of the humerus misplaced out of the socket toward the chest.

The signs of dislocation are drooping shoulder, a depression on the front of the shoulder and loss of function at the joint. The sling and swathe provides a simple and effective splint. If the shoulder is immobile at an awkward angle, padding may be necessary to support the arm away from the chest.

The Collarbone

The clavicle acts as a strut, propping the back of the shoulder. It can be fractured by a direct blow to the shoulder or by a blow transmitted up an extended arm. A broken collarbone is a common mountain bike injury. Deformity and tenderness can often be found by feeling the entire clavicle from sternum to shoulder. Typically, a patient with an injured clavicle will be unable to use the arm on the injured side. Splint with a sling and swathe, immobilizing the shoulder and arm.

The Pelvis

The pelvis is a bowl-shaped structure consisting of three bones fused with the sacrum, the lower portion of the vertebral column. The upper part of the femur meets the pelvis at a shallow socket and forms the hip joint.

A broken pelvis is a serious injury. It takes considerable force to break a pelvis; such force can cause associated internal injuries, including rupture of the bladder and blood loss. Treat this patient as if he has a back injury, and immobilize the trunk and legs. A backboard, Stokes litter or packframe litter is necessary to immobilize and carry the patient.

The Femur and Hip

A dislocated hip is usually the result of a high-velocity mechanism such as a fall from height. A leg with a dislocated hip is generally shortened with the foot turned out. If the hip is dislocated for more than a few hours, the blood supply to the head of the femur can be compromised and permanent damage to the bone can occur. Splint hip fractures or dislocations with a U-shaped foamlite tube, immobilizing the entire leg.

Muscles surrounding the fracture of long bones may contract spastically, causing the bone ends to override. This increases pain and soft tissue damage as well increasing the possibility of artery and nerve injury. Spasm of the large thigh muscles is of special concern in fractures of the femur. A femur fracture can bleed as much as two liters into the surrounding tissues, causing life-threatening shock. The leg may appear shortened and the thigh swollen. The femur is best splinted with traction.

Traction Splints
Traction splints place tension on the muscles surrounding a fracture, reducing pain and spasm and helping with realignment. Traction splints for femur fractures in the wilderness can be complex in design, and the traction straps require constant attention to make sure they are not causing reduced blood flow to the foot. Even with these considerations, traction is the treatment of choice for the midshaft femur fracture.

How to Construct A Traction Splint
Before you begin constructing the traction splint, splint the injury with a full-leg foamlite splint. The leg splint will provide support, insulation and padding. Follow this by applying padding at the ankle.

1. To prepare for applying traction, attach traction straps over the boot or padded ankle. Fold two cravats into long, narrow bandages. Fold length-wise, and pass one over and one behind the ankle, making sure the ends of each bandage are facing in opposite directions. Now pull the ends of each bandage through the loop in the other bandage. The bandages should fit snugly and flat against the ankle. The toes should remain visible or at least accessible for assessing blood flow and nerve function.

2. To construct the traction splint, place ski poles, tent poles or any pole-like object a foot longer than the leg against the outside of the leg. Anchor the pole using a well-padded strap over the thigh at the hip.

3. Apply traction on the thigh by pulling the traction straps. Maintain traction by securing the traction straps to the end of the splint. Tie the traction splint to the leg splint.

TRACTION

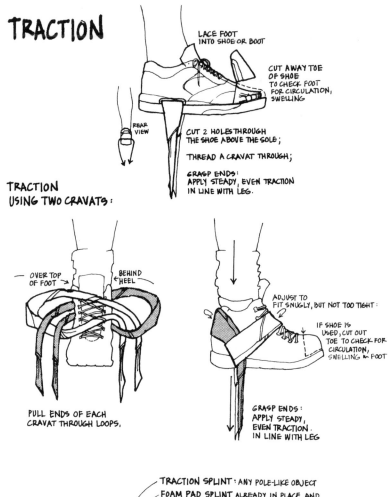

LACE FOOT
INTO SHOE OR BOOT

CUT AWAY TOE
OF SHOE
TO CHECK FOOT
FOR CIRCULATION,
SWELLING

REAR
VIEW

CUT 2 HOLES THROUGH
THE SHOE ABOVE THE SOLE;

THREAD A CRAVAT THROUGH;

GRASP ENDS:
APPLY STEADY, EVEN TRACTION
IN LINE WITH LEG.

TRACTION
USING TWO CRAVATS:

OVER TOP
OF FOOT

BEHIND
HEEL

PULL ENDS OF EACH
CRAVAT THROUGH LOOPS.

ADJUST TO
FIT SNUGLY, BUT NOT TOO TIGHT:

IF SHOE IS
USED, CUT OUT
TOE TO CHECK FOR
CIRCULATION,
SWELLING IN FOOT

GRASP ENDS:
APPLY STEADY,
EVEN TRACTION.
IN LINE WITH LEG

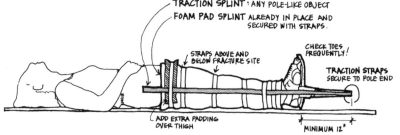

TRACTION SPLINT: ANY POLE-LIKE OBJECT
FOAM PAD SPLINT ALREADY IN PLACE AND
SECURED WITH STRAPS.

STRAPS ABOVE AND
BELOW FRACTURE SITE

CHECK TOES
FREQUENTLY!

TRACTION STRAPS
SECURE TO POLE END

ADD EXTRA PADDING
OVER THIGH

MINIMUM 12"

The Knee

It may be difficult to tell if the femur, the tibia or the knee is injured. Assume the worst and splint the femur. Most knee injuries can be wrapped with an elastic bandage and taped or stabilized with a foamlite splint in such a way that the patient can walk out without further damage. A grossly unstable knee with major ligament rupture will be accompanied by severe pain, inability to move the joint or bear weight, swelling and obvious deformity. This injury requires a simple splint and a litter evacuation.

The Lower Leg

The lower ends of the tibia and fibula are the prominent knobs on the sides of the ankle. The thin layers of skin over the tibia make open fractures common. Splint both the knee and the ankle in a roll of foamlite.

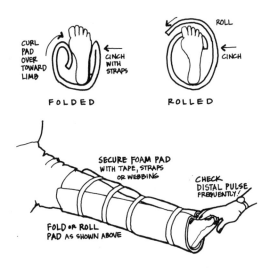

The Ankle

It can be difficult to differentiate between a fracture or a sprain to the ankle. The injury can be immobilized with a stirrup of foamlite and wrapped with clothing for insulation and padding. Knee and ankle injuries are also addressed in Chapter 15 (Athletic Injuries).

Final Thoughts

Fractures and dislocations are not common in wilderness activities, but they do occur, and the first-aider should be prepared. Splinting is a basic skill by which the first-aider can reduce the patient's pain and suffering. Practice improvising splints with available materials.

Summary: Fractures and Dislocations

Fracture: a break in a bone. Skin over an open fracture is broken, exposing bone to infection. Skin over a closed fracture remains intact.

Dislocation: The displacement of a bone from its normal position at a joint.

Signs and Symptoms
Consider the mechanism of injury
Pain and tenderness
Crepitus
Swelling and discoloration
Deformity
Loss of function at a joint (dislocation)
Loss of function at a bone (fracture)

Assessment
Assess the bone or joint
Remove clothing, visualize the injury
Look for deformity, swelling, discoloration
Feel for tenderness, deformity, swelling
Assess circulation
Distal pulse in wrist or foot
Temperature and color in the hand or foot

Assess nerve
  Ask the patient to move fingers or toes
  Test for sensation to touch or pain

Treatment
Immobilize the injury
  Bones above and below dislocations
  Joints above and below fractures
Clean and dress wounds
Remove jewelry, watches and tight clothing
Splint before moving
Elevate to reduce swelling
Assess circulation, temperature and sensation
    before and after splinting
Assess for other injuries
Treat for shock

Consider relocation of a dislocation or angulated fracture if:
  the femur is fractured
  the limb is unsplintable or untransportable in its
      current position
  pulse/sensation is absent

Basic Splints:
  Upper Extremity–sling and swathe
  Lower Extremity–U-shaped foamlite tube

CHAPTER 6
HEAD AND SPINAL CORD INJURIES

Introduction

Head injuries are among the leading causes of death for people between ages one and 42. Each year in the United States, two million people suffer head injury. Of these, 100,000 die and 90,000 become permanently disabled. The care, treatment and rehabilitation of head-injured persons costs tens of billions of dollars annually. The primary cause of head injury is motor vehicle accidents, but outdoor recreational activities including climbing and whitewater boating carry the risk of head injury.

Central Nervous System Anatomy

Together, the brain, spinal cord and peripheral nerves monitor and control all body functions.

The brain governs thoughts, emotions, senses, memory and movement, as well as basic physiological functions. The brain processes information from our senses, initiates motor responses, remembers, solves problems and makes judgments.

The three main divisions of the brain are the cerebrum, the cerebellum and the brain stem. The cerebrum is the largest part of the brain, the center for our "higher" cognitive functions: problem solving, memory, speech, hearing, sight, etc. The cerebellum, in the lower rear of the skull, regulates posture, coordination and motor responses. The brain stem, at the base of the brain, maintains consciousness, heart rate, blood pressure and breathing.

The skull houses and protects the brain. The brain is covered by three layers of tissue, known collectively as the meninges: the dura mater, the pia mater and the arachnoid. Cerebral spinal fluid (CSF), nourishing and cushioning the brain, flows within these layers. Blood vessels are located within the brain and the meninges.

Central nervous system tissue is extremely sensitive to oxygen deficiency. Depriving the brain of oxygen for only a few minutes can result in permanent damage.

Head Injuries

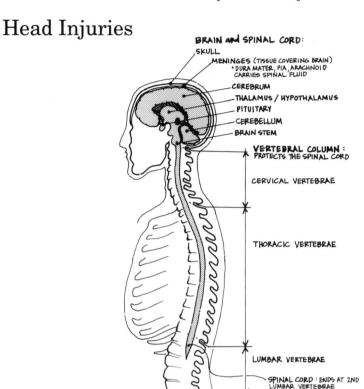

BRAIN and SPINAL CORD:

SKULL

MENINGES (TISSUE COVERING BRAIN)
• DURA MATER, PIA, ARACHNOID
CARRIES SPINAL FLUID

CEREBRUM

THALAMUS / HYPOTHALAMUS

PITUITARY

CEREBELLUM

BRAIN STEM

VERTEBRAL COLUMN :
PROTECTS THE SPINAL CORD

CERVICAL VERTEBRAE

THORACIC VERTEBRAE

LUMBAR VERTEBRAE

SPINAL CORD : ENDS AT 2ND
LUMBAR VERTEBRAE

SACRUM (FUSED)

COCCYX TAILBONE

Head injuries include scalp, skull and brain injuries. A large
blood supply feeds the scalp, causing it to bleed profusely when
cut. A bruised or lacerated scalp can therefore mask underlying
injury to the skull or brain. Examine scalp injuries carefully to see if
bone or brain is exposed or if an indentation, which might be a
depressed fracture, is present. Bleeding from the scalp can be controlled by applying gentle pressure on the edges of the wounds, being
careful to avoid direct pressure on possibly unstable central areas.

The skull consists of 22 fused bones. The strongest are the bones
forming the top and sides of the protective box encasing the brain.
Fractures of the skull are not in themselves life-threatening

except when associated with underlying brain injury or spinal cord injury, or when the fracture causes bleeding by tearing the blood vessels between the brain and the skull. Many serious head injuries occur without skull fractures.

Skull fractures can be open or closed. Open skull fractures, in addition to indicating that the head has been hit hard, expose the brain to infection. A crack to the floor of the skull is called a basal skull fracture.

Brain injury can be fatal when it disrupts heartbeat and breathing. In the long term, a severe brain injury may leave the patient physically immobile or mentally incompetent, with severely impaired judgment and problem solving ability or an inability to process or communicate information properly.

The brain can be injured by a direct blow to the head or by twisting forces, which cause deformation and shearing against the inside of the skull. Some movement between brain and skull is possible. A blow to the head can make the brain "rattle" within the skull, tearing blood vessels in the meninges or within the brain itself.

A concussion is temporary brain dysfunction or loss of consciousness following a blow to the head. There may be no accompanying brain injury. Contusions (bruising of brain tissue) and hemorrhages or hematomas (bleeding within the brain) are more serious injuries that can lead to increased pressure in the skull. Encased in the rigid box, a swelling or bleeding brain will press against the skull; the body has no mechanism to avoid or release such an increase in pressure. As pressure rises, blood supply is shut off by compression of swollen vessels and brain tissue is deprived of oxygen. The brain stem can be squashed by the pressure, affecting heart and lung function.

Signs and Symptoms

Signs and symptoms of head injury depend on the degree and progression of injury. Some indications of head injury appear immediately from the accident; others develop slowly over time.

Signs and Symptoms of Head Injury

Changes in level of consciousness
  Unconsciousness
  Disorientation, confusion, incoherence, irrationality
Headache
Vision disturbances
Loss of balance
Nausea and vomiting
Paralysis
Seizures
Combativeness
Blood or CSF from ears, mouth or nose
Soft tissue injury to skull
Obvious skull fracture
Raccoon sign, Battle's sign
Slow pulse, rising blood pressure, irregular respirations

Changes in Level of Consciousness (LOC)

Loss of consciousness may be short or may persist for hours or days. The patient may alternate between periods of consciousness and unconsciousness or be conscious but disoriented, confused and incoherent–exhibiting changes in behavior and personality or verbal or physical combativeness. The patient may be unconscious but respond to commands, unconscious but respond to pain or totally unconscious and unresponsive.

Headache, Vision Disturbances, Loss of Balance, Nausea and Vomiting, Paralysis, Seizures

Headache, vision problems, loss of balance, nausea and vomiting and paralysis may accompany head injury. In serious cases, the patient may assume abnormal positions with the legs and arms stiff and extended or arms clutched across the chest. A brain-injured patient may have seizures.

Combativeness

A head-injured patient may become combative, striking out randomly and with surprising strength at the nearest person. If the brain is oxygen-deprived, supplemental oxygen and airway maintenance may help alleviate such behavior. Restraint may be necessary to protect the patient and the rescuers.

Blood or CSF, Soft Tissue Injury to Skull, Obvious Skull Fracture, Raccoon Sign, Battle's Sign

Blood or clear fluid (CSF) leakage from ears, mouth or nose is a sign of a skull fracture, as are pain, tenderness and swelling at the injury site or obvious penetrating wounds or depressed fractures. Two other signs of skull fracture–bruising around the eyes (called raccoon sign) and bruising behind the ear (Battle's sign)–usually appear several hours after the injury.

Slow Pulse, Rising Blood Pressure, Irregular Respirations

Changes in vital signs that indicate a serious brain injury are a slow pulse, rising blood pressure and irregular respiratory rate. These contrast with the rising pulse, falling blood pressure and rapid regular respiratory rate seen with shock.

Assessment

Initial assessment of brain injury can be difficult. The symptoms of a concussion, which is the least severe of brain injuries, are similar to those seen in more serious brain injuries. The assessment may also be complicated when the patient's level of consciousness is affected by drugs, alcohol or other traumatic injuries.

Assessment of a head injury begins with checking airway, breathing, circulation (ABC), bleeding and the cervical spine. A patient with a head injury is at high risk for cervical spine injury. Avoid movement of the neck. If you suspect head or neck injury, use the jaw thrust to open the airway.

After a thorough physical assessment, including vital signs, evaluate the nervous system. Note the level of consciousness and the patient's ability to feel and move extremities. Use the

AVPU (conscious and *Alert,* unconscious and responsive *Verbally,* unconscious and responsive to *Pain* or *Unresponsive*) system to assess level of consciousness. Question the patient or bystanders as to a loss of consciousness. Was it immediate, or was there a delay before loss of consciousness? Has the patient been awake but drowsy, sleepy, confused or disoriented? Has the patient been going in and out of consciousness?

Watch any head-injured patient carefully even if the injury does not at first appear serious. Consciousness may progress into disorientation, confusion and, eventually, unconsciousness.

Treatment

An urgent evacuation is required for any patient who has become unconscious, even for a minute or two, or who exhibits vision or balance disturbances, irritableness, lethargy, or nausea and vomiting after a blow to the head. A patient who experiences a brief episode of unconsciousness but who awakens without any other symptoms may be walked out of the mountains with a support party capable of quickly evacuating the patient if the brain condition worsens.

Treatment for Head Injury

ABCs

Assume cervical spine injury

If patient is vomiting, position on side

Control scalp bleeding

Do not control internal bleeding or drainage

Elevate head

Record neurological assessment

ABCs

An injured brain needs oxygen. Ensuring an open airway is the first step in treatment.

If Vomiting, Position Patient on Side

Head-injured patients have a tendency to vomit. Log-rolling the patient onto his/her side while maintaining cervical spine stabilization will help drain vomit while maintaining the airway. Use the jaw thrust to open the airway.

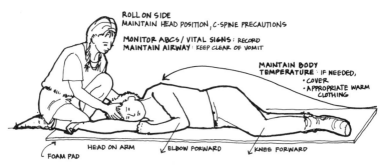

CARING FOR A BRAIN-INJURED PATIENT

Control Scalp Bleeding

Cover open wounds with sterile dressings as a barrier against infection. While it is acceptable to clean scalp wounds, cleaning open skull injuries may introduce infection into the brain, so leave them as you find them. Stabilize impaled objects in place.

Do Not Control Internal Bleeding or Drainage

Do not attempt to prevent drainage of blood or clear cerebral spinal fluid from the ears or nose. Blocking the flow could increase pressure within the skull.

Elevate Head

Keep the patient in a horizontal or slightly head-elevated position. Do not elevate the legs, as this might increase pressure within the skull.

Record Neurological Assessment

Watch the patient closely for any changes in level of consciousness. These observations will be valuable to the receiving physician. Record changes in your patient report.

Spinal Cord Injuries

As with head injuries, spinal cord injuries primarily involve young people, with most cases occurring in men between the ages of 15 and 35. An estimated 10,000 new spinal cord injuries occur each year in the United States, and because central nervous tissue does not regenerate, victims are left permanently disabled–half as paraplegics and half as quadriplegics. Motor vehicle accidents account for the majority of spinal injury cases, followed by diving, motorcycle wrecks and falls.

The spinal cord is the extension of the brain outside the skull. A component of the central nervous system, the spinal cord is the nervous connection between the brain and the rest of the body.

The spinal cord is protected within the vertebrae, 33 of which form the backbone, or spine. A force driving the spine out of its normal alignment can fracture or dislocate the vertebrae, thereby injuring the spinal cord. However, there can be vertebral fractures or ligament and muscle damage to the backbone without damage to the spinal cord. Fractured or dislocated vertebrae can pinch, bruise or cut the spinal cord, damaging the nervous connections.

The smallest vertebrae with the greatest range of motion are in the neck, the most vulnerable part of the spine. From there, the vertebrae become progressively larger as they support more weight. The location of damage to the spinal cord determines whether the patient may die or be left paralyzed from the neck down (quadriplegia) or the waist down (paraplegia).

Assessment

Always assume spinal cord injuries on unconscious accident victims, head-injured patients or anyone who has fallen from a height, undergone a high-velocity skiing fall, diving accident or blow to the head. If the patient is alert and well-oriented, has no other injuries or numbness, weakness or tingling in the extremities and has no complaints of pain or tenderness in the spine, a cervical spine injury is unlikely.

Check for strength, sensation, ability to move and weakness or numbness in the hands and feet. Ask the patient to wiggle fingers or toes, push his feet against your hands or squeeze your hands with theirs. Ask the patient to identify which toe or finger you are touching. If the patient is unconscious, check for sensation by applying a painful stimulus at the toes and fingers (a pinprick or pinch) and watching the patient's face for a grimace.

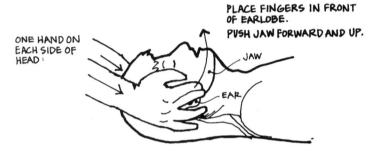

JAW THRUST AIRWAY OPENING FOR SUSPECTED C-SPINE PATIENTS :
- *DO NOT MOVE NECK OR SPINE.*
- *DO NOT TILT HEAD BACK*

PLACE FINGERS IN FRONT OF EARLOBE.
PUSH JAW FORWARD AND UP.

ONE HAND ON EACH SIDE OF HEAD :

JAW

EAR

Signs and Symptoms

Signs and symptoms of spinal cord injury include weakness, loss of sensation or ability to move, numbness and tingling in the hands and feet, soft tissue injury over or near the spine and tenderness on the spine.

Signs and Symptoms of Spinal Cord Injury

Mechanism of injury

Weakness in extremities

Loss of strength or ability to move in extremities

Loss of sensation in extremities

Tenderness in spine

Numbness and tingling in hands and feet

Treatment

Treatment for a spinal cord injury is to stabilize the spine to prevent further damage. While it may be necessary to move a spine-injured patient, your first choice should be on-scene stabilization.

Treatment of Spinal Cord Injury
Stabilize the spine
    Hands on patient's head
    Clothing or blanket roll
Move with log roll or 4-person lift
Immobilize the spine
    Cervical collar
    Backboard

Stabilize the Spine

Before spinal immobilization devices become available, one person should always be at the head of the patient, maintaining stabilization of the neck. A clothing or blanket roll may be used as an improvised cervical collar to aid in stabilization, freeing rescuers for other tasks. A strap of cloth or bandage across the forehead secured with rocks wrapped in clothing protects the head and neck.

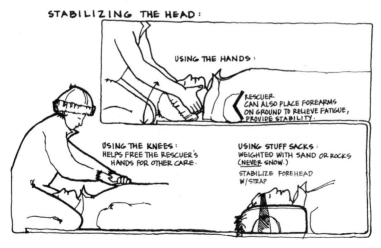

STABILIZING THE HEAD:

USING THE HANDS:

RESCUER CAN ALSO PLACE FOREARMS ON GROUND TO RELIEVE FATIGUE, PROVIDE STABILITY.

USING THE KNEES: HELPS FREE THE RESCUER'S HANDS FOR OTHER CARE.

USING STUFF SACKS: WEIGHTED WITH SAND OR ROCKS (NEVER SNOW.)

STABILIZE FOREHEAD W/STRAP

Move with Log Roll or Four-Person Lift

Assume that the patient may have to be moved at least twice during the rescue—once to place insulation underneath his body to prevent hypothermia and a second time to place him on a litter or backboard. Two common techniques for moving the patient are the log roll and the lift. Practice these under the guidance of an emergency care instructor.

A patient can be assessed and immobilized while lying face down or on his back or side. Unless airway, breathing or bleeding problems are present, you should take the time required to carry out the log roll or lift and to explain your actions to the patient.

Immobilize the Spine

Ideally, the patient should be moved as few times as possible and preferably after immobilization on a backboard, Kendrick Extrication Device, SKED litter, cervical collar or other spine immobilization device. Until such equipment arrives, insulate and shelter the patient. Wilderness treatment may require caring for a patient during prolonged immobilization.

How To Perform a Four-Person Log Roll

The Concept:

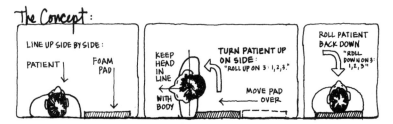

1. The rescuers take positions:
Rescuer #1 maintains stabilization of the head throughout the procedure and gives the commands.

Rescuer #2 kneels beside the patient's chest and reaches across to the shoulder and upper arm of the patient.

Rescuer #3 kneels beside the patient's waist and reaches across to the lower back and pelvis.

Rescuer #4 kneels beside the patient's thighs and reaches across to support the legs with one hand on the patient's upper thigh, the other behind the knee.

Techniques :

RESCUER POSITIONS :

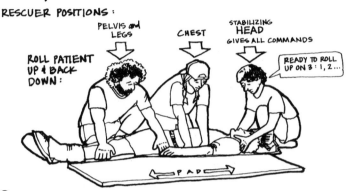

2. The rescuers roll the patient onto his side:
Rescuer #1, at the head, gives the command, "Roll on 3; 1, 2, 3," and the rescuers slowly roll the patient toward them, keeping the patient's body in alignment. Rescuer #1 supports the head and maintains alignment with the spine. Once the patient is on his side, a backboard or foamlite pad can be placed where the patient will be lying when the log roll is complete.

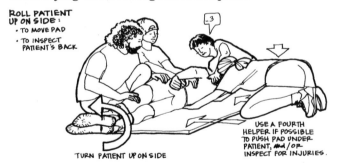

3. The rescuers roll the patient onto his back:
When Rescuer #1 gives the command, "Lower on 3; 1, 2, 3," the procedure is reversed, and the patient is slowly lowered onto the backboard or foamlite pad while the rescuers keep the spine in alignment.

Lifting Technique

The patient can be lifted by four people, enabling a fifth person to slide a backboard, foamlite pad or litter underneath. The rescuer at the head again maintains stabilization during the entire procedure and gives the commands. The other three rescuers position themselves at the patient's sides, one kneeling at chest level and another at pelvis level on the same side while the third rescuer kneels at waist level on the opposite side. Before lifting, the rescuers place their hands over the patient to visualize their hands in position under the chest, lower back, pelvis and thighs. They then slide their hands in accurate position underneath the patient as far as they can without jostling the patient. On command, "Lift on 3; 1, 2, 3," rescuers lift the patient six to eight inches into the air, then lower him onto the pad or litter.

THE LIFT

The Concept:

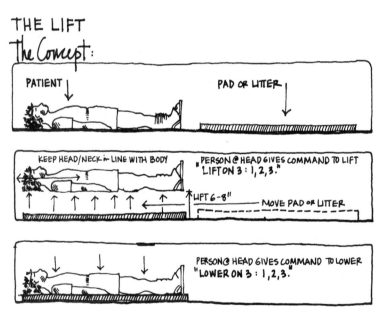

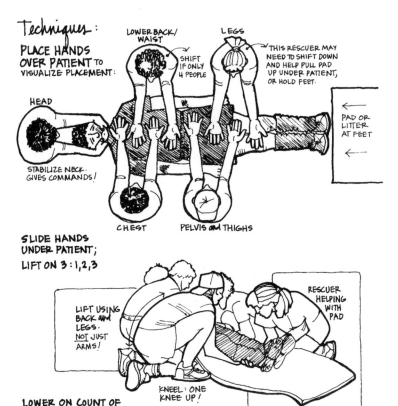

Techniques:
PLACE HANDS OVER PATIENT TO VISUALIZE PLACEMENT:

LOWER BACK/ WAIST

LEGS

SHIFT IF ONLY 4 PEOPLE

THIS RESCUER MAY NEED TO SHIFT DOWN AND HELP PULL PAD UP UNDER PATIENT, OR HOLD FEET.

HEAD

PAD OR LITTER AT FEET

STABILIZE NECK. GIVES COMMANDS!

CHEST

PELVIS and THIGHS

SLIDE HANDS UNDER PATIENT; LIFT ON 3: 1,2,3

LIFT USING BACK and LEGS. NOT JUST ARMS!

RESCUER HELPING WITH PAD

KNEEL: ONE KNEE UP!

LOWER ON COUNT OF 3 WHEN PAD OR LITTER IS IN PLACE.

Final Thoughts

Airway maintenance, cervical spine precautions and patient assessment are important treatments for the head and spine injured, but they are only stopgap measures. Head injury is one of this country's leading killers and disablers of children and young adults. A quarter of head and spine injuries result in death or permanent disability. The cost of treating a serious head injury is staggering. In urban settings, first aid for brain or spine injuries includes rapid transport to neurological hospitals, an impossibility in a wilderness setting.

Prevention is the best treatment: Wear a helmet!

Summary: Head and Spinal Cord Injuries

Head Injuries include scalp, skull and brain injuries. A concussion is temporary brain dysfunction and loss of consciousness following a blow to the head. Contusions, bruising or bleeding into the brain are more serious injuries.

Signs and Symptoms of Head Injury
Changes in level of consciousness
    Unconsciousness
    Disorientation, confusion, incoherence, irrationality
Headache
Vision disturbances
Loss of balance
Nausea and vomiting
Paralysis or numbness/weakness in the extremities
Seizures
Combativeness
Blood or CSF from ears, mouth or nose
Soft tissue injury to skull
Obvious skull fracture
Raccoon sign, Battle's sign
Slow pulse, rising blood pressure, irregular respirations

Treatment of Head Injury
ABCs
Assume cervical spine injury
If vomiting, position patient on side
Control scalp bleeding
Do not control internal bleeding or drainage
Elevate head
Record neurological assessment

The Spinal Cord is the nervous connection between the brain and the rest of the body. Damage to the spinal cord can cause paralysis.

Signs and Symptoms of Spinal Cord Injury
Mechanism of injury
Weakness in extremities
Loss of strength or ability to move in extremities
Loss of sensation in extremities
Tenderness in spine
Numbness and tingling in hands and feet

Treatment of Spinal Cord Injury
Stabilize spine
    Hands on patient's head
    Clothing or blanket roll
Move with log roll or 4-person lift
Immobilize spine
    Cervical collar
    Backboard

CHAPTER 7
CHEST INJURIES

Introduction

Accidents in North American Mountaineering has documented more than a few instances of mountaineers who've suffered serious chest and lung injuries from falls or have punctured their chests with ice axes. Paddlers experience chest injuries from impact with rocks or from blows by the bow of kayaks. Horsepacking and backcountry skiing are other wilderness activities in which there are mechanisms—falls and collisions—for chest trauma. In the backcountry, our role is to recognize the injury, support the patient and organize a rapid evacuation.

Anatomy and Physiology

Chest injuries can be serious if they compromise the respiratory or cardiovascular systems. The respiratory system provides oxygen to and removes carbon dioxide from the body. The cardiovascular system transports these gases as well as nutrients and waste products to and from the cells. Contained within the chest cavity are some of the structures responsible for these processes: the airway passages, lungs, heart and major vessels, vena cava and aorta.

The clavicles, rib cage and diaphragm form the boundaries of the chest cavity. The rib cage consists of 12 pairs of ribs. All the ribs are attached to the spine in the back. The upper seven pairs are attached to the sternum by cartilage; the next three pairs are attached to cartilage only; and the lowest two pairs ("floating ribs") are attached to the spine and not to anything in the front.

The Respiratory System

The components of the respiratory system are the nose, mouth, pharynx, larynx, epiglottis, trachea, bronchi, bronchioles and alveoli. The diaphragm and muscles of the chest wall move air in and out of the lungs.

The average healthy adult breathes twelve to twenty times per minute, moving half a liter of air with each breath. Respiratory rate increases with exercise, altitude, illness or injury. A person in good aerobic shape may breathe only six to eight times a minute.

PARTS OF THE RESPIRATORY SYSTEM :

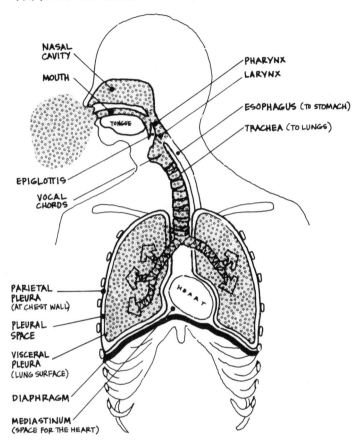

NASAL CAVITY
MOUTH
TONGUE
PHARYNX
LARYNX
ESOPHAGUS (TO STOMACH)
TRACHEA (TO LUNGS)
EPIGLOTTIS
VOCAL CHORDS
HEART
PARIETAL PLEURA (AT CHEST WALL)
PLEURAL SPACE
VISCERAL PLEURA (LUNG SURFACE)
DIAPHRAGM
MEDIASTINUM (SPACE FOR THE HEART)

Nose, Mouth, Pharynx, Larynx

As air enters the nose or mouth it is warmed and humidified by mucous membranes that line the respiratory tract. The mucus produced by the membranes and the cilia (hair-like structures) helps keep foreign material out of the lungs. Air passes from the nose or mouth into the pharynx, past the larynx and into the trachea. The larynx consists of tiny bones, muscles, cartilage and two vocal cords. Air forced past the vocal cords causes them to vibrate, producing sound.

The Epiglottis

The epiglottis sits above the larynx and prevents food from entering the trachea by closing over the larynx during swallowing. If solids or liquids inadvertently enter the larynx, the vocal cords spasm, causing us to cough.

The Trachea

The trachea is approximately five inches long and is composed of cartilage, which prevents the trachea from collapsing. At the bottom of the trachea the tube divides into the right and left bronchi. After air enters the lungs via the bronchi, it follows smaller passageways called bronchioles until it enters the alveoli.

The Alveoli

The alveoli are small air sacs surrounded by capillaries where red blood cells release carbon dioxide and pick up oxygen. Blood then flows into the pulmonary veins, which carry it to the heart and the rest of the body.

The Lungs

The lungs, one on each side of the chest cavity, occupy most of the cavity. Each lung is enclosed by a double-layered membrane called the pleura. The layer that attaches to the lung is called the visceral pleura and the layer attached to the chest wall is called the parietal pleura.

Between the two layers is a thin film of fluid which lubricates the membranes and allows them to move freely. This area is called the pleural space, and under normal conditions it is a potential space under negative pressure. If air enters the pleural space as in a pneumothorax, the potential space becomes an actual space, and the lung collapses.

Inspiration is the active motion of breathing. The diaphragm moves downward, and the intercostal muscles (muscles between the ribs) move the chest wall outward. As the ribs move outward, the negative pressure in the lungs increases and air is sucked into the lung. When the pressure within the lungs and the atmospheric pressure are equal, air stops entering the lungs. At this point the diaphragm and chest muscles relax, elastic recoil reduces lung size, and air is exhaled (expiration).

The Diaphragm

The diaphragm is a specialized muscle that works both voluntarily and involuntarily. The level of carbon dioxide in the blood determines how fast and deeply we breathe. If the level of carbon dioxide in the blood increases, the respiratory center in the brain tells the diaphragm to increase the respiratory rate. If the level of carbon dioxide is too low, the brain tells the diaphragm to slow down. We can directly control the diaphragm by taking deep breaths or by holding our breath but only for short periods of time, after which the involuntary control centers of the brain take over again.

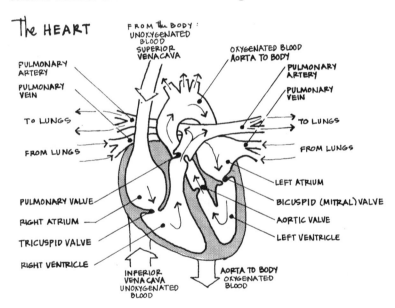

The HEART

FROM the BODY: UNOXYGENATED BLOOD SUPERIOR VENA CAVA

OXYGENATED BLOOD AORTA TO BODY

PULMONARY ARTERY

PULMONARY VEIN

TO LUNGS

FROM LUNGS

PULMONARY ARTERY

PULMONARY VEIN

TO LUNGS

FROM LUNGS

LEFT ATRIUM

BICUSPID (MITRAL) VALVE

AORTIC VALVE

LEFT VENTRICLE

PULMONARY VALVE

RIGHT ATRIUM

TRICUSPID VALVE

RIGHT VENTRICLE

INFERIOR VENA CAVA UNOXYGENATED BLOOD

AORTA TO BODY OXYGENATED BLOOD

The Heart

The heart lies under and to the left of the sternum in the mediastinum—the area between the lungs. The pericardial sac surrounds the heart and contains 20 to 60 milliliters of fluid. The fluid allows the heart to beat freely within the sac.

The heart is about the size of an adult fist. It has four chambers: two atria and two ventricles. Unoxygenated blood flows from the superior and inferior venae cavae into the right atrium. It then enters the right ventricle and travels to the lungs via the pulmonary artery. After picking up oxygen in the lungs, the blood flows back into the left atrium via the pulmonary vein, then into the left ventricle and leaves the heart via the aorta.

The myocardium (heart muscle) is an involuntary muscle under the control of the central nervous system. The heart increases or decreases its pumping rate according to signals from the brain. The heart also has an electrical conduction system of its own. The heart can continue to beat indefinitely if only the higher (thought) centers of the brain are damaged. If the respiratory and cardiac centers stop sending signals, for example, as in drowning, the heart may only continue beating for a few minutes.

An average resting pulse rate for an adult is 60 to 80 beats per minute. A person in good aerobic shape will have a lower pulse rate; a person who is ill or injured may have a higher rate. Tachycardia is when the resting pulse rate is greater than 100/minute; bradycardia, when the resting pulse rate is below 50.

Injuries to the Ribs

Injuries to the chest can be divided into two categories: injuries to the ribs and injuries to the lungs. With all chest injuries, coughing is painful and difficult. Nonetheless, encourage the patient to cough frequently to help move secretions out of the lung and prevent pneumonia. Splinting the chest with the hand or a stuff sack filled with clothes will help the pain when coughing.

Evacuate the patient. If the patient is not in respiratory distress or in danger of further injuring the rib by falling, he can walk out. If the patient is in respiratory distress or suffering from a flail chest, he will need to be carried out.

Rib Fractures

The most commonly fractured ribs are ribs five through 10. Ribs one through four are protected by the shoulder girdle and are rarely fractured. The floating ribs—ribs 11 and 12—are more flexible and will give before breaking.

Signs and Symptoms
Rib fractures cause deformity and/or discoloration over the injured area. The patient complains of tenderness over the fracture (point tenderness) when touched. Breathing or coughing causes sharp, stabbing pain at the site of the fracture. Respiratory rate increases, as the patient breathes shallowly in an attempt to decrease the pain. The patient may clutch the chest on the fractured side in an attempt to splint it. Carefully observe rib fracture victims for other injuries.

**Signs and Symptoms
of Rib Fractures**

Point tenderness over the fracture

Sharp, stabbing pain

Increased, shallow respiratory rate

Treatment
A single fractured rib that is not displaced (simple rib fracture) does not require splinting. Non-narcotic pain medication (acetaminophen or ibuprofen) may be all the treatment necessary. Avoid narcotics (such as codeine and Percodan), as they may depress respiration.

**Treatment
for Rib Fractures**

Tape the fracture site on one side of chest

Elastic bandage around chest

Tape the Fracture Site on One Side of Chest
If the pain is severe, tape the fractured side from sternum to spine with four or five pieces of one- to two-inch adhesive tape. This decreases movement at the fracture site and diminishes pain. Tape should never be wrapped completely around the chest as this can restrict breathing.

Elastic Bandage Around Chest

Alternatively, wrap an elastic bandage around the entire chest. The bandage should be loose enough to allow easy inhalation. At altitudes above 10,000 feet, taping or wrapping the chest may compromise carbon dioxide and oxygen exchange. If a bandage is necessary to control pain, the patient's breathing and color should be watched closely.

Flail Chest

A flail chest occurs when three or more adjacent ribs are broken in two or more places, loosening a segment of the chest wall. When the patient breathes in, the increased negative pressure pulls the flail segment inward and the lung does not fill with air as it should. When the patient breathes out, the opposite occurs, and the flail segment may be pushed outward. The flail segment moves in a direction opposite of normal breathing, thus the term "paradoxical respirations."

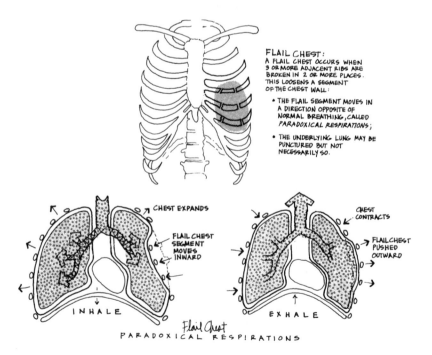

FLAIL CHEST:
A FLAIL CHEST OCCURS WHEN 3 OR MORE ADJACENT RIBS ARE BROKEN IN 2 OR MORE PLACES. THIS LOOSENS A SEGMENT OF THE CHEST WALL:

• THE FLAIL SEGMENT MOVES IN A DIRECTION OPPOSITE OF NORMAL BREATHING, CALLED PARADOXICAL RESPIRATIONS;

• THE UNDERLYING LUNG MAY BE PUNCTURED BUT NOT NECESSARILY SO.

CHEST EXPANDS

FLAIL CHEST SEGMENT MOVES INWARD

INHALE

CHEST CONTRACTS

FLAIL CHEST PUSHED OUTWARD

EXHALE

Flail Chest
PARADOXICAL RESPIRATIONS

Signs and Symptoms

A flail chest develops only with a massive chest injury such as a heavy fall against a rock or a rockfall onto the chest. The patient is in immediate respiratory distress. Put your hands under the patient's shirt and you will feel a part of the chest moving in while the opposite part of the chest is moving out. This is also clearly visible upon inspection.

Signs and Symptoms of Flail Chest

Paradoxical chest movement

Respiratory distress

Treatment for Flail Chest

There are four ways to stabilize a flail segment so that normal respiratory function can continue:

1. Position the patient on the injured side with a rolled-up piece of clothing underneath the flailed segment.

2. Apply pressure with your hand to the flailed area. This works only as a temporary measure, as it is difficult to hold pressure while transporting the patient.

3. Apply a weighted object, such as a small plastic bag filled with sand, to the injured area.

4. Tape a large pad firmly over the flail segment.

Treat the patient for shock and evacuate.

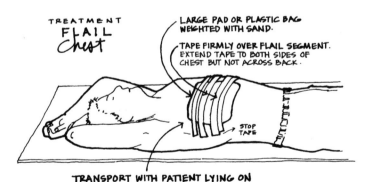

TREATMENT
FLAIL
Chest

LARGE PAD OR PLASTIC BAG WEIGHTED WITH SAND.

TAPE FIRMLY OVER FLAIL SEGMENT. EXTEND TAPE TO BOTH SIDES OF CHEST BUT NOT ACROSS BACK.

STOP TAPE

TRANSPORT WITH PATIENT LYING ON AFFECTED SIDE NOT ON HEALTHY LUNG SIDE.

Injuries to the Lungs

In addition to injuries to the ribs, the underlying lungs may be damaged. Blood vessels can be ruptured and torn, causing bleeding into the chest, and lungs can be punctured causing air to leak into the chest.

Pneumothorax/Hemothorax

Pneumothorax occurs when air leaks into the pleural space creating negative pressure that collapses the lung. Pneumothorax can be caused by a fractured rib that lacerates the lung (traumatic pneumothorax), a weak spot on the lung wall that gives way (spontaneous pneumothorax) or an open chest wound.

Hemothorax occurs when lacerated blood vessels cause blood to collect in the pleural space. The source of blood can be a fractured rib or lacerated lung. A hemothorax, if more than one liter, may compromise lung function by compressing the lung and cause shock from blood loss.

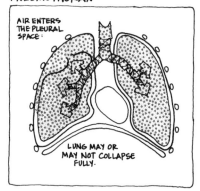

PNEUMOTHORAX

AIR ENTERS THE PLEURAL SPACE:

LUNG MAY OR MAY NOT COLLAPSE FULLY.

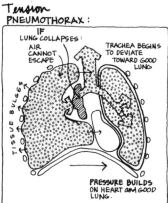

Tension PNEUMOTHORAX:

IF LUNG COLLAPSES:
AIR CANNOT ESCAPE

TRACHEA BEGINS TO DEVIATE TOWARD GOOD LUNG

TISSUE BULGES

PRESSURE BUILDS ON HEART and GOOD LUNG.

Spontaneous Pneumothorax

A congenital weak area of the lung may rupture creating a spontaneous pneumothorax. The highest incidence occurs in tall, thin, healthy men between the ages of 20 and 30. Eighty percent of spontaneous pneumothoraxes occur while the person is at rest. The patient complains of a sudden, sharp pain in the chest and increasing shortness of breath.

Tension Pneumothorax

If a hole opening into the pleural space serves as a one-way valve – allowing air to enter but not to escape– a tension pneumothorax develops. With each breath, air enters the pleural space, but it cannot escape with expiration. As pressure in the pleural space increases, the lung collapses into a ball two to three inches in diameter. Pressure in the pleural space eventually causes the mediastinum to shift to the unaffected side, putting pressure on the heart and good lung. If the pressure in the pleural space exceeds that in the veins, blood cannot return to the heart and death occurs.

As pressure builds, you may see the trachea deviate toward the unaffected side, tissue between the ribs bulge and the neck veins distend. Respirations become increasingly rapid. The pulse is weak and rapid; cyanosis occurs. Listening to both sides of the chest (ear on chest wall) may indicate that air is entering only one side. Tapping on the injured side may produce a drum-like sound.

Open Chest Wounds

If a wound through the chest wall breaks into the pleural space, air enters, creating a pneumothorax. If the wound remains open, air moves in and out of the pleura causing a sucking noise.

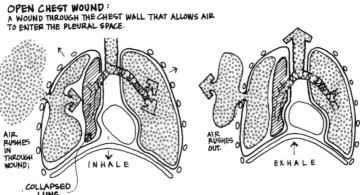

OPEN CHEST WOUND:
A WOUND THROUGH THE CHEST WALL THAT ALLOWS AIR TO ENTER THE PLEURAL SPACE.

AIR RUSHES IN THROUGH WOUND; INHALE

COLLAPSED LUNG

AIR RUSHES OUT. EXHALE

The goal of treatment is to limit the size of the pneumothorax. Quickly seal the hole with any non-porous material—a plastic bag or petroleum jelly-impregnated gauze, for example. Tape the bag or gauze down on all sides to complete the seal. If a tension pneumothorax develops, you can remove the bag or gauze long enough to allow air to exit the wound, then immediately reapply the dressing. You may need to repeat this process several times during the evacuation.

Pulmonary Contusion

A pulmonary contusion is a bruise of the lung. Fluid and blood collect at the site of the bruise interfering with gas exchange. Large pulmonary contusions can cause severe respiratory distress.

Usually the patient has undergone a blow to the chest. The chest wall may be bruised. The patient will be short of breath. Signs and symptoms of shock may be present with large contusions. The patient may cough up blood during the next few days after injury. A severe contusion is almost always associated with several fractured ribs.

Pulmonary Embolism

A pulmonary embolism occurs when a clot (usually from a leg vein) breaks loose and lodges in the blood vessels of the lung. Fat embolism occurs when fat globules are released from broken bones (usually the femur), enter the circulatory system via a lacerated vessel and lodge in the vessels of the lung. The clot or globules impair normal blood flow resulting in shock if the obstruction is severe. Decreased mobility–lying in a tent waiting out a storm, for example–may predispose a person to blood clots.

The patient complains of a sudden onset of shortness of breath and pain with inspiration. Respiratory rate and pulse will be elevated.

> ### Assessment of Injury to the Lungs
>
> General
> Obvious chest trauma
> Shortness of breath

General (Cont.)
  Rapid, shallow respirations
  Cyanosis
  Shock
  Coughing up blood
Pneumothorax/pulmonary embolism
  Sudden, sharp chest pain
Tension pneumothorax
  Tracheal deviation
Open chest wound
  Sucking noise

Treatment for
  Injury to the Lungs

  Maintain an open airway
  Stop the bleeding
  Quickly seal open chest wounds
  Stabilize impaled objects
  Position of comfort for the patient
  Evacuate

Hyperventilation Syndrome

Hyperventilation syndrome is an increased respiratory rate caused by an overwhelming emotional stimulus. The patient becomes apprehensive, nervous or tense. For example, he may normally have a fear of heights, and the thought of rock climbing triggers a hyperventilation episode, or he may fall and suffer a minor injury but begin to hyperventilate out of fear and anxiety. The hyperventilation can quickly become the major condition affecting the patient.

CARPOPEDAL SPASMS
HYPERVENTILATION SYNDROME :

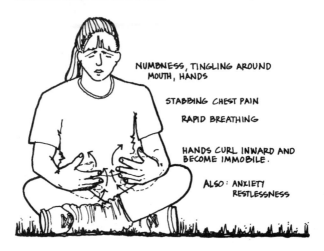

NUMBNESS, TINGLING AROUND MOUTH, HANDS

STABBING CHEST PAIN

RAPID BREATHING

HANDS CURL INWARD AND BECOME IMMOBILE.

ALSO: ANXIETY RESTLESSNESS

Signs and Symptoms

Signs and symptoms of hyperventilation include a high level of anxiety, a sense of suffocation without apparent physiological basis, rapid and deep respiration, rapid pulse, dizzyness and/ or faintness, sweating and dry mouth.

As the syndrome progresses, the patient may complain of numbness or tingling of the hands or around the mouth. Thereafter painful spasms of the hands and forearms— carpopedal spasms—may occur. The hands curl inward and become immobile. The patient may complain of stabbing chest pain. Rapid respiration increases loss of carbon dioxide, which causes the blood to become alkaline. The alkaline blood causes the carpopedal spasms.

Treatment

To treat hyperventilation syndrome, attempt to resolve the emotional concern, and treat the respiratory problem. Your objectives are to increase the carbon dioxide level in the blood and slow the patient's respiratory rate. Breathing into a stuff sack, or any bag, will make the patient re-inhale exhaled carbon dioxide. Reassure the patient by explaining what you are doing and why.

Injuries to the Heart

In addition to the lungs, the heart may also be damaged by blows to the chest. Contusion or bruises to the heart muscle, bleeding into the pericardial sac or damage to the ventricles are grave injuries. Signs of shock and respiratory distress will be evident. In the wilderness, our treatment is supportive—airway, treating for shock and evacuation.

Final Thoughts

Chest injuries range from the painful, but not life-threatening, simple rib fracture to serious injuries of the chest wall, lungs and heart. Chest injuries are often complicated by other injuries as well.

Respiratory Distress

Respiratory distress is an overall term that covers any situation in which a patient is having difficulty breathing. Respiratory distress can occur after an injury, an illness such as pneumonia, during a heart attack or an asthma attack or after inhalation of a poisonous gas.

Signs and symptoms of respiratory distress are anxiety and restlessness, shortness of breath, rapid respirations and pulse, signs of shock, including pale, cool and clammy skin and cyanosis of the skin, lips and fingernail beds, and labored breathing using accessory muscles of the neck, shoulder and abdomen to achieve maximum effort. The patient is usually more comfortable sitting than lying.

Respiratory distress is a frightening experience for both the patient and the rescuer. If the underlying cause is emotional, as in hyperventilation syndrome, a little reassurance may be all that's needed to alleviate the problem. If a chest injury with underlying lung damage or an illness such as pneumonia or a pulmonary embolus occurs, treatment in the field is difficult. Evacuation is the course of action. The airway can be maintained, the patient positioned in the most comfortable position for breathing, the injury splinted or taped, wounds dressed and the patient treated for shock.

Summary: Chest Injuries

Injury to the Ribs

Assessment

Rib fracture
Point tenderness
Sharp pain
Increased, shallow breathing
Flail chest
Paradoxical chest movement
Respiratory distress

Treatment

Rib fracture
Tape the fracture site
Flail chest
Position patient on injured side
with chest supported
Tape a large pad over the flail chest

Injury to the Lungs

Assessment

General
Obvious chest trauma
Shortness of breath
Rapid, shallow respirations
Cyanosis
Shock
Coughing up blood

Pneumothorax/pulmonary embolism
Sudden, sharp chest pain

Tension pneumothorax
Tracheal deviation

Open chest wound
Sucking noise

Treatment

Maintain an open airway
Stop the bleeding
Quickly seal open chest wounds
Stabilize impaled objects
Position of comfort for the patient
Evacuate

Chapter 8
ABDOMINAL INJURIES

Introduction

Abdominal Anatomy and Physiology

Abdominal Illness

Kidney Stones

Appendicitis

Peritonitis

Hemorrhoids

Gastric and Duodenal Ulcers

Gastroenteritis — "Traveler's Diarrhea"

Abdominal Trauma

Abdominal Assessment

Final Thoughts

Summary: Acute Abdominal Pain

Introduction

The abdomen contains the major blood vessels supplying the lower extremities and the digestive, urinary and reproductive systems. A lot can go wrong in the belly, and deciding how serious a problem is can be difficult even for a physician. As first-aiders, our role is ultimately simple–to decide if the problem is an "acute abdomen," and if so, to support and evacuate the patient from the backcountry. Knowledge of the location and function of the abdominal organs and some of the common abdominal problems can make this determination easier.

Abdominal Anatomy and Physiology

The digestive tract processes food to nourish the cells of the body. Secretions within the digestive tract break down food into basic sugars, fatty acids and amino acids. These products of digestion cross the wall of the intestine and travel to the liver via the veins for detoxification. From the liver, blood circulates nutrients to the individual cells of the body.

The Abdominal and Pelvic Cavities

The abdominal cavity, like the chest, is lined by a slippery membrane, called the peritoneum, which covers the organs. The area behind the peritoneum between the abdominal organs and the muscles of the back is called the retroperitoneum. The diaphragm separates the chest from the abdomen.

The liver, gallbladder, stomach, spleen, pancreas, appendix and large and small intestines lie in the abdominal cavity. The kidneys, ureters, adrenals, pancreas, aorta and inferior vena cava are retroperitoneal. The female reproductive organs, bladder, lower end of the large intestine and rectum are located in the pelvic cavity.

The Digestive Tract

The digestive tract starts at the mouth, where food mixes with saliva–a combination of mucus, water, salts, digestive enzymes and organic compounds. As food is swallowed, it passes from the mouth into the pharynx. The pharynx divides into the trachea and esophagus. The trachea lies in front of the esophagus. Food could easily go into the trachea, but a thin flap of cartilage, the epiglottis, closes the entrance to the trachea with each swallow.

The esophagus is a 10-inch muscular tube extending from the larynx to stomach. Contractions of the esophagus–peristalsis –propel food to the stomach.

The Stomach
The stomach is a J-shaped organ approximately 10 inches long located in the upper left quadrant of the abdomen. The major function of the stomach is to intermittently store food and move it into the intestine in small amounts. Every 15 to 25 seconds stomach contractions mix food with gastric juice, turning it into chyme, a thin liquid. Water, salts, alcohol and certain drugs are absorbed directly by the stomach.

ORGANS OF THE
ABDOMINAL Cavity:

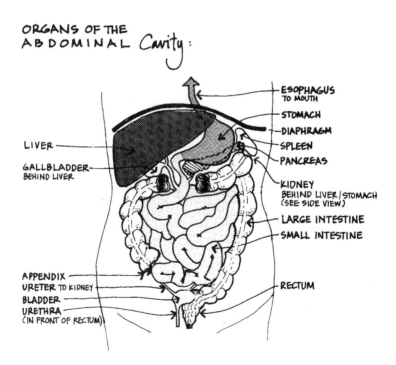

LIVER

GALLBLADDER-
BEHIND LIVER

APPENDIX
URETER TO KIDNEY
BLADDER
URETHRA
(IN FRONT OF RECTUM)

ESOPHAGUS
TO MOUTH
STOMACH
DIAPHRAGM
SPLEEN
PANCREAS
KIDNEY
BEHIND LIVER / STOMACH
(SEE SIDE VIEW)
LARGE INTESTINE
SMALL INTESTINE
RECTUM

The Small and Large Intestines
From the stomach, chyme passes into the small intestine—a tube 21 feet long and one inch in diameter. Within the first foot of the small intestine, food mixes with secretions from the pancreas and gallbladder. Ninety percent of the products of digestion (proteins, fats, carbohydrates, vitamins and minerals) are absorbed in the lower end of the small intestine. Peristalsis moves food through the intestines.

Chyme passes from the small intestine to the large intestine—a tube five feet long and 2-1/2 inches in diameter. The appendix is located just below the junction of the small and large intestines. The large intestine absorbs water, forming a solid stool.

The rectum is where feces are stored. The last two inches of the intestinal tract forms the anus, which consists of a series of sphincters that move the feces out of the body.

The Liver
The liver lies beneath the diaphragm in the upper right quadrant. At four pounds in weight, it is the largest solid organ in the abdomen and the one most often injured. There are 500 functions of the liver, among them: detoxifying the products of digestion, converting glycogen, fat and proteins into glucose, storing vitamins and producing bile.

The Gallbladder
Bile, essential for fat digestion and absorption, is stored in the gallbladder, a pear-shaped organ 3/4 of an inch long. The gallbladder responds to the presence of food (especially fats) in the small intestine by constricting and emptying bile into the intestine.

The Pancreas
The pancreas is an oblong organ located in back of the liver. It contains two types of glands. One produces pancreatic juice, which aids in the digestion of fats, carbohydrates, starches and proteins. The juice flows directly into the small intestine via the pancreatic duct. The other gland secretes chemicals, including insulin, that regulate sugar metabolism.

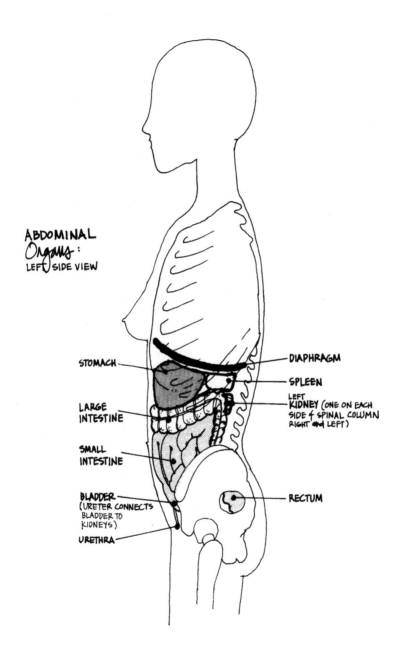

ABDOMINAL
Organs :
LEFT SIDE VIEW

STOMACH

LARGE
INTESTINE

SMALL
INTESTINE

BLADDER
(URETER CONNECTS
BLADDER TO
KIDNEYS)

URETHRA

DIAPHRAGM

SPLEEN

LEFT
KIDNEY (ONE ON EACH
SIDE of SPINAL COLUMN
RIGHT and LEFT)

RECTUM

The Spleen

The spleen, located in the upper left quadrant, beneath the diaphragm, is the only abdominal organ not involved in digestion. The spleen produces blood cells and destroys worn-out red blood cells.

The Urinary System

The urinary system—kidneys, ureters, bladder and urethra— discharge waste materials filtered from the blood. The two kidneys rid the blood of toxic wastes and control water and salt balance. If the kidneys fail to function, toxic waste will concentrate in the blood, causing death.

Urine flows from the kidneys to the bladder via the ureters. The bladder can hold up to 800 milliliters of urine. At 200 to 400 milliliters we feel the urge to void. The bladder empties to the outside via the urethra. In women the urethra is about 1-1/2 inches long; in men, approximately eight inches.

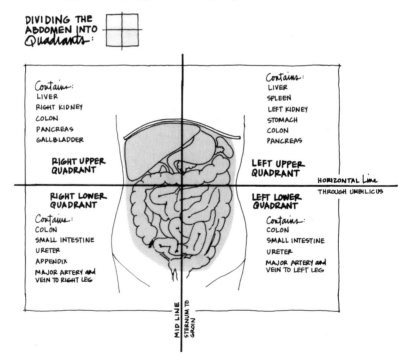

DIVIDING THE ABDOMEN INTO Quadrants:

Contains:
LIVER
RIGHT KIDNEY
COLON
PANCREAS
GALLBLADDER

RIGHT UPPER QUADRANT

Contains:
LIVER
SPLEEN
LEFT KIDNEY
STOMACH
COLON
PANCREAS

LEFT UPPER QUADRANT

HORIZONTAL Line THROUGH UMBILICUS

RIGHT LOWER QUADRANT

Contains:
COLON
SMALL INTESTINE
URETER
APPENDIX
MAJOR ARTERY and VEIN TO RIGHT LEG

LEFT LOWER QUADRANT

Contains:
COLON
SMALL INTESTINE
URETER
MAJOR ARTERY and VEIN TO LEFT LEG

MID LINE
STERNUM TO GROIN

Abdominal Illness

Kidney Stones

Kidney stones occur when minerals precipitate from the urine in the kidney. Approximately 3/4 of kidney stones are crystallized calcium. Predisposing factors for kidney stones include urinary tract infections, dehydration, an increase in dietary calcium, too much vitamin D, and cancer.

Signs and Symptoms

As a stone passes down the ureter, the patient experiences excruciating pain that comes and goes with increasing intensity. The pain usually begins at the level of the lowest ribs on the back and radiates to the lower abdomen and/or groin. The patient is pale, sweaty, nauseated and "writhing" in pain. There may be pain with urination and blood in the urine. Chills and fever will not be present. The duration of the pain depends upon the location of the stone. Pain is severe while a stone is passing from kidney to bladder and stops after the stone has dropped into the bladder. The pain may last as long as 24 hours but the duration is usually shorter.

Treatment

Drinking copious amounts of water may help the patient pass the stone. Pain medication such as Tylenol with codeine or Percocet may relieve some of the pain. If pain continues for more than 48 hours or if the patient is unable to urinate, evacuate.

Appendicitis

Appendicitis is an inflammation of the appendix usually caused by a kinking of the appendix or by a hardened stool obstructing the opening. Due to the obstruction, mucus builds within the appendix causing pressure, swelling and infection. The highest incidence of appendicitis occurs in men between the ages of 10 and 30.

Signs and Symptoms

The classic symptoms of appendicitis are pain behind the umbilicus (the navel), anorexia, nausea and vomiting which develop gradually over one to two days. The pain then shifts to the lower right quadrant, halfway between the umbilicus and right hip bone. The patient may have one or two bowel movements but will usually not have diarrhea. When you apply pressure with your hand over the appendix, the patient may complain of pain when you remove your hand. This is called rebound tenderness. A fever and elevated pulse may be present. Due to infection and pain, the patient may lie on his side or back with legs tucked onto the abdomen (fetal position).

Before the appendix ruptures, the skin over the appendix will be hypersensitive. If you stroke the skin surface with a pin or grasp the skin between the thumb and forefinger and pull upward, the patient may complain of pain. If the appendix ruptures, the pain temporarily disappears but soon reappears as the abdominal cavity becomes infected (peritonitis). If infection remains localized (abscess) the patient may only run a low fever and complain of not feeling well. The abscess may not rupture for a week or more.

Treatment
Appendicitis is a surgical emergency. The patient must be evacuated.

Peritonitis
Peritonitis is an inflammation of the peritoneum. Causes include penetrating abdominal wounds, abdominal bleeding or ruptured internal organs that spill digestive juices into the abdominal cavity.

Signs and Symptoms
Signs and symptoms of peritonitis vary depending on whether the infection is local or general. The patient lies very still, as movement increases pain. He may complain of nausea, vomiting, anorexia and/or fever. The abdomen is rigid and tender. The infection causes peristaltic activity of the bowel to stop, so the patient will have no bowel movements. Shock may be present. The patient appears very sick.

Treatment
Peritonitis is a severe infection beyond our capability to treat in the wilderness; treat the patient for shock and evacuate.

Hemorrhoids

Hemorrhoids are varicose veins of the anal canal. They may be internal or external. Constipation, straining during elimination, diarrhea and pregnancy can cause hemorrhoids. External hemorrhoids can be very painful. Internal hemorrhoids tend not to be painful but bleed during bowel movements. The stool may be streaked on the outside with blood. The patient may complain of itching around the anus.

Treatment

Apply moist heat to the anal area. This can be done with a bandana dipped in warm water. Rest, increased liquid and fruit intake to keep the stools soft, and/or anesthetic ointments (such as Dibucaine Ointment, Preparation H or Anusol) will help decrease pain and bleeding.

Gastric and Duodenal Ulcers

Decreased resistance of the stomach lining to pepsin and hydrochloric acid or an increase in the production of these chemicals may result in ulcers. Stress, smoking, aspirin use, caffeine, alcohol and heredity are possible causes.

Signs and Symptoms

The patient complains of a gnawing, aching or burning in the upper abdomen at the midline one to two hours after eating or at night when gastric secretions are at their peak. The pain may radiate from the lowest ribs to the back and frequently disappears if the patient ingests food or antacids.

Is it indigestion or is it an ulcer? Indigestion symptoms tend to be associated with eating. The patient complains of fullness and heartburn and may belch or vomit small amounts of food. Indigestion worsens when more food is ingested. As time passes and the stomach empties, symptoms disappear. Indigestion tends to be related to a single meal.

Treatment

The primary treatment for ulcers is to take antacids one hour after meals, eat small, frequent meals and avoid coffee, alcohol and spicy foods, which increase the secretions of the stomach. Long-term treatment includes rest and counseling to decrease stress. If the ulcer perforates the wall of the stomach, symptoms of peritonitis occur.

Gastroenteritis—"Traveler's Diarrhea"

Gastroenteritis is an inflammation of the stomach and intestines caused by bacteria, viruses or protozoa. These organisms normally live in our intestines; we develop resistance to the particular strains from our home environment. When exposed to unfamiliar strains, we become sick. These organisms are most commonly transmitted through fecal contamination of water or food.

Signs and Symptoms

The patient experiences nausea, vomiting, diarrhea, headache, abdominal cramps and/or generalized muscular aching. Fever and chills are not usually present. The illness usually lasts two to five days.

Treatment

The goal of treatment is to prevent dehydration and replace electrolytes that are lost in the stools. Diarrhea can cause loss of large amounts of potassium and bicarbonate and varying amounts of sodium and chloride causing an electrolyte imbalance.

The first solid foods the patient takes following an episode of diarrhea should be bland—plain rice, plain oatmeal, dry bread or dry pancakes. See Chapter 19 (Hydration) for more information on preventing dehydration.

Prevention

Always wash your hands with soap and water before preparing meals and after urinating or defecating in order to decrease the risk of transmitting bacteria from the urine or stool to the mouth. See Chapter 17 (Hygiene and Water Disinfection) for further details on hygiene, food-borne illness and proper care when handling food.

Abdominal Trauma

Abdominal organs are either solid or hollow. When hollow organs are perforated, they spill their contents into the abdominal cavity. Solid organs tend to bleed when injured. Either bleeding or spillage of digestive juices causes peritonitis.

Hollow Organs	Solid Organs
stomach	liver
small and large intestine	spleen
gallbladder	pancreas
ureters	kidneys
urinary bladder	

Blunt Trauma
Inspect the abdomen for bruises; consider how the injury occurred to diagnose what, if any, organs may have been damaged. Pain, signs and symptoms of shock and a significant mechanism of injury are reasons to initiate an evacuation.

Penetrating Wounds
Assume any penetrating wound to the abdomen has entered the peritoneal lining. Treat the patient for shock and evacuate.

Impaled Objects
Leave any impaled object in place; removal will increase bleeding. Stabilize the object with dressings. If there is bleeding, apply pressure bandages around the wound. Evacuate the patient by the gentlest means to minimize movement of the impaled object.

Evisceration
An evisceration is a protrusion of abdominal organs through a laceration in the abdominal wall. Cover the eviscerated bowel with dressings that have been soaked in disinfected water. These should be moistened every two hours to prevent the loops of bowel from becoming dry. Several more layers of thick dressings should be applied to the wound to minimize heat loss. Change the dressings daily. Treat for shock and evacuate the patient immediately.

Monitor vital signs hourly for the first 12 hours after treating a patient who has sustained a blow to the abdomen. Check the urine for blood. To do this, have the patient urinate into a water bottle and let the urine settle for at least two hours. Look for reddish fluid near the bottom of the bottle, which indicates the presence of blood in the urine. Report your findings to the physician when you evacuate the patient.

Abdominal Assessment

The first-aider needs a few simple skills to be able to evaluate the condition of a patient with an abdominal problem.

1. Inspect the abdomen. Position the patient in a warm place, lying down. Remove clothing so you can see the entire abdomen. A normal abdomen is slightly rounded and symmetrical. Look for old scars, areas of bruising, rashes, impaled objects, eviscerations and distention. Check the lower back for the same. Look for any movement of the abdomen—wave-like contractions may indicate an abdominal obstruction.

2. Listen to the abdomen in all quadrants. Place your ear on the patient's abdomen and listen for bowel sounds (gurgling noises). An absence of noise indicates an injured or ill bowel. You must listen for at least two to three minutes in all quadrants before you can properly say no bowel sounds are present.

3. Palpate the abdomen. With the palms down, apply gentle pressure with the pads of your fingers. Make sure your hands are warm and that you palpate in all the quadrants. Cold fingers or jabbing can cause the patient to tighten his abdominal muscles, thereby impeding the assessment. The abdomen should be soft and not tender. Abnormal signs include localized tenderness, diffuse tenderness and stiff, rigid muscles ("board-like abdomen").

4. Discuss the patient's condition with him. Ask about pain: Where is it located, where does it radiate to, and what is the severity and frequency? What aggravates/alleviates the pain?

Are there patterns to the pain (at night, after meals, etc.)? Observe facial expressions. Do the patient's facial expressions conflict with his answers? Ask the patient about his past history. Any allergies, past surgery, diagnosis, treatment, or injuries? Have any relatives had abdominal problems? Any problems with swallowing, digestion, bowel, bladder or reproductive organs? Any back or circulation problems?

Final Thoughts

There are many medical problems that cause acute abdominal pain. Determining the actual source of the pain and the urgency of the condition can be difficult, even for a physician. As leader of a wilderness trip, your task is not to make a diagnosis; it is to decide if the pain indicates an "acute abdomen," a possible surgical emergency requiring further evaluation. Severe and prolonged pain indicates a need for evacuation. Pain associated with prolonged vomiting or cramping, fever, inability to move and tenderness and guarding of the abdominal wall reinforces this determination.

Summary: Acute Abdominal Pain

Assessment (Indications for Evacuation)
Severe and prolonged abdominal pain
Pain associated with vomiting, fever
Tenderness or guarding of the abdominal wall
Inability to move

Treatment
Treat for shock
No food/fluids by mouth
Evacuation

CHAPTER 9
COLD INJURIES

Introduction

On a snowy subzero morning in early November, after two days of searching, a lost hunter was found in the Wind River Mountains south of Lander, Wyoming. His nose, hands, feet and stomach were severely frostbitten and he showed limited signs of life. After several hours of evacuation by snow litter and four-wheel drive, rescuers delivered him to the emergency room with a rectal temperature of 74°F.

His ordeal was not over yet. The hypothermia caused his heart to stop, and only after three hours of rewarming and CPR did he begin to recover. His story was presented by the media as one of "miraculous" survival. He was lucky, and he knows it. Today, this man is a strong advocate of prevention.

Knowledge of causes, assessment and treatment of cold injuries is an essential component of wilderness medicine. Hypothermia is usually associated with cold climates, but hypothermia can set in even in warm climates, as it has on NOLS sea kayaking courses in Mexico. If you spend enough time outdoors, you will almost certainly gain firsthand experience with cold injuries such as hypothermia, frostbite and immersion foot.

The Physiology of Temperature Regulation

Humans are warm-blooded animals who maintain a relatively constant internal temperature regardless of the environmental temperature. We do this by producing heat internally by metabolizing food and by adjusting the amount of heat we lose to the environment.

Human cells, tissues and organs operate efficiently only within narrow temperature limits. If our temperature rises 2°F above the normal of 98.6°F, we become ill. If it rises 7°F, we become critically ill. If our temperature decreases 2°F, we feel cold. A 7°F decrease puts our life in jeopardy.

Human beings are designed to live in tropical climates, so our heat loss mechanisms are highly developed. Our insulation mechanisms, however, are less efficient. To adapt structurally to cold, our bodies would have to grow thick insulating hair all over and develop greater reserves of fat. Rather than remaining angular and cylindrical, which promotes heat loss, our body shape would become rounder and shorter to prevent heat loss. This would especially affect our ability to tolerate lower body temperatures and near-freezing temperatures in our fingers and toes.

Physiological adaptations to cold might also include the ability to dramatically increase heat production through fat metabolism and changes in metabolic rate, as well as to develop chemicals that could act like antifreeze in our cells.

As it is, human beings can live in the cold because our intellectual responses enable us to deal effectively with environmental stress. Much of what students learn on NOLS courses is how to live comfortably in extreme environmental conditions by employing skill, disciplined habits and quality equipment. We compensate for our physical deficiencies with behavioral responses such as eating and drinking and creating microclimates through the use of clothing, fire and shelter. The diminished intellectual response evident in early stages of hypothermia, as well as altitude sickness, heat illness and dehydration, dangerously impairs our ability to react to the environment.

Mechanisms of Heat Production
The three main physiological means for producing heat are our metabolic rate, exercise and shivering.

Mechanisms of Heat Production
Resting Metabolism
Exercise
Shivering

Resting Metabolism

The biochemical reactions keeping us alive produce heat as a by-product. Our basal metabolic rate is a constant internal furnace. The rate increases slightly when we are exposed to cold for long periods of time but not enough to satisfy our body's entire heat requirements in winter conditions.

Exercise

Exercise is an important method of heat production. Muscles, which make up 50 percent of our body weight, produce 73 percent of our heat during work. Short bursts of hard physical effort can generate tremendous amounts of heat, while moderate levels of exercise can be sustained for long periods. This valuable source of heat does have its limitations. Physical conditioning, strength, stamina and fuel in the form of food and water are necessary to sustain activity.

An important heat source for infants and hibernating mammals is the oxidation of brown fat from deposits on their abdomen, in their armpits and behind their shoulders. Oxidizing or burning brown fat produces considerable heat—of particular significance for infants, who because of their small size have a large surface area for heat loss. Brown fat cells are almost completely absent in adult humans.

Shivering

Shivering–a random, inefficient quivering of our muscles– produces heat at a rate five times greater than our basal metabolic rate. It is our first defense against cold. Shivering occurs when temperature receptors in the skin and brain sense a decrease in body temperature and trigger the shivering response.

As with all forms of work, the price of shivering is fuel. How long and how effectively we shiver is limited by the amount of carbohydrates stored in muscles and by the amount of water and oxygen available. In order to shiver, we have to pump blood into our muscles. Warm blood flowing close to the surface reduces our natural insulation and increases heat loss.

Shivering also hinders our ability to perform the behavioral tasks necessary to reduce heat loss and increase heat production. It is difficult to zip up your parka, start your stove or ski to camp during violent shivering. On the other hand, vigorous physical activity can override the shivering response, causing a person to cool past the point of shivering without experiencing the response.

Mechanisms of Heat Loss

The core of the body contains the organs necessary for survival: the heart, brain, lungs, liver and kidneys. The shell consists of the muscles, skin and superficial tissues. The ebb and flow of blood from core to superficial tissues is a constant process. As our temperature rises, blood volume shifts and carries heat to the outer layers of the skin. As we cool, less blood flows to the periphery, preserving heat for the vital organs.

Our mechanisms for heat loss are so well developed that we lose heat in all but the hottest and most humid conditions. If on a warm day we do not lose most of the heat our bodies produce, our temperature rises. The primary means of heat loss is through the skin. Warm, flushed skin can dispose of the heat through radiation, convection, conduction or evaporation.

Mechanisms of Heat Loss
Conduction
Convection
Radiation
Evaporation

Our circulatory system controls heat by regulating the volume of blood flowing to the skin and superficial muscles. When we are resting comfortably, only a small percentage of blood flows directly to the skin. During heat stress, however, the blood vessels open up and blood flow to the skin may increase a hundredfold.

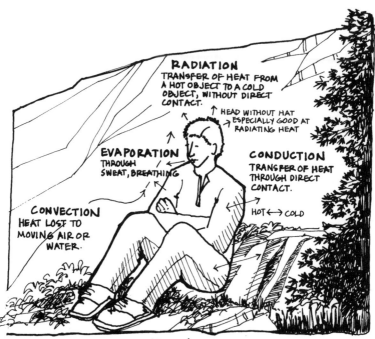

MECHANISMS OF Heat Loss

During cold stress, blood is shunted from the periphery to the core, reducing the heat lost to the environment. Constricted blood vessels can reduce blood flow to the skin by 99 percent.

Conduction

Conduction is transfer of heat through direct contact between a hot and a cold object. Heat moves from the warmer to the colder object. We lose heat when we lie on the cold, wet ground. We gain heat when we lie on a hot beach or rock. The rate of heat transfer is determined by the temperature difference between the two objects, the surface area exposed to the cold surface and the effectiveness of the insulation between the body and the cold surface. The more efficient the insulation, the less heat is transferred. Warm, still air is an effective insulator. Water is a good conductor. Immersion in cold water is a profound threat to temperature balance.

Convection
Convective heat transfer occurs when the medium of transfer moves. Whether through moving air or water, heat escapes from the surface of the body by convection. Moving air (wind chill), besides cooling us directly, strips us of the microclimate of air heated by the body. The loss of this insulating layer next to the body further accelerates heat loss.

Moving water carries heat directly from the surface of the body. To discover the cooling power of moving water, place your fingers in a bowl of cold water. Slowly swirl your fingers. The increase in heat loss is immediately perceptible.

Heat is transferred convectively through the body by the blood. As we cool and the body shunts blood away from the skin, the superficial tissues—especially in our fingers and toes—no longer gain heat from the blood, which increases the likelihood of frostbite.

Radiation
Radiation is the transfer of infrared, or heat radiation, from a hot object to a cold object. In winter, with a normal body temperature of 98°F, we lose heat to the environment through radiation. We can receive radiative heat input from fires, from the sun or from reflection off snow, water or light-colored rocks.

Clear winter nights tend to be colder than cloudy ones. Cloud cover reflects much of the earth's radiative heat back to the ground, reducing the severity of the nighttime temperature drop. Reflected, radiated heat waves bouncing off the walls and snowfields of a cirque during bright sunshine increase warmth—and the possibility of sunburn.

When exposed to the environment, the skin acts as a radiator. Unlike in the rest of the body, the blood vessels in the head do not constrict and reduce the blood supply flowing to the scalp. The head is therefore an excellent radiator of heat, eliminating from 35 to 50 percent of our total heat production. The effectiveness of garments designed to reflect and conserve radiative heat is not agreed upon universally, but the effectiveness of dry insulation, especially on the head, is undeniable.

Evaporation
Heat is necessary to the evaporation of perspiration from the skin's surface. Evaporative heat loss accounts for 20 percent of the body's normal total heat loss. When we become overheated, though, evaporation becomes our major mechanism for heat loss. Evaporation can liberate as much as 1,000 kilocalories an hour.

Sweating accounts for roughly two thirds of our evaporative heat loss. The remaining one third is lost through breathing. Inhalation humidifies air and warms it to body temperature. During exhalation, evaporation of moisture from the surface of the lungs and airways uses heat and cools the body. The rate and depth of breathing and humidity of the air determine the amount of heat and moisture lost. The colder and dryer the air and the faster the breathing rate, the greater the heat loss. To reduce heat loss through evaporation, avoid hard breathing and sweating. Sweating in cold environments is a bad habit. It wets insulation and cools the body.

A constant balance of heat gain and loss is required to maintain a stable body temperature. The adjustments the body makes are designed to keep our vital organs—heart, brain, lungs, kidneys and liver—within a temperature range in which they operate effectively. If core temperature rises above normal, potentially life-threatening conditions—heat stroke or high fever—develop. When core temperature drops below normal, hypothermia may be the result.

Hypothermia
Hypothermia occurs when body temperature drops to 95°F or lower, a condition that is not exclusive to the winter environment. Hypothermia can develop whenever heat loss exceeds heat gain and is as common during the wind, rain and hail of summer as it is during winter. Immersion in cold water can cause hypothermia. If body temperature drops as low as 80°F, death is likely.

Signs and Symptoms

The signs and symptoms of hypothermia change as body temperature falls. Mental functions tend to go first, and the patient loses his ability to respond appropriately to the environment. Muscular functions deteriorate until he is too clumsy to walk or stand. Biochemical processes become slow and deficient as the body cools.

Signs and Symptoms of Hypothermia

Mental

  Deterioration in decision making ability

  Slow and improper response to cold

  Apathy, lethargy

  Increased complaints, decreased group cooperation

  Slurred speech, disorientation progressing to incoherence
      and irrationality and possible unconsciousness

Muscular

  Shivering

  Loss of fine motor ability progressing to stumbling,
      clumsiness and falling

  Muscle stiffness and inability to move
      (in severe cases)

Hypothermia in which body temperatures remain above 90°F is classified as mild to moderate. Hypothermia below 90°F is severe. A healthy adult with a body temperature of 93°F is dangerously cold, but chances are good that rewarming will be successful. If the same person has a temperature of 90°F or less, rewarming in the backcountry can be difficult, and the patient's life may be in grave danger.

Early signs and symptoms of hypothermia can be difficult to recognize and may easily go undiagnosed. The patient does not feel well. You may assume he is tired, not hypothermic. Yet this is the stage in which successful rewarming in the wilderness is possible if our awareness is such that we catch the problem.

On the other hand, hypothermia in its later stages may be more obvious. The patient collapses, slurs his words, is semi-conscious, grossly uncoordinated or unconscious and unresponsive. This stage of hypothermia is easier to recognize, yet much harder to treat in the wilderness.

Mild Hypothermia

In the early stages of hypothermia the patient feels chilled. The skin may be numb with goose bumps. Minor impairment of muscular performance is evident in stiff and clumsy fingers. Shivering begins. Mental deterioration occurs at the same time. Responses are slow and/or improper, such as not changing into dry clothes or failing to wear a rain jacket, wind garments or hat.

Shivering is the first response to cold. It reaches its maximum when body temperature has fallen to 95° to 93°F. Shivering stops when the temperature falls to 92° to 90°F. During the fast cooling phase, the pulse rate increases to as high as 150 per minute. Later, as the body becomes cooler, pulse rate and blood pressure falls. Respirations slow and may finally cease around 78°F.

Moderate Hypothermia

As body temperature drops into the mid-nineties, muscular coordination deteriorates. The patient may stumble, walk slowly, lack energy and become apathetic and lethargic. He talks less and may become uncooperative and complaining. Responses to questions may be inappropriate; the patient may exhibit slurred speech and confusion about time or place.

As body temperature approaches the low nineties, gross muscular incoordination becomes obvious: stumbling, falling, and inability to use hands. The patient may become cantankerous or forgetful and display inappropriate behavior.

Severe Hypothermia

When body temperature drops below ninety, shivering stops. Energy reserves are depleted and obvious mental deterioration is present, along with incoherence, disorientation and irrationality likely. Exposed skin is very cold and may be blue.

In the mid-to-low eighties, severe muscular rigidity may occur. The patient may become unconscious and exhibit dilated pupils. His pulse may be undetectable and he may appear to have stopped breathing or to have already died.

Recognizing Hypothermia (Assessment)

Hypothermia is easily overlooked in the wilderness and has been mistaken for fatigue, irritability, dehydration and mountain sickness. It may be associated with illnesses such as diabetes, stroke and drug overdose.

The most important diagnostic tools in the backcountry are the first-aider's awareness of and suspicion concerning the condition and his attention to the patient's mental state. Oral or axillary temperatures may not reflect the status of the core organs; a rectal temperature is the most accurate temperature available in the field. However, obtaining a rectal temperature reading on a cold and confused patient can be awkward. Also, exposing the patient in order to obtain a rectal reading may cause further cooling. Whether you can obtain a rectal temperature or not, if you suspect hypothermia, treat it immediately and aggressively.

Conventional thermometers read only to 94°F. Low-reading thermometers should be included in the first aid kits of cold weather rescue units or of any outdoor group traveling in a potentially cold environment.

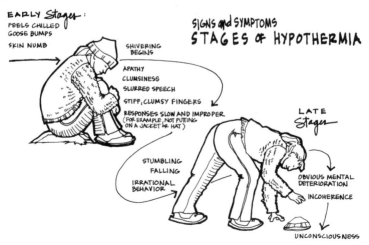

EARLY *Stages* :
FEELS CHILLED
GOOSE BUMPS
SKIN NUMB

SHIVERING BEGINS
APATHY
CLUMSINESS
SLURRED SPEECH
STIFF, CLUMSY FINGERS
RESPONSES SLOW AND IMPROPER
(FOR EXAMPLE, NOT PUTTING ON A JACKET OR HAT)

STUMBLING
FALLING
IRRATIONAL BEHAVIOR

SIGNS and SYMPTOMS
STAGES OF HYPOTHERMIA

LATE *Stages*

OBVIOUS MENTAL DETERIORATION
INCOHERENCE

UNCONSCIOUSNESS

Anyone in a cool or cold environment is at risk for hypothermia. Persons with altered mental status (confused, slurred speech, disoriented) in the outdoors may be hypothermic. Any ill or injured person may have difficulty maintaining proper body temperature.

Assessment of Hypothermia

Above 90°F (Mild and Moderate)
    Conscious
    Shivering
    Able to walk
    Alert

Below 90°F (Severe)
    Abnormal level of consciousness
    No shivering
    Unable to walk
    Decreased mental awareness

Treatment for Hypothermia

Prevention of hypothermia is simple. Treatment is not. Rewarming can be a long and complex process taking hours, and it may be impossible in the backcountry.

Mild to Moderate Hypothermia

A mildly hypothermic patient may be rewarmed in the field. In the absence of a serious underlying medical condition, the chances for successful rewarming are good. The patient in early hypothermia may respond well to removal of the cold stress. While we cannot change the air temperature, we can replace wet clothing with dry, protect the patient from the wind, add layers of insulation and apply heat.

Severe Hypothermia

A severely hypothermic patient produces little or no heat and in the absence of external heat sources may cool further. A cold heart is susceptible to abnormal rhythms such as ventricular fibrillation, a random quivering of the heart that fails to pump blood. Jarring or bouncing, almost inevitable in transport from the backcountry, can trigger this rhythm.

There may be complications from an underlying medical condition or trauma and complex disturbances in the body's biochemical balance. For these reasons a patient with severe hypothermia must be rewarmed in a hospital.

Evacuation of the severely hypothermic patient must occur simultaneously with attempts to prevent further cooling. If you do not apply heat to the patient during transport, further cooling is almost certain. Monitor ABCs and vitals and carry the patient as gently as possible.

Treatment for Hypothermia

Above 90°F (Mild and Moderate)
Prevent further heat loss
Remove from cold
Dry
Insulate
Actively rewarm
Sleeping bags
Heat sources
Hydrate, hot drinks

Below 90°F (Severe)
Evacuate to rewarm
Dry, insulate
Prevent further heat loss (apply heat)
ABCs
Handle gently

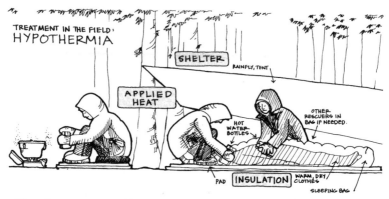

TREATMENT IN THE FIELD:
HYPOTHERMIA

Backcountry Rewarming Techniques

Most rewarmings are simple. We dry the patient, dress him in warm clothes, give him a hot drink and everything works out fine. If the patient is more seriously cold, we usually place him in a sleeping bag with warmers inside, build a fire and take other aggressive actions as necessary.

Backcountry Rewarming Techniques*

Simple Rewarming (Prevent Further Heat Loss)

　Remove from the cold environment

　Dry the patient, dress in dry clothing

　Insulate the head and neck

Complex Rewarming

　Feed and hydrate the patient, if conscious and alert

　Place patient in sleeping bag(s) with other person(s)

　Place hot water bottles on torso

　Use fires as heat sources

　Feed, hydrate and rotate the warmers

　Be persistent; rewarming takes time

　Monitor ABCs

　Handle the patient gently

*These are options for rewarming hypothermic patients in the backcountry. "Simple" and "complex" do not necessarily correspond with "mild or moderate" (above 90°) and "severe" (below 90°).

Prevent Further Heat Loss

Remove the patient from the cold environment and make sure he is dry. Dress him in dry clothing, especially a hat to reduce heat loss from the head and neck. For mild hypothermia, this and a hot drink are often all the treatment that's needed.

Feed and Hydrate the Patient, if Conscious and Alert

Hot drinks are a good source of heat, fluid and sugar. Again, be careful of burning the patient. The patient must be conscious and alert to drink. Hydrate and feed with hot drinks and simple foods, such as candy bars, followed by a good meal after he is rewarmed. A rewarmed patient should not return to the cold until his energy and fluid reserves have been replenished. A fatigued or dehydrated patient is a strong candidate for another episode of hypothermia.

Place the Patient in Sleeping Bag with Other Person(s)

A sleeping bag is the backcountry's most tried and true rewarming tool. Place the patient in one or more bags with at least one other person as a heat source. If the patient is left alone in the bag, he will only be insulated at his current body temperature, since the hypothermic patient has lost the ability to produce heat himself. In fact, further cooling may occur.

Clothing placed over the opening of zipped-together sleeping bags helps reduce heat loss. Several sleeping bags placed over the patient and the warmers will also help. The more humid environment inside the sleeping bag reduces respiratory heat loss as does loosely wrapping a scarf or other article of clothing across the patient's mouth and nose.

In our experience, it's best to keep the rewarmed patient in the sleeping bag for a good night's sleep and to give him a good hot meal and several liters of water.

Place Hot Water Bottles on Torso

Hot water bottles applied to the chest, abdomen, neck and groin—areas close to the core and containing large blood vessels—are an excellent source of heat. Be careful not to burn the patient. Apply the hot water bottles to yourself before applying them to your patient. Wrap them in socks to insulate them from direct contact with the patient.

Use Fires as Heat Sources

Fires are an excellent source of heat. Position the patient in the sleeping bag next to or between two fires. Use a space blanket as a reflector. If you are without a sleeping bag, dress the patient in dry clothes for insulation. One or more individuals huddling around or hugging the patient will provide insulation and heat. A windproof outer layer will reduce the patient's convective and evaporative heat loss.

Feed, Hydrate and Rotate the Warmers

Warmers expend energy to rewarm the patient and in the process themselves become potential hypothermia victims. Watch the warmers, they need to be fed and hydrated or they may become hypothermic.

Be Persistent; Rewarming Takes Time

Individuals such as the hunter described in the Introduction have recovered from prolonged, profound hypothermia. Newspaper headlines occasionally describe "frozen and dead" people who were successfully rewarmed. The adage to remember about hypothermia treatment is that "the victim is never dead until he is warm and dead."

Monitor ABCs

It may be difficult to find the pulse or respiration rate of a cold patient. A severely cold patient may have a heart rate of 20 to 30 beats per minute and be breathing only three to four times a minute. Cold reduces metabolic demands; a patient can sustain life with these abnormally low rates. Take your time during assessment.

The Wilderness Medical Society advises not to start CPR on a hypothermia victim if the chest wall is frozen. Prognosis is poor for patients with a core temperature below 82°F, patients who have been underwater for more than 40 minutes, or have life-threatening injuries, or if transport time to a hospital is more than four hours. If you do start CPR on a hypothermic patient, you are committed to continuing it until the patient is rewarmed.

Because of the cold patient's reduced physiological processes, some experts advise delaying CPR until the patient's core temperature reaches at least the high eighties and reducing the rate of compressions and ventilations to half of normal. Check with your local physician to see if protocols for CPR and hypothermia have been established in your area.

Frostbite

Frostbite acts locally on areas such as fingers, toes and ears. It is not life-threatening, but tissue damage from frostbite can result in loss of function or, in serious cases, gangrene and amputation.

Frostbite occurs when tissue is frozen. As blood flow declines, cooling can progress to freezing. The fluid between cells freezes. The formation of ice crystals draws water out of the cells, dehydrating them. Mechanical cell damage also occurs as the crystals rub together. Blood clots in small vessels and circulation stops, further damaging cells.

A second phase of injury occurs during rewarming. Damaged cells release substances that promote constriction and clotting in small blood vessels, impairing blood flow to the tissues.

Causes of Frostbite

Cold stress
Low temperatures
Wind chill
Moisture
Poor insulation
Contact with supercooled metal or gasoline
Interference with circulation of blood
Cramped position
Tight clothing (gaiters, wristwatches, etc.)
Local pressure
Tight fitting or laced boots
Dehydration

Low temperatures, contact with moisture and wind chill accelerate heat loss and increase the likelihood of frostbite. Metal and petroleum products can cool well below the point of freezing. Skin contact with metal or supercooled gasoline will cause immediate freezing. Constriction of an extremity, as caused by tight boots, gaiters or watchbands, or confinement in a cramped position may reduce blood flow and increase the likelihood of frostbite.

Remember: blood brings oxygen and nutrients to the tissue, as well as heat. Dehydration and hypothermia impair circulation to the extremities by reducing the available fluid and by promoting constriction of blood vessels to preserve heat in the core.

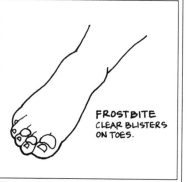

FROSTBITE
CLEAR BLISTERS
ON TOES.

Frostnip

Simple classification of frostbite includes frostnip, superficial frostbite and deep frostbite. Many experts classify frostbite only after it has thawed and the extent of the damage is apparent.

With frostnip only the outer layer of skin is frozen. It appears white and waxy or possibly gray or mottled. Frostnip may occur from contact with a cold metal or a supercooled liquid or from exposure to severe wind chill. High winds together with cold temperatures create conditions for frostnip on exposed areas of the face, nose, ears and cheeks.

Frostnip is similar in physiology to a first degree burn and is sometimes called first degree frostbite. After the nipped area is rewarmed, the layer of frozen skin becomes red. Over a period of several days the dead skin will peel. As it heals, the appearance of the injury is similar to that of sunburn, a first degree burn.

Warm frostnip immediately. Placing a warm hand on a cheek, placing cold fingers into an armpit or warm (100° to 108°F) water will rewarm the frozen area. Covering up from the wind and cold, thereby reducing the exposure, should prevent further injury.

Superficial Frostbite

Superficial frostbite injures a partial thickness of the skin, similar to a second degree burn. This injury has progressed from frostnip into the underlying tissues. Externally it appears as a white, mottled or gray area. It feels hard on the surface, soft and resilient below. Blisters usually appear within 24 hours after rewarming.

Treatment for second degree or superficial frostbite is rapid rewarming by immersion in warm (100° to 108°F) water. This injury extends into the underlying tissues and is more extensive than frostnip. Unlike frostnip, the injury should not be rewarmed by simple application of heat. Proper rewarming is crucial to healing.

Deep Frostbite

The most serious form of frostbite is deep or third degree frostbite. The injury extends from the skin into the underlying tissues and muscles. The external appearance is the same as frostnip and superficial frostbite, but the frozen area feels hard. After thawing the area may not blister or may blister only where deep frostbite borders on more superficial damage.

Differentiating superficial from deep frostbite before thawing is difficult. Blisters containing clear fluid, extending to the tips of the digits and forming within 48 hours of rewarming suggest superficial frostbite. Blood-filled blisters that don't reach the tips of the digits, delayed blisters or the lack of blisters indicates deep frostbite. Like superficial frostbite, deep frostbite is rewarmed by immersion in warm water.

Treatment for Frostbite

Dangerous folk remedies for frostbite include rubbing the frozen part with snow, flogging the area to restore circulation and exposing it to an open flame. The treatment of choice is rapid rewarming in warm water.

Treatment for Frostbite

Delay rewarming until it can be done once and done well
Rapidly rewarm in warm water
  The water should be between 100° and 108°F
  Completely immerse the frozen tissue
  Use a large basin
  Thaw completely

Post-thaw care
  Protect the thawed tissue from trauma
  Elevate to reduce swelling
  Place pads between toes and fingers
  Do not constrict the extremity
  Prevent refreezing

Delay Rewarming

Try to keep the injury frozen until rewarming can be carried out correctly. Many people, including this author, have traveled long distances with frozen feet in order to reach a place where rewarming could be done once and done well. How long the area can be kept frozen without increasing the damage is a matter of controversy. Tissue damage does seem related to the length of time the tissue stays frozen.

There are several problems with keeping a frostbitten extremity frozen while evacuation takes place. If the injury occurred from exposure to extreme cold, lack of proper clothing or in conjunction with hypothermia, the frostbitten area may rewarm as the problem that caused it is corrected. The activity of traveling may generate enough heat to begin thawing, thus increasing the possibility of further injury from refreezing or bruising. Unintentional slow rewarming is common.

If the injury is confined to a small area of the body, tips of toes or fingers, slow thawing is likely, and field rewarming should be started. If the injury is extensive, thawing will be difficult. Try to keep the area frozen. Adjustments in clothing and work rate will be necessary.

Rapidly Rewarm In Warm Water

Treatment for frostbite, best done in a hospital, is rapid rewarming in water between 100° to 108°F. Use a thermometer to ensure that the water is the proper temperature. For a rough estimate, 105°F is hot tap water. Water colder than 100°F will not thaw frostbite rapidly. Water hotter than 108°F may burn the patient.

Water temperature should remain constant throughout the procedure. This requires a source of hot water and several containers large enough to contain the entire frozen part. Do not pour hot water over the frozen tissue. Rather, immerse the frozen area, being careful not to let it touch the sides or bottom of the container. When the water cools, remove the frostbitten part, quickly rewarm the water and re-immerse the part.

Thawing frozen fingers generally takes 45 minutes. There is no danger of overthawing, but underthawing can leave tissue permanently damaged. A flush of pink indicates blood returning to the affected site. Rewarming frostbite is generally very painful. Aspirin or ibuprofen are appropriate for pain relief. If hypothermia is present, it takes priority in treatment.

Post-Thaw Care
Air dry the extremity carefully; don't rub. Swelling will occur, along with blister formation. Inserting gauze between the fingers or toes will keep these areas dry as swelling occurs. Blisters may be drained with a sterile syringe and then dressed with aloe vera ointment. Once the tissue is thawed, it is extremely delicate and seemingly minor trauma can damage it.

Prevent refreezing after thawing. The freeze-thaw-freeze sequence will produce permanent tissue damage. The seriousness of frostbite injury is increased if freeze-thaw-freeze has occurred or if it is accompanied by fracture or soft tissue injury.

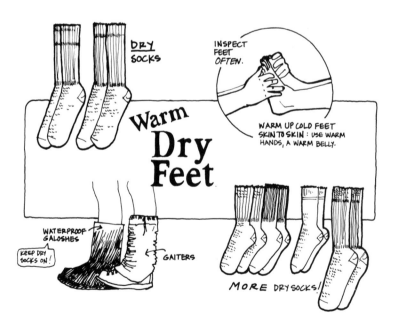

Immersion Foot

Immersion foot is a local, non-freezing cold injury that occurs in cold, wet conditions, usually in temperatures of 30° to 40°F. At least 12 hours' exposure to cold, wet conditions is necessary to produce the injury. People have contracted immersion foot in hip waders and vapor barrier boots. Dry socks and feet provide total protection.

Immersion foot occurs when cold, wet conditions constrict blood vessels. Reduced blood flow to the extremity deprives cells of needed oxygen and nutrients. Permanent muscle and nerve damage may result.

Signs and Symptoms of Immersion Foot

The extremity appears cold, swollen and mottled. Cyanosis is usually present. Tactile sensitivity is reduced, as is capillary refill time. The foot may look shiny. The patient may describe the foot as feeling wooden.

When the extremity rewarms, the skin becomes warm, dry and red. The pulse is bounding. The injury is painful. The injured area may itch, tingle and exhibit increased sensitivity to cold, possibly permanently. The recovery period can last weeks. Nerve damage may be permanent. The development of blisters, ulcers and gangrene is possible. Loss of a foot or lower leg is also possible.

Signs and Symptoms of Immersion Foot

Cold, mottled extremity
Foot feels "wooden, numb, pins and needles"
When rewarmed, the foot becomes red, dry and painful
    with bounding pulses

Prevention
    Rotate socks as needed to keep feet dry
    Check feet daily
    Sleep with feet warm and dry

Treatment for Immersion Foot

Warm an immersion foot slowly at room temperature. In serious cases swelling, pain and blister formation will prevent walking. In most cases the extremity will be sore. Avoid walking on injured feet, and elevate the feet to reduce the swelling. Bed rest, along with avoiding trauma, is necessary until the injury heals.

Treatment for Immersion Foot
Remove the feet from the cold, wet environment
Air dry
Do not constrict the extremity
Protect the feet from trauma
Elevate the feet to reduce the swelling

Final Thoughts: Prevention

The possibility of cold injury is our constant companion on wilderness trips. You can successfully treat hypothermia, frostbite and immersion foot 24 hours a day by practicing prevention.

Summary: Cold Injuries

Hypothermia is a lowering of the core body temperature occurring when heat loss exceeds heat production. It is a dangerous disturbance of body function. Mild hypothermia (above 93°F–patient conscious, shivering, able to walk) is treatable in the field. Severe hypothermia (below 93°F–patient unconscious, not shivering, unable to walk) requires rewarming in a hospital.

Signs and Symptoms of Hypothermia
Mental
    Deterioration in decision making ability
    Slow and improper response to cold
    Apathy, lethargy
    Increased complaints, decreased group cooperation
    Slurred speech, disorientation progressing to incoherence
        and irrationality and possible unconsciousness
Muscular
    Shivering
    Loss of fine motor ability progressing to stumbling,
        clumsiness and falling
    Muscle stiffness and inability to move
        (in severe cases)

Treatment for Hypothermia
Mild Hypothermia
    Prevent Further Heat Loss
        Dry
        Remove from cold
        Insulate
    Actively Rewarm
        Hydrate, Hot Drinks
        Food
        Sleeping Bags

Summary: Cold injuries, Cont.

Severe Hypothermia
    Evacuate to Rewarm
        Dry, insulate
        Prevent further heat loss (apply heat)
        ABCs
        Handle gently

Frostbite is a local freezing injury classified as frostnip, superficial or deep. Frostbitten tissue is cold, gray, white or mottled. Frostnip only affects the skin and is easily treated with immediate rewarming. Superficial and deep frostbite progress into underlying tissue layers and should be rewarmed rapidly in warm water.

Treatment for Frostbite
Delay rewarming until it can be done once and done well
Rapidly rewarm in warm water
    The water should be between 100° and 108°F
    Completely immerse the frozen tissue
    Use a large basin
    Thaw completely
Post-thaw care
    Protect the thawed tissue from trauma
    Elevate to reduce swelling
    Place pads between toes and fingers
    Do not constrict the extremity
    Prevent refreezing

Immersion foot is a local, non-freezing injury. Signs and symptoms are swollen, cyanotic and mottled feet with slow capillary refill.

Treatment for Immersion Foot

Remove the feet from the cold, wet environment

Air dry

Do not constrict the extremity

Protect the feet from trauma

Elevate the feet to reduce the swelling

MORE DRY SOCKS!

CHAPTER 10
HEAT ILLNESS

Introduction

Our bodies produce heat constantly. When heat production exceeds heat loss, body temperature rises. Factors that reduce heat loss include high environmental temperature, excessive clothing and inability to sweat. To survive in a hot environment, human beings must eliminate enough heat to keep the body temperature within acceptable limits—97°F to 100°F. Vital organs are irreversibly damaged when the body temperature stays at or above 107°F for any length of time.

Heat illness is unusual on NOLS courses because we are diligent and aggressive with prevention. Outdoor leaders should be knowledgeable about the causes, recognition and treatment of heat illness. Preventing heat illness, like preventing hypothermia, frostbite, altitude illness and dehydration, is a 24-hour-a-day task.

Physiology

The body generates 2,000 to 5,000 kilocalories (kcal) of heat per day. Every metabolic function, blink of the eye and beat of the heart produces heat. Basal metabolism alone would raise the body temperature 1.5°F per hour if heat were not dissipated.

Organs responsible for heat loss are the skin, cardiovascular system and respiratory system. As discussed in Chapter 9 (Cold Injuries), the four main mechanisms by which the body loses heat are radiation, evaporation, convection and conduction. Of these, radiation and evaporation are the body's primary two avenues of heat loss.

Radiation

Under heat stress, the body dilates superficial blood vessels, increases heart rate and cardiac output and directs more blood to the skin. Normally one third to one half a liter of blood per minute is shunted to the skin and superficial tissues. The body can increase skin blood flow to four liters per minute when it is heat stressed.

Radiation accounts for 65 percent of the heat lost when the air temperature is lower than body temperature. In hot environments radiation is a major source of heat gain. The body can gain up to 300 kcal per hour when exposed to the sun.

Evaporation

Sweating by itself does not cool skin. Evaporation of perspiration cools the body because heat is necessary to change water from liquid to vapor. A heat-acclimatized person can sweat as much as two liters per hour for a total loss of one million kilocalories of heat.

Acclimatization

Acclimatizing to heat entails increasing the rate of sweating, decreasing the sweating threshold, improving vasodilation and decreasing electrolyte loss in the sweat. When acclimatized, we sweat faster and sooner and lose fewer electrolytes in the sweat.

To become acclimatized to a hot environment, the body requires one and a half to two hours of exercise in the heat daily for approximately 10 days to two weeks. To remain acclimatized requires one and a half to two hours of exercise per week.

Predisposing Factors in Heat Illness

Increased heat production, decreased heat dissipation and a lack of salt and water are the basic factors that produce heat illness.

Other factors in the development of heat illness are age, general health, use of medications or alcohol, fatigue and a prior history of heat illness. Patients with underlying problems (illness or injury) may not be able to tolerate heat. Underdeveloped physical mechanisms contribute to the incidence of heat illness in children. Individuals with compromised heart function will be less able to adjust when stressed by heat. A study conducted by the U.S. Army demonstrated a correlation between lack of sleep, fatigue and the development of heat illness.

Antihistamines, antipsychotic agents, thyroid hormone medications, amphetamines and alcohol are among the drugs that have been implicated in the development of heat illness. Some interfere with thermoregulation; others increase metabolic activity or interfere with sweating.

Heat Illness

A continuum of signs and symptoms gives evidence of heat illnesses that range from heat syncope and cramps to heat exhaustion and heat stroke. Symptoms of heat illness, like those of hypothermia and altitude illness, may be subtle and remain unrecognized until a sudden collapse occurs.

Heat Syncope

Heat syncope is fainting due to heat stress. Shunting of blood to the periphery decreases blood flow to the brain through vasodilation and pooling of blood in the large leg veins. Standing for long periods of time (soldier on parade syndrome) is a common cause of heat syncope.

Heat Syncope
Sudden fainting episode in the heat
Usually self-limited
Aggravated by dehydration
Aggravated by standing for long periods

Signs and Symptoms of Heat Syncope
Tunnel vision, vertigo, nausea, sweating, weakness
Sudden fainting

Treatment for Heat Syncope
Lie flat, elevate legs
Hydrate

Assessment and Treatment
Prior to fainting the person may complain of tunnel vision, vertigo, nausea, sweating or feeling weak.

Heat syncope is self-limiting; leave the patient lying flat and he will regain consciousness. Conduct a primary and secondary survey to check for any injuries that may have occurred as a result of the fall.

Heat Cramps

Heat cramps are painful muscle contractions that follow exercise in hot conditions. They are caused by a lack of salt and occur in muscles fatigued by exercise. People who sweat profusely and drink only water to replace lost fluids are more susceptible to heat cramps.

Heat Cramps
Usually occur after exercise
Affect fatigued muscle groups

Treatment for Heat Cramps
Rest, lie flat, elevate legs
Hydrate

Assessment and Treatment
Calf, abdominal and thigh muscles can be affected, and muscle spasms in the abdomen can be severe. Treat by moving the patient to a cool spot and replenishing the lost salt. Mix one quarter to one half teaspoon of salt in a liter of fluid and have the patient drink it slowly. Avoid salt tablets and massaging the muscles. Salt tablets tend to make people nauseous and massaging the muscles increases the pain.

Heat Exhaustion and Heat Stroke

The distinction between heat exhaustion and stroke is not completely clear. Some authorities consider heat exhaustion an early stage of a progression to heat stroke. Sweating, body temperature and other symptoms may not be distinct between the two illnesses. The prevailing thought is that a patient with altered brain function—bizarre behavior, confusion, delirium, ataxia, seizure or unconsciousness—should be considered to have heat stroke.

Heat stroke is caused by a failure of the body to dissipate heat. There are two broad classifications of heat stroke: classic and exertional. Classic heat stroke affects the chronically ill, the elderly and infants. It develops slowly and is common during heat waves. Exertional heat stroke is more likely to affect healthy, fit individuals and to develop rapidly during exercise or hard physical work.

**Risk Factors for
Exertional Heat Stroke**
Overweight
Overdressing
Fatigue
Dehydration
Alcohol use
Medications
Exertion
High humidity
High temperature
Not acclimatized
Young athlete

Assessment
The signs and symptoms of heat exhaustion are caused by a lack of salt and water. The patient complains of weakness, fatigue, frontal headache, vertigo, thirst, nausea, vomiting, muscle cramps and faintness. The body temperature is between 102°F and 104°F. The patient may or may not be sweaty. Pulse and respiratory rate are elevated. Urine output is decreased due to dehydration.

In contrast to heat exhaustion, the onset of heat stroke is usually rapid. The patient becomes delirious or comatose. The pulse and respiratory rate are elevated. Only 20 percent of patients with heat stroke will demonstrate any prodromal

signs and symptoms prior to becoming delirious or unconscious. Prodromal signs and symptoms are confusion, drowsiness, disorientation, irritability, anxiety and ataxia, as well as
the signs and symptoms of heat exhaustion. Heat stroke
victims usually have a rectal temperature above 104°F.

Assessment of
Heat Exhaustion and Heat Stroke

Heat Exhaustion   *Heat Stroke*

Heat Exhaustion	Heat Stroke
Weakness	Delirious
Fatigue	Comatose
Headache	Rapid pulse
Vertigo	Rapid respiratory rate
Thirst	Temperature above 104°F
Nausea/vomiting	
Slightly elevated temp.	
Temperature 102°-104°F	
Faintness	

Treatment
Treatment for heat exhaustion and stroke is rapid cooling.
Both the temperature reached and the length of time it is
sustained can affect the long-term outcome of the disease.

Treatment for Heat Exhaustion and Heat Stroke
Cool environment
Remove clothing
Rest, lie flat
Cool water and fan
Hydrate
Monitor temperature
Evacuate (for heat stroke)

Provide a Cool Environment, Lie the Patient Flat,
Remove His Clothing, Cool with Water and Fanning
Shade the patient or move him from direct heat. Position him
lying flat and remove his clothing. Immerse the patient in cool
water, or spray him with water and fan the body to enhance
evaporation. Apply cool cloths to the patient's trunk, armpits,
abdomen and groin, where large blood vessels lie near the skin
surface. If you immerse the patient in cool water, remove him
when the body temperature reaches 102°F. Continue to cool by
spraying and fanning.

Monitor Temperature
Hypothermia becomes possible with such precipitous cooling,
so monitor the patient's temperature for hypothermia as well
as rebound hyperthermia. Document how long the temperature was elevated, how high it was and how long it took to cool
the patient. Body temperature may remain unstable even
after cooling. Evacuate the heat stroke patient, keeping a close
watch on his temperature.

Hydrate
Do not give fluids by mouth until the patient is mentally alert
enough to hold the glass and drink. If the patient is unconscious, make sure the airway is open and the patient is
breathing. If the patient is seizing, protect him from harming
himself; do not restrain the patient, but remove objects that
may cause harm.

Aspirin and acetaminophen will not lower the body temperature in heat illness and should not be given. High body
temperatures decrease the ability of blood to clot, and aspirin
further exacerbates this problem.

Evacuate (For Heat Stroke)
Any patient you suspect of having heat stroke should be
evacuated immediately for further evaluation. Internal organ
damage may not present itself for several days following the
episode of heat stroke.

Sun-Related Illnesses

Most skin damage is caused by short wavelengths of ultraviolet radiation. Longer ultraviolet wavelengths increase the thickness and pigmentation of the skin, which protects the skin by reducing the penetration of harmful ultraviolet radiation. The ozone layer blocks the shortest and most damaging wavelengths. As the earth's ozone layer decreases, the incidence of skin cancer is predicted to increase.

Two-thirds of ultraviolet radiation is received during the hours of 10:00 a.m. to 2:00 p.m. At high altitude, the thin atmosphere filters out less ultraviolet radiation, and the skin is damaged more quickly. Snowfields reflect 70 to 85 percent of the ultraviolet radiation. Water reflects 2 percent when the sun is directly overhead and more when the sun is lower. Finally, grass reflects 1 to 2 percent. Mountaineering at high altitudes, especially on snow, increases the risk of sun-related problems.

Sunburn

People with fair skin, usually blonds and redheads, are susceptible to burning even if exposed for only a little while. Dark skin contains more of the protective pigment melanin. Certain drugs, such as sulfonamides (Bactrim, Septra), tetracyclines (Vibramycin), oral diabetic agents, tranquilizers (Thorazine, Compazine, Phenergan, Sparine) and barbiturates, increase the skin's sensitivity to sunlight.

Unprotected skin can receive first or second degree burns from the sun. Fever blisters or cold sores often follow sunburning of the lips or extensive exposure to skin. These are herpes simplex (viral) infections and can be quite painful. A patient with extensive sunburn may complain of chills, fever or headache.

Phototoxic Reactions

A phototoxic reaction is an abnormally severe sunburn related to the ingestion of a drug, plant or chemical or the application of a drug, plant or chemical to the skin.

Treatment for Sunburned Skin
Cold, wet dressings or dressing soaked in a solution of boric acid (one teaspoon per liter of water) will relieve some of the pain. Anesthetic sprays and ointments may relieve the pain but increase the risk of a phototoxic reaction. Long-sleeved shirts and pants protect skin from the sun and prevent further burning.

Sunscreens
Exposure to the sun in small doses promotes tanning, which protects the skin from burns. Unfortunately, degenerative changes will still occur in the skin, so it is best to use sunscreens.

Sunscreens are rated by their sun protection factor (SPF). The SPF number is a guideline for the multiplied length of time a person wearing the sunscreen can spend in the sun. SPF is based on the minimal "erythemal dose," or the length of time before the exposed skin becomes red. For example, a person without sunscreen may be able to spend 30 minutes safely in the sun. Applying a sunscreen with an of SPF of 10 should allow the same person to spend 10 times as long in the sun, or 300 minutes, before the skin turns red. This system assumes that the sunscreen is not washed off by water or sweat and is used in adequate amounts.

Creams that completely block ultraviolet radiation (zinc oxide, A-Fil and Red Veterinary Petrolatum) are good for areas that are easily burned, such as the nose, ears and lips. Sunscreens should be applied on cloudy or overcast days as well as on sunny ones. The ultraviolet radiation that penetrates cloud cover is often great enough to burn the skin.

Snow Blindness
The burning of the cornea and conjunctiva is called snow blindness. The eyes feel dry and as if they are full of sand. Moving, blinking or opening the eyes is painful. The eyes will be red and tear excessively. Symptoms may not develop for eight to 12 hours after the eyes have been exposed to the sun.

Treatment

Snow blindness will heal spontaneously in several days. Cold compresses, pain medication and a dark environment relieve the pain. Don't rub the eyes or put anesthetics in the eyes. These can damage the cornea.

Sunglasses, especially those with side blinders, decrease the ultraviolet radiation received by the eyes and prevent snow blindness. If a person loses his sunglasses, make temporary ones from two pieces of cardboard with slits cut to see through. Wear sunglasses on cloudy or overcast as well as sunny days.

Final Thoughts: Prevention

Prevention of sunburn and heat-related illness is, of course, the best treatment. Leaders need to be alert for signs of developing heat illness in their groups. Environmental risk factors of high heat and humidity, coupled with dehydration, exertion and overdressing should raise caution. The vague symptoms of fatigue, headache, weakness, irritability and malaise should be recognized as indicators of dehydration and heat illness.

Tips For Preventing Heat Illness

1. Shade the head and back of the neck to decrease heat gain from the sun.

2. Drink lots of fluids: one half liter prior to strenuous exercise and a fourth of a liter every 20 minutes during exertion. It has been shown that a person will only voluntarily replace two-thirds of his lost fluids, therefore, fluids must be forced on a regular basis. The best way to tell if you're hydrated is by the color of your urine. The urine should be clear to pale yellow. Dark urine indicates dehydration.

3. Make sure your diet contains an adequate amount of salt. The average American diet contains 10 to 12 grams of salt per day, which should be adequate for exercising in hot environments. One study found that men working in the heat averaged

seven liters of sweat lost per day and adapted successfully on a diet that contained six grams of salt per day.

4. Wear loose fitting, light colored clothes. This maximizes heat loss by allowing convection and evaporation to take place.

5. Exercise cautiously in conditions of high heat and humidity. Air temperatures exceeding 90°F and humidity levels above 70 percent severely impair the body's ability to lose heat through radiation and evaporation.

6. Recognize the diseases and drugs that impair heat dissipation.

7. Know the warning signs of impending heat illness–dark colored urine, dizziness, headache and fatigue.

8. Acclimatize. It takes 10 days to two weeks to acclimatize to a hot environment.

Tips for Preventing Sun-Related Illness: Don't Sunburn!

1. Apply sunscreen 30 minutes before going out and reapply it frequently.

2. Apply sun block to your lips, nose and other sensitive areas.

3. Wear a hat with a brim.

4. Wear sunglasses even on cloudy days.

5. Minimize sun exposure between 10 a.m. and 3 p.m.

6. Wear a long-sleeved shirt and pants.

7. Examine your skin, and see a physician if you notice a mole changing shape, color or size or if you have a "sore" that won't heal.

Summary: Heat Illness

Heat Syncope: characterized by a sudden fainting episode in the heat. It is aggravated by dehydration and by standing for long periods. It is usually self-limited.

Assessment for Heat Syncope
Tunnel vision, vertigo, nausea, sweating, weakness
Sudden fainting

Treatment for Heat Syncope
Lie flat, elevate legs
Hydrate

Heat Cramps: usually occur after exercise and affect fatigued muscle groups.

Treatment for Heat Cramps
Rest, lie the patient flat, elevate legs
Hydrate

Heat Exhaustion and Heat Stroke

Assessment

Heat Exhaustion	*Heat Stroke*
Weakness	Delerious
Fatigue	Comatose
Headache	Rapid pulse
Vertigo	Rapid respiratory rate
Thirst	Temperature above 104°F
Nausea/vomiting	
Slightly elevated temp.	
Temperature 102°-104°F	
Faintness	

Treatment

Cool environment	Cool water and fan
Remove clothing	Hydrate
Rest, lie flat	Monitor temperature
Evacuate (for heat stroke)	

CHAPTER 11
POISONS, STINGS AND BITES

Introduction

A poison is any substance–solid, liquid or gas–that impairs health when it comes into contact with the body. Poisoning ranks fifth in causes of accidental death in the United States, responsible for approximately 5,000 deaths a year. Approximately one million cases of non-fatal poisoning from substances such as industrial chemicals, cleaning agents, medications and insect sprays occur each year.

Virtually any substance can be poisonous if consumed in sufficient quantity. For example, vitamins can be highly toxic in overdose. A snakebite that kills a child may only produce illness in an adult. Accidental overdoses of aspirin kill more children each year than substances we commonly consider poisons.

A venom is a poison excreted by certain animals. Venomous animals have specialized glands that produce toxic substances for injection into adversaries and prey. All venoms are poisons, but not all poisons are venoms. Most animal venoms are complex mixtures of toxic and carrier (non-toxic) substances. The toxins in various venoms vary in potency, effect and chemical makeup. They may impair nerve function, destroy cells or affect the heart or blood.

Much information has been disseminated about the treatment of serpent, spider and scorpion bites—much of it inaccurate. Outside the United States there are snakes, spiders and insects that carry deadly venoms. In the U.S., however, snakes and spiders cause relatively few deaths each year. This is not to undersell the potency of these poisons, rather to emphasize that ill-informed and misguided treatment can be as harmful to the patient as the venom.

Poisons

Poisons enter the body through ingestion, inhalation, absorption and injection. In general, treat ingested poisoning in the backcountry by dilution and vomiting. Treat absorbed poisons, if dry, by brushing off the skin and, if wet, by flushing with water. Move the victim of an inhaled poison to fresh air and maintain his airway. As systemic symptoms of poisoning appear, provide the basics of care, including: ABCs, continuous evaluation and evacuation to a medical facility.

Ingested Poisons

Examples of ingested poisons include drugs, toxic plants and bacterial toxins on contaminated food. The use of poorly labeled fuel bottles as water bottles has led to accidental ingestion of gasoline. Poisons absorbed from the stomach into the general circulation can affect several body systems. Treatment involves diluting the poison and/or removing it from the stomach before it is absorbed.

Treatment for Ingested Poisons

If you suspect an ingested poison, induce vomiting—but only if the patient is fully conscious. If the patient is stuporous, unconscious or having seizures, his airway may become obstructed with vomit.

Do not induce vomiting for ingested corrosive chemicals or petroleum products. Vomiting can increase the corrosive damage, as these chemicals burn both on the way down and on the way back up the esophagus. Also extremely harmful if they enter the lungs, these substances can cause a chemical pneumonia.

Treatment for Ingested Poisons
Induce vomiting:
Give 2 tbs of syrup of ipecac with half a liter of water
Repeat dose if no vomiting occurs after 20 minutes
After vomiting ceases, give 5 tbs activated charcoal

If ipecac is unavailable:
    2 tbs mild soap or mustard
    tickle back of throat

Do not induce vomiting if:
    corrosive or petroleum products
    altered levels of consciousness
    seizures

If syrup of ipecac and activated charcoal are available:
Syrup of ipecac stimulates vomiting, and charcoal is a potent
diluent and absorbent. If available, give an adult two tablespoons (15-30ml) of ipecac with half a liter of water. If vomiting
does not occur within 20 minutes, the dose of ipecac and water
may be repeated once. After vomiting has ceased, give activated charcoal, five tablespoons in a water slurry. The charcoal
absorbs residual stomach contents.

If syrup of ipecac and activated charcoal are unavailable:
Often on wilderness expeditions the available treatment is to
give the patient two tablespoons of mild soap, such as Campsuds
or Dr. Bronner's, or a teaspoonful of dried mustard to swallow
with half a liter of water. Tickling the back of the throat to
stimulate the gag reflex may also induce vomiting.

In current practice, if more than 30 minutes has passed since
ingestion many physicians use activated charcoal instead of
ipecac. In the backcountry, vomiting should be induced even if
considerable time has passed, provided the patient remains
conscious and has not ingested corrosive or petroleum products. After the patient has vomited, he should drink at least a
half liter of water to dilute the poison. Save a sample of the
poison and a sample of the vomit for later analysis.

In the backcountry, people have died after mistakenly eating
poisonous plants and mushrooms. An expert should identify any
vegetation you intend to eat. If you suspect ingested plant
poisoning, treat by dilution and induced vomiting. Save samples
for identification after a plant causes poisoning.

Common Poisonous Plants in Western United States	
Name	*Genus*
Arnica	Arnica
Bleeding Heart	Dicentra
Buttercup	Ranunculus
Clematis	Clematis
Coyotillo	Karwinskia

Nightshade	Atropa
Larkspur	Delphinium
Camas	Zigadenus
Desert Potato	Jatropha
False Hellebore	Veratrum
Foxglove	Digitalis
Iris	Iris
Jimson Weed	Datura
Lily of the Valley	Guaiacum
Monkshood	Aconitum
Mountain Laurel	Kalmia
Poison Hemlock	Conium
Groundsel	Senecio
Sweet Pea	Lathyrus
Locoweed	Oxytropus
Water Hemlock	Cicuta

Inhaled Poisons

In 1986, two climbers on Denali (Mt. McKinley) died from carbon monoxide poisoning caused by using a stove in a poorly ventilated tent. Carbon monoxide is an odorless and colorless gas produced from incomplete combustion and is the most frequently encountered inhaled poison in the United States. Automobiles, portable stoves, lanterns and heaters are all sources of carbon monoxide.

Carbon monoxide combines with hemoglobin in the blood, displacing oxygen and reducing the oxygen carrying capacity of the blood. This can happen rapidly and without warning. At high altitudes, where less oxygen is available, the potential for poisoning increases. Signs and symptoms of carbon monoxide poisoning range from lightheadedness and headache to coma, seizures and death.

Treatment for Inhaled Poisons

The immediate treatment for any inhaled poisoning is to remove the patient from the source of the poison. Maintain the airway and move the patient to fresh air. Although not readily available in the wilderness, administration of oxygen is standard treatment. The patient who experiences a notable disturbance in alertness or coordination, complains of breathing difficulty or loses consciousness should be evacuated to a physician for evaluation.

Prevent inhaled poisoning by keeping tent or snow shelter well ventilated during cooking, or better yet, by cooking outside.

Carbon Monoxide Poisoning

Signs and symptoms
    Lightheadedness, dizziness, throbbing headache
    Nausea and vomiting
    Irritability, impaired judgment
    Altered level of consciousness
    Seizures, respiratory failure, coma

Treatment
    Move patient to fresh air
    Maintain airway
    If possible, administer oxygen

Absorbed Poisons

Poisons can enter the body through the skin or mucous membranes. Pesticide sprays absorbed through the skin are a common source of poisoning. Toxins secreted into the skin by sea cucumbers and some species of exotic reptiles can cause serious reactions.

Treatment for Absorbed Poisons

If the poison is dry, brush it off, then flush the area with large volumes of water. If the poison is wet, flush the site thoroughly with water, then wash with soap and water. Exceptions are lye and dry lime, which react with water to produce heat and further corrosion. Do not rinse lye or dry lime, but brush the powder off the skin.

**Treatment for
Absorbed Poisons**
Dry poisons: brush off, then rinse with water
Wet poisons: rinse thoroughly with water

Injected Poisons

The poisons that enter the body via the injected venoms of stinging insects and reptiles are often complex systemic poisons with multiple toxins. The injected poisons that most concern us in the wilderness are the venoms of snakes, bees, wasps, spiders and scorpions.

Bees and wasps cause more deaths in the U.S. than snakes— approximately 100 deaths a year, which usually result from acute allergic reaction known as anaphylactic shock.

Venomous Snakes

Imagine yourself trying to catch a small mammal for dinner, equipped only with a long, limbless body. You might develop the ability to leap quickly to your victim. You might also develop a venom to immobilize the victim. This is how a rattlesnake makes its living: striking quickly and accurately and immobilizing or killing its victims with venom.

Approximately 45,000 snakebites occur in the U.S. each year, 8,000 of them from venomous snakes. Twelve to 15 people die a year from these bites, mostly the young, elderly and infirm. Bites commonly occur on the arms below the elbow and on the legs below the knee. In most cases, the snake is provoked by being handled, antagonized or inadvertently stepped upon.

Prevent snakebite by watching closely where you step. Never reach into concealed areas. Shake out sleeping bags and clothing before use. One NOLS student was bitten on the hand when he attempted to pick up a rattlesnake. Never handle snakes, even if you think they are dead.

There are two families of venomous snakes in the United States: Elapidae, represented by the coral snake, and Crotalidae, represented by the rattlesnake, copperhead and cottonmouth, or water moccasin. Elapidae venom primarily affects the nervous system, causing death by paralysis and respiratory failure. Crotalidae venom is a complex mix of substances affecting the nerves, the heart, blood clotting and other functions.

Coral Snake
The coral snake averages 23 to 32 inches in length, is thin and brightly colored, with adjacent red/yellow bands. It is the creature referred to in the old saw "red and yellow kill a fellow, red and black, venom lack." Coral snakes live in the southern and southwestern states, inhabiting dry, open brushy ground near water sources. They are docile and bite only when provoked. Their short fangs generally limit their bites to fingers, toes and loose skin folds.

The signs of systemic poisoning by the neurotoxic venom, which may occur several hours after the bite, include drowsiness, weakness, nausea, rapid pulse and rapid respiration progressing to respiratory failure.

CORAL SNAKE

THIN, BRIGHTLY COLORED

23-32" LONG

└ ADJACENT RED/YELLOW BANDS

SYMPTOMS:

- LITTLE PAIN OR SWELLING

- NEUROTOXIC VENOM POISONING MAY LEAD TO DROWSINESS, WEAKNESS AND OTHER SYMPTOMS and PROGRESS TO POSSIBLE RESPIRATORY FAILURE.

Rattlesnake

Rattlesnakes have triangular heads, thick bodies, and pits between the eyes and nostrils. Coloring and length varies with the species. Most are blotched and colored in earthy browns, grays or reds. Four feet is an average length, although large eastern diamondback rattlesnakes have reached six and a half feet in length. The number of rattles varies with the snake's age and stage of molt. Oftentimes the rattlers do not rattle before a strike. Rattles are thought to have evolved as a warning device to prevent hoofed mammals from stepping on the snake.

Rattlesnake fangs retract when the mouth is closed and extend during a strike. Rattlesnakes periodically shed their fangs. At times, two fangs are present on each side. One will be potent, the other not. Venom release is under the snake's control. A rattler can apparently adjust the volume of venom injected to match its victim's size. The age, size and health of the snake affect venom toxicity. The same factors affect the victim's response to the venom.

Multiple strikes are possible, and depth of the bite varies as does the amount of venom injected. Fang marks are not a reliable sign of envenomization, as 20 to 30 percent of bites do not envenomate. Pain at the site with rapid swelling and bruising is a better sign that venom has been injected.

Signs and symptoms of venomous poisoning include swelling, pain and tingling at the bite site, tingling and a metallic taste in the mouth, fever, chills, blurred vision and muscle tremors.

Treatment for Rattlesnake Bites*
Clean wound with antiseptic soap
Apply sterile dressing
Remove rings and other constrictive items
Keep limb at or below level of heart
Keep patient quiet, hydrated and comfortable
Suction with Sawyer Extractor

Also cottonmouth or copperhead bites.

Gently clean the wound with an antiseptic soap and apply a sterile dressing. The goal of treatment is safe and rapid transport to a hospital for evaluation. Keep the affected limb at heart level or below. Keep the patient quiet, hydrated and comfortable during evacuation. Activity and anxiety accelerate the absorption of the venom. Ideally, immobilize and carry the victim. Walking is acceptable if the patient feels up to it and if no other alternative is available.

A healthy adult may become ill from the envenomization, but he probably will not die. The patient is often at greater danger from the effects of treatment by misinformed rescuers. Pressure bandages, tourniquets, electric shock, ice and incision of the area can permanently damage tissue that might otherwise remain unaffected. Pressure bandages are appropriate treatment for some exotic snakebites but not for rattlesnake envenomizations, in which local concentration of venom from a tourniquet can cause tissue damage.

Studies show that suction devices, such as the Extractor by Sawyer Products, can remove up to 30 percent of venom if applied within three minutes. The suction from the Extractor is applied without incision.

Bee Stings

The venom apparatus of most species of bees, located on the posterior abdomen, consists of venom glands, a venom reservoir and structures for stinging or injection. The stinger and venom are used in defense and subjugation of prey.

Multiple stings are more dangerous than single stings, and those occurring closely in time are more dangerous than those occurring over a longer duration. Multiple stings, which often result from disturbing a nest, can be life-threatening.

Treatment for Bee Stings
Scrape or flick off stinger
Clean wound with antiseptic soap
Ice/cool compress may relieve pain
If necessary, treat for anaphylaxis

RATTLESNAKES

GENERAL CHARACTERISTICS:

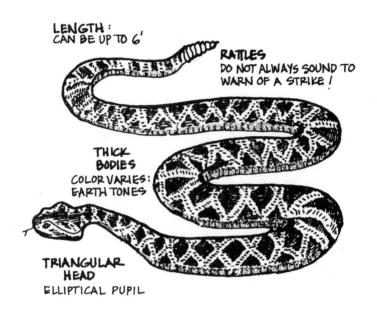

LENGTH:
CAN BE UP TO 6'

RATTLES
DO NOT ALWAYS SOUND TO
WARN OF A STRIKE!

**THICK
BODIES**
COLOR VARIES:
EARTH TONES

**TRIANGULAR
HEAD**
ELLIPTICAL PUPIL

MECHANISMS OF A RATTLESNAKE BITE:

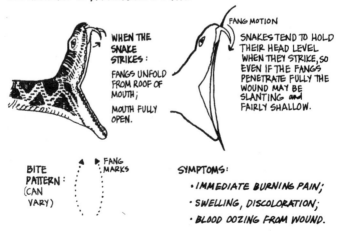

**WHEN THE
SNAKE
STRIKES:**

FANGS UNFOLD
FROM ROOF OF
MOUTH;

MOUTH FULLY
OPEN.

FANG MOTION

SNAKES TEND TO HOLD
THEIR HEAD LEVEL
WHEN THEY STRIKE, SO
EVEN IF THE FANGS
PENETRATE FULLY THE
WOUND MAY BE
SLANTING and
FAIRLY SHALLOW.

**BITE
PATTERN:**
(CAN
VARY)

FANG
MARKS

SYMPTOMS:

- *IMMEDIATE BURNING PAIN;*
- *SWELLING, DISCOLORATION;*
- *BLOOD OOZING FROM WOUND.*

Stings from bees and wasps usually cause instant pain, swelling and redness. If the stinger remains in the skin, scrape or flick it out. A barb prevents the bee from withdrawing the stinger, so the bee's muscular venom reservoir continues to inject until the stinger is scraped away. Avoid squeezing the attached venom sac.

Gently clean the wound with an antiseptic soap. Ice or cool compresses may help relieve pain and swelling. The patient should avoid scratching, as scratching the stings can cause secondary infections. Applying meat tenderizer to relieve the pain is a folklore remedy not supported by any scientific study.

Bee stings cause more anaphylaxis than do the stings of any other insect. Individuals who are allergic to the sting of one species of bee or wasp may also be allergic to that of a different species.

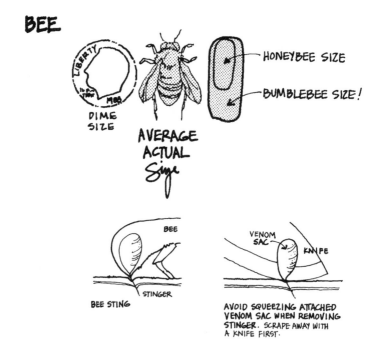

Arachnids

Arachnids are mostly terrestrial and wingless and have four pairs of legs. Spiders, scorpions, tarantulas and ticks are arachnids. There are over 30,000 spider species worldwide. They live in a variety of habitats and all are carnivores.

Poisonous spiders inject venom through hollow fangs. The fangs are primarily for subduing and killing prey, secondarily for defense. The venoms are fast-paralyzing agents which contain enzymes to predigest prey, which is then sucked up.

Treatment for Spider and Scorpion Bites
Clean wound with antiseptic soap
Ice/cool compress to relieve pain

If systemic symptoms of envenomization develop:
ABCs and supportive care
Evacuate to antivenin

Black Widow Spider
The black widow spider has a sinister name, yet kills only four to six persons a year in the U.S. A member of the genus Lactrodectus, the venomous adult female is four centimeters long and is shiny black with a red "hourglass" marking on the bottom of the abdomen. The adult male is not venomous. There are five species of "widow" spiders, all of which have some type of red marking on the underside of the abdomen but only three of which are black. Black widows are typically found under stones and logs. They are common in desert overhangs, crawl spaces, outhouses and barns; rare in occupied buildings.

The black widow usually bites only when its web is disturbed. The bite is not initially painful–a pinprick sensation with slight redness and swelling followed by numbness. Ten to 60 minutes may pass before the onset of toxic symptoms. The venom is primarily a nerve toxin that stimulates muscle contraction, causing large muscle cramps. The abdomen may become board-like and excruciatingly painful. Weakness, nausea, vomiting and anxiety are common. Systemic signs include hypertension, breathing difficulty, seizures and, in the very young or old, cardiac arrest.

The pain generally peaks in one to three hours and can continue over several days. The natural course of the illness is general recovery after several days. Local cleansing and ice may retard pain and venom absorption. Antivenin is available, as are agents to counteract muscle spasm.

Brown Spider

The brown spider, genus Loxosceles, is rare in the West, especially in Wyoming and Colorado; most abundant in the South and Midwest. It has a violin-shaped mark on its head. The spiders average 1.2cm in length with a 5cm leg span. Unlike the black widow, both sexes are dangerous.

Brown spiders live in hot, dry, undisturbed environments, such as vacant buildings and woodpiles. They are nocturnal hunters of beetles, flies, moths and other spiders, and they are most active from April to October, hibernating in fall and winter. They will attack humans only as a defensive gesture.

The venom of the brown spider causes cell and tissue injury. Signs and symptoms vary from a transient irritation to painful and debilitating skin ulcers. Although the bite can be sharply painful, it is often painless. Nausea and vomiting, headache, fever and chills may be present. In severe envenomizations, redness and blisters form within six to 12 hours. Within one to two weeks an area of dying skin—a necrotic ulcer—forms and may leave a crater-like scar.

The injury can be difficult to diagnose. The bite often goes unnoticed until a skin ulcer develops. Clean the bite site with an antiseptic soap and evacuate the patient to a physician.

Tarantulas

Except for some species found in the tropics, tarantulas are not dangerous. The tarantula's fangs are too weak to penetrate very deeply, and the effects of the bite are limited to a small local wound. Tarantula bites are rare.

BROWN SPIDER:

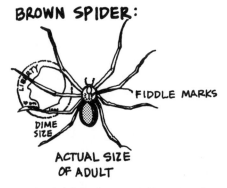

FIDDLE MARKS

DIME SIZE

ACTUAL SIZE
OF ADULT

- VIOLIN SHAPED MARKS ON TOP OF HEAD
- BOTH MALE and FEMALE ADULTS VENOMOUS

BLACK WIDOW SPIDER:

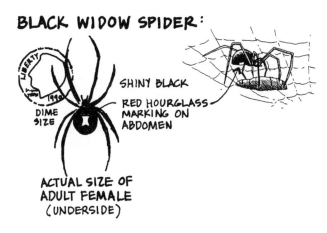

SHINY BLACK

RED HOURGLASS
MARKING ON
ABDOMEN

DIME SIZE

ACTUAL SIZE OF
ADULT FEMALE
(UNDERSIDE)

- FEMALE ADULTS VENOMOUS;
- LOOK FOR DISTINCTIVE RED HOURGLASS
  MARKING ON THE UNDERSIDE OF
  ABDOMEN !

Scorpions

Scorpions first appeared on the earth 300 million years ago. Grasslands and deserts are primary habitat for more than 600 species of scorpions, some of which carry deadly venoms. In North America, most species are relatively harmless, their stings producing effects similar to those of bee stings.

Only one type of scorpion, a small yellowish species of the genus Centruroides, is dangerous. It lives in Mexico, Arizona and New Mexico and has been reported in Southern Utah. Fatalities from its venom occur mostly in the young and old.

Scorpions feed at night on insects and spiders, injecting their prey with multiple toxins from a stinger at the tip of their tails. Scorpions like to hide in dark places during the day; beware when reaching into woodpiles or under rocks. Develop a habit of shaking out shoes, clothes and sleeping bags when in scorpion country.

A scorpion sting produces a pricking sensation. Typical symptoms include burning pain, swelling, redness, numbness and tingling. The affected extremity may become numb and sensitive to touch.

Treat the sting by applying ice or cool water to relieve the local symptoms. Clean the wound with an antiseptic soap. In the case of a severe poisoning, signs and symptoms include impaired speech resulting from a sluggish tongue and tightened jaw, muscle spasms, nausea, vomiting, convulsions, incontinence, and/or respiratory and circulatory distress. Immobilize the extremity and transport the patient to a hospital. An antivenin is available.

Ticks

The bites of mosquitoes, black flies, midges, horseflies and deerflies tend to be relatively minor. Usually only localized irritation occurs, although anaphylaxis is a possibility. This group is more significant for its capacity to act as vectors of diseases such as malaria and yellow fever. Worldwide, only the mosquito transmits more disease than the tick. Ticks carry a

SCORPIONS

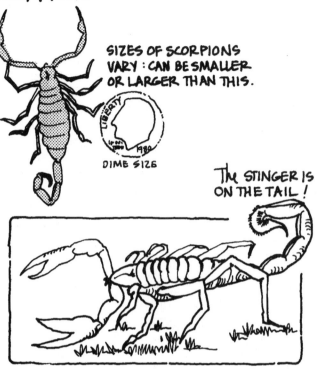

SIZES OF SCORPIONS VARY : CAN BE SMALLER OR LARGER THAN THIS.

DIME SIZE

The STINGER IS ON THE TAIL !

TICKS

DIME SIZE

ACTUAL SIZE OF ADULT

GENUS DERMACENTOR
COMMON WYOMING TICK

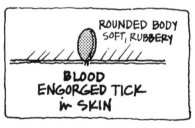

ROUNDED BODY
SOFT, RUBBERY

BLOOD
ENGORGED TICK
in SKIN

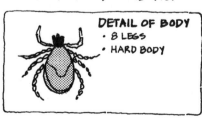

DETAIL OF BODY
• 8 LEGS
• HARD BODY

variety of diseases, including Tick Fever, Relapsing Fever, Spotted Fever, Tularemia, Babesiosis and Lyme Disease.

Ticks are relatives of spiders and scorpions, and there are two major families of ticks: hard ticks and soft ticks. Most common in the Rockies is the hard tick, genus Dermacentor. As with all ticks, it requires blood meals to molt from larva to nymph and from nymph to adult. The various diseases the tick carries are transmitted to the host during the blood meal. Tick season in Wyoming is April through July, although ticks are active throughout the warm months.

LIFE CYCLE of the TICK:

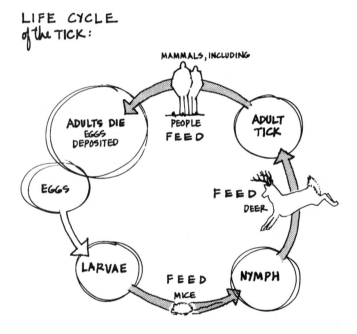

Preventing exposure is essential in tick-infested areas. Topical tick repellent is available; look for the chemical ingredient "premethrin." A visual inspection of all body parts at least twice daily is recommended, as adult ticks generally stay on the body for a few hours before attaching. Even after a tick has attached itself, prompt removal may prevent the transmission of disease.

Diagnosis of tick-caused illness in the field is difficult. A tick bite accompanied by a rash, fever, flu symptoms or continued muscle aches and pains should be seen by a physician.

To remove a tick, grasp it as close to the skin as possible with tweezers or gloved fingers. Pull the tick out with steady pressure, being careful not to squeeze body fluids out of the tick and into the wound. Clean the bite site thoroughly with an antiseptic soap. Traditional tick removal methods (a hot match head, nail polish or alcohol) may induce the tick to regurgitate into the wound.

Treatment for Tick Bites
Promptly remove the tick with a gentle, steady pull
Clean the bite site with soap and water
In cases of rash, fever, flu, or muscle aches following a tick bite, the patient should be seen by a physician

---

Anaphylaxis

The mechanisms causing anaphylactic shock are associated with the immune system. An anaphylactic response is a massive, generalized reaction of the immune system that is potentially harmful to the body.

Our immune system recognizes foreign substances and produce antibodies to those substances. Antibodies are then present to neutralize the invader the next time it appears. In an allergic person, reintroduction of the foreign material results in an overreaction of the immune system and an abnormal, massive release of histamine. The histamine causes fluid to leak from blood vessels, causing edema and swelling. It also dilates blood vessels and can obstruct the airway.

For most people the allergic response is mild, though often irritating. Hay fever is one example of a mild allergic response. Hay fever sufferers complain of a runny nose, sneezing, swollen eyes, itching skin and possibly hives. Antihistamines and decongestants are the usual treatment.

Common triggers of anaphylaxis are bee stings or other insect bites, penicillin and other drugs, and some foods. Instead of the mild symptoms of hay fever, anaphylaxis produces asphyxiating edema of the larynx, rapid pulse, a rapid fall in blood pressure, rash, itching, hives and flushed skin, swollen, red, and teary eyes, swelling of the feet and hands, nausea, vomiting and abdominal pain. The airway obstruction and shock may be fatal. Onset usually occurs within a few minutes of contact with the triggering substance, although the reaction may be delayed.

Treatment of anaphylaxis is immediate administration of epinephrine to counteract the effects of the histamine. Epinephrine is a prescription medication. Persons who know they are vulnerable to anaphylactic shock usually carry injectable epinephrine in an Anakit or Epipen.

Final Thoughts: Prevention

Tips for Preventing Poisoning Emergencies

1. Read labels for information on toxic substances
2. Cook outside or in well-ventilated tents or snow shelters
3. Identify plants before you eat them
4. Be aware of foot placement
5. Look before you reach under logs or overhangs or onto ledges
6. Shake out clothing, footwear and sleeping bags

The following table provides some perspective on the likelihood of death from bee stings and snakebites in the U.S. and worldwide. It also shows how this might compare with the likelihood of death from some of the other fearsome animals that routinely appear in movies, news bites and our darkest dreams.

Estimated Yearly Human Deaths from Animal Attack

Species	United States	Worldwide
Bees	100	unknown
Venomous snakes	15	60,000
Wolves	0	50
Sharks	4	15
Crocodilians	2	1,000
Grizzly bear	2	—
Lions, tigers, pumas	unknown	1,700

Adapted from: Callahan, M. *Wilderness Management of Injuries Caused by North American Animals.* Syllabus Annual Meeting Wilderness Medical Society [Snowbird, UT] 1990.

Summary: Poisons, Stings and Bites

Treatment for Ingested Poisons: plants, drugs.
Give 2 tbs of syrup of ipecac with 1/2 liter of water
Repeat dose if no vomiting occurs within 20 minutes
After vomiting ceases, give 5 tbs activated charcoal.

If ipecac is unavailable:
    2 tbs mild soap or mustard
    tickle back of throat

Do not induce vomiting if:
    corrosive or petroleum products
    altered levels of consciousness
    seizures

Treatment for Carbon Monoxide Poisoning
Move to fresh air
Maintain airway
If possible, administer oxygen

Treatment for Absorbed Poisons
Dry poisons: brush off, then rinse with water
Wet poisons: rinse thoroughly with water

Injected Poisons: bees, wasps, spiders, snakes, scorpions

Treatment for Bee and Wasp Stings
Scrape or flick off stinger
Clean wound with antiseptic soap
Ice/cool compress may relieve pain
If necessary, treat for anaphylaxis

Treatment for Spider and Scorpion Bites

Clean wound with antiseptic soap
Ice/cool compress to relieve pain

If systemic symptoms of envenomization develop:
    ABCs and supportive care
    Evacuate to antivenin

Treatment for Rattlesnake Bites

Clean wound with antiseptic soap
Apply sterile dressing
Remove rings and other constrictive items
Keep limb at or below level of heart
Keep patient quiet, hydrated and comfortable
Suction with Sawyer Extractor

Treatment for Tick Bites

Promptly remove the tick with a gentle, steady pull
Clean the bite site with soap and water
In cases of rash, fever, flu, or muscle aches following
a tick bite, the patient should be seen by a physician

CHAPTER 12
MARINE ENVENOMATIONS

Injuries From Marine Animals

Marine Spine Envenomations

Signs and Symptoms

Treatment for Marine Spine Envenomations

Zebra Fish, Stone Fish and Scorpion Fish

Sea Urchins

Starfish

Cone Shells

Stingrays

Nematocyst Sting Envenomations

Signs and Symptoms

Treatment for Nematocyst Sting Envenomations

Anemones

Jellyfish

Portuguese Man-Of-War

Fire Coral

Hard Coral

Sea Cucumbers

Final Thoughts

Summary: Marine Envenomations

Injuries From Marine Animals

Injuries from marine organisms are rarely the result of an aggressive, unprovoked attack. Most injuries occur as a result of accidental contact or when a threatened animal reacts in self-defense. This chapter discusses two broad categories of injuries from aquatic animals; marine spine envenomations and nematocyst sting envenomations. Treatment for these two types of injuries is also very different: injuries from spines are treated with hot water immersion; stings are rinsed in vinegar.

Marine Spine Envenomations

Marine animals with venom known to be harmful to people include the zebra fish, scorpion fish, stone fish, sea urchins and stingrays, which deliver venom through spines, and the cone shells, which inject venom through a proboscis. Envenomation may cause life-threatening injury or mild irritations, depending on the species, the number of punctures, the amount of venom, the health of the victim and other factors.

Signs and Symptoms

Signs of marine venom injury include local discoloration, cyanosis and laceration or puncture wound. Symptoms include numbness, tingling and intense local pain. In serious envenomations nausea, vomiting, paralysis, respiratory distress, heart rhythm irregularities and shock can occur.

Treatment for Marine Spine Envenomations

Treat marine envenomations by controlling bleeding, removing imbedded spines, cleaning the wound and controlling pain with hot water soaks.

Treatment for Marine Spine Envenomations

Control bleeding

Immerse the injury in water as hot as the patient can tolerate (usually 115° to 120°F) for 30-90 minutes or until the pain is gone

---

Remove imbedded spines
Irrigate the wound
Clean the wound
Elevate the extremity to help control swelling
Monitor for signs of infection or envenomation
Medications for pain are appropriate

Immerse the injury in water as hot as the patient can tolerate (usually 115° to 120°F) for 30 to 90 minutes or until the pain is gone. This therapy is thought to inactivate heat-sensitive proteins in the venom. Immersion in a large pot or a plastic bag filled with hot water is best, but hot compresses can also be used.

Clean the wound with irrigation. Remove obvious imbedded spines carefully. Elevate the extremity to help control swelling. Remedies such as meat tenderizer, papain or mangrove sap are not scientifically confirmed and may irritate the wound.

Removing imbedded spines is against standard treatment for impaled objects; however, the spines are a source of infection and a continued source of venom. Their presence also retards healing and may cause further injury. This is often difficult; the spines are brittle and break easily, leaving a foreign body that may cause infection. Use tweezers or fingers (wear gloves) to remove the spines. If the spine is hard to remove, leave it in place and evacuate the patient to a physician. Medications to control pain are appropriate.

Monitor the patient for signs of generalized envenomation. With severe envenomations, signs and symptoms of shock and respiratory distress will develop. In these cases, our treatment is supportive care and evacuation.

Zebra Fish, Stone Fish and Scorpion Fish

There are three genera in this family—stone fish, zebra fish and scorpion fish—and several hundred species. The stone fish, inconspicuous and possessing a highly toxic venom, is considered to be among the most dangerous of all venomous creatures.

Zebra fish are spectacularly colored, while stone fish are less so. All members of the family are found in shallow waters. Zebra fish are free swimmers, while stone fish often hide in cracks, near rocks or among plants. The stone fish may bury itself under sandy or broken coral bottoms. A dead stone fish is still dangerous! Its venom remains active for 48 hours after death.

The immediate intense pain of stone fish envenomation peaks in 60 to 90 minutes and can persist for days, despite treatment. Stone fish wounds are slow to heal and prone to infection.

Sea Urchins

Sea urchins are non-aggressive, nocturnal, omnivorous feeders who move slowly across the ocean bottom and are often found on rocky bottoms and burrowed in sand and small crevices. The hard spines protecting their vital organs can envenomate victims if the urchin is stepped on, handled or inadvertently bumped. Their grasping organs, called pedicellariae, can also envenomate.

Symptoms are usually local and mild; however, infections are possible if pieces of imbedded spines remain in the skin or joint capsules. Spines imbedded into joints or large fragments left in soft tissues should be evaluated by a physician. Severe reactions are rare.

Spines lodged in the skin often turn it a brownish purple color. This reaction is harmless and can be seen regardless of whether a spine has broken off and remains imbedded or not.

Starfish

The venomous crown-of-thorns starfish is found in the Indo-Pacific area, the Red Sea, the eastern Pacific and the Sea of Cortez. Starfish are scavengers that feed on other echinoderms, mollusks, coral and worms. The upper surface of the crown-of-thorns starfish is studded with sharp, poisonous spines that can penetrate even the best diving gloves.

Cone Shells

The shells of these animals, which live in shallow waters, reefs and tide pools, are beautiful but hide a nasty sting. Cone shells project a long proboscis from the narrow end of the shell and inject venom from its tip. Toxicity to humans varies but rarely produces death. Do not handle cone shells. Drop them immediately if the proboscis is observed. Almost all reported envenomations have come from collectors handling the shells. The injury resembles a bee sting with pain, burning and itching. Serious envenomations produce cyanosis and numbness at the injury site which progresses to numbness around the mouth, then generalized paralysis.

CONE SHELL:

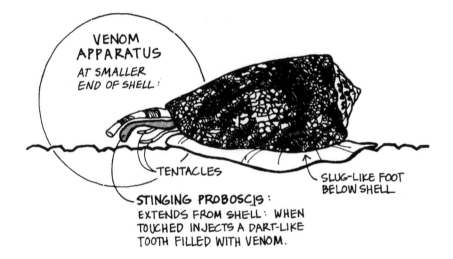

VENOM APPARATUS AT SMALLER END OF SHELL:

TENTACLES

SLUG-LIKE FOOT BELOW SHELL

STINGING PROBOSCIS: EXTENDS FROM SHELL: WHEN TOUCHED INJECTS A DART-LIKE TOOTH FILLED WITH VENOM.

Treatment of cone shell stings is largely supportive. Clean and thoroughly irrigate the puncture wound. Use of hot water soaks is unproved but may provide pain relief. Likewise, use of circumferential pressure bandages is also unconfirmed but may slow the spread of the venom.

Stingrays

Stingrays are bottom feeders, often found in shallow waters, lying on top of or partially buried under sandy bottoms. Most stingray envenomations occur when the careless swimmer or wader steps on the buried ray. The stingray's tail whips up, and its serrated barbs inflict a nasty wound. Such defensive attacks usually cause wounds to the leg or ankle, and pieces of barbs may remain imbedded in the wound. Wounds often take the form of bleeding soft tissue lacerations or punctures. Intense local pain may last up to 48 hours.

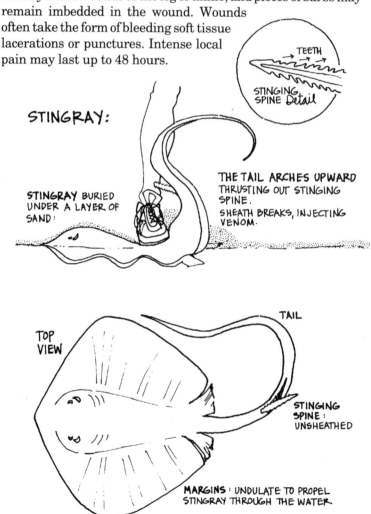

TEETH

STINGING SPINE Detail

STINGRAY:

STINGRAY BURIED UNDER A LAYER OF SAND:

THE TAIL ARCHES UPWARD THRUSTING OUT STINGING SPINE.
SHEATH BREAKS, INJECTING VENOM.

TOP VIEW

TAIL

STINGING SPINE: UNSHEATHED

MARGINS: UNDULATE TO PROPEL STINGRAY THROUGH THE WATER.

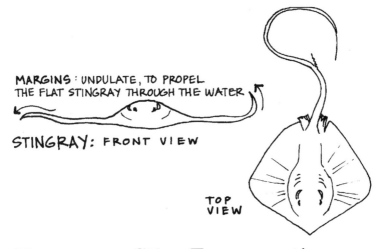

MARGINS : UNDULATE, TO PROPEL
THE FLAT STINGRAY THROUGH THE WATER

STINGRAY: FRONT VIEW

TOP VIEW

Nematocyst Sting Envenomations

Nematocysts are specialized stinging capsules found in members of the phylum Coelenterata, which includes the sea anemones, jellyfish, Portuguese man-of-wars and some corals. The nematocyst discharges an incapacitating venom, allowing the animal to kill and digest its prey. Some nematocysts produce a sticky venomous substance, while others deliver a barbed, venomous stinger.

Nematocyst discharge is triggered by contact with the skin or by changes in osmotic pressure, as can occur when the nematocyst is rinsed with fresh water. Nematocysts are generally found around the coelenterate's mouth or on the tentacles, and nematocysts from dead jellyfish can still envenomate.

Signs and Symptoms

Signs and symptoms range from mild skin irritations to rapid death and vary considerably with the envenomating species. In general, contact with a nematocyst produces painful local swelling, redness and a stinging, prickling sensation that progresses to numbness, burning and throbbing pain. Pain may radiate from extremities to the groin, abdomen, or armpit. The contact site may turn a reddish brown-purple color, marked by swelling. In more serious cases, blisters may occur.

Severe envenomations may produce headaches, abdominal cramps, nausea, vomiting, muscle paralysis and respiratory or cardiac distress.

Treatment for Nematocyst Sting Injury

Treat nematocyst injury first by protecting yourself and second by inactivating and removing nematocysts from the skin. Rinse the injury with sea water to begin removing remaining nematocysts. Do not scrape, rub or rinse with fresh water, as this will cause any nematocysts on the skin to release more venom. Soak the injury in vinegar for at least 30 minutes. Alcohol, meat tenderizer and baking soda are less effective, although a baking soda slurry is effective in treating the sting of the Chesapeake sea nettle.

After soaking, remove all visible tentacles with tweezers. Sticky tentacles may be easier to remove if you first apply a drying agent such as baking soda, talc or sand. Nematocysts can also be removed with adhesive tape or by shaving gently with a razor and shaving cream and then rinsed in vinegar. Remember: be careful. Rescuer injury is common both in the water and when removing nematocysts on shore.

Treatment for Nematocyst Sting Envenomations
Rinse with sea water to remove remaining nematocysts
Soak in vinegar for at least 30 minutes
After soaking, remove all visible tentacles

Anemones

Stinging cells surround the mouths of these sessile organisms. Contact often occurs from accidentally brushing into the anemone. Anemone nematocysts usually produce only very mild local symptoms.

Jellyfish

These animals vary in size from tiny (2mm) to big (2 meters with 40-meter tentacles). Most produce mild local signs and symptoms; however, some produce very potent venom. The box jellyfish–*Chironex fleckeri*–found in the Pacific Ocean off Western Australia, can cause death within one minute.

Portuguese Man-Of-War

This large colony of animals usually lives on the surface of the open ocean, its long, transparent tentacles dangling for prey. It is transported by winds and currents, and the animal or pieces of its tentacles can sometimes be pushed into coastal waters. Contact with pieces of tentacle usually causes only mild, superficial reactions. However, contact with a large number of tentacles from an intact animal can provoke massive envenomations and cause serious reactions.

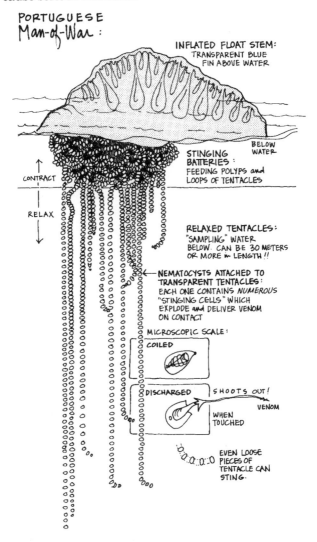

PORTUGUESE Man-of-War :

INFLATED FLOAT STEM:
TRANSPARENT BLUE FIN ABOVE WATER

BELOW WATER

STINGING BATTERIES :
FEEDING POLYPS and LOOPS OF TENTACLES

↑ CONTRACT
↓ RELAX

RELAXED TENTACLES:
"SAMPLING" WATER BELOW. CAN BE 30 METERS OR MORE in LENGTH !!

NEMATOCYSTS ATTACHED TO TRANSPARENT TENTACLES:
EACH ONE CONTAINS NUMEROUS "STINGING CELLS" WHICH EXPLODE and DELIVER VENOM ON CONTACT

MICROSCOPIC SCALE :

COILED

DISCHARGED | SHOOTS OUT !
VENOM
WHEN TOUCHED

EVEN LOOSE PIECES OF TENTACLE CAN STING.

Fire Coral

Fire corals are so named because they make you feel as if you've touched hot coals. They are found in coral reefs in tropical waters. Their nematocyst sting causes immediate pain, often described as burning, and small raised red areas on the skin. The localized pain usually lasts one to four days.

Hard Coral

Hard corals are not highly venomous but often have very sharp edges that can cause abrasions or even lacerations. The wounds heal slowly, especially if pieces of coral are imbedded in the skin. Some species can cause rashes. Vigorous irrigation of the wound is helpful to remove coral pieces. Imbedded pieces of coral often cause slow healing wound infections known at NOLS as "Coast Disease."

Sea Cucumbers

These creatures are bottom scavengers found in both shallow and deep water. Sea cucumbers often feed on nematocysts, so they may secrete coelenterate venom as well. They also produce a liquid toxin that causes skin irritations and often severe inflammatory reactions (swelling, raised patches, itching, oozing). To treat, rinse the skin thoroughly with water, and soak the injured area in vinegar as for coelenterates.

Traumatic Wounds

Wounds in a marine environment are treated as any other soft tissue wound, with an emphasis on cleansing and prevention of infection. See Chapter 3 (Soft Tissue Injuries). Research shows that sea water contains many potentially dangerous contaminants. Soft tissue wounds in sea or fresh water should be vigorously cleaned to reduce the chance of infection.

Final Thoughts

Learn to identify marine animals and to understand their habits. When wading, shuffle your feet to alert stingrays to your presence. Touching marine animals or coral formations is not necessary to enjoy them. When swimming and diving, avoid standing or walking on coral reefs or banging against them. A minimum-impact approach protects not only you, but the fragile underwater environment as well.

Summary: Marine Envenomations

Treatment for Marine Spine Envenomation
(stone fish, scorpion fish, cone shell, stingray or sea urchin)
Immerse the affected area in hot water (usually 115° to 120°F) for 30-90 minutes or until pain is relieved

Treatment for Nematocyst Sting Envenomation
(jellyfish, anemone, coral, possibly a sea cucumber)
Soak the affected area in vinegar for 30 minutes
Remove all visible tentacles with tweezers
Remove obvious imbedded spines
Rinse and irrigate the wound thoroughly
Monitor closely for signs and symptoms of systemic involvement. If these are present, consider evacuation

---

Chapter 13
COLD WATER IMMERSION AND DROWNING

Introduction

NOLS students participating in river crossings, sea kayaking, sailing, whitewater rafting and kayaking, sail boarding, snorkeling and canoeing are exposed to the hazards associated with being on or by water. These hazards include cold water immersion, immersion hypothermia and drowning.

Cold Water Immersion

The body's responses to cold water immersion are many. Sudden immersion in cold water causes a gasp for air, constriction of blood vessels in the extremities and an increase in breathing and heart rate. The initial gasp may result in water inhalation, and the rapid breathing rate makes it more difficult to hold the breath underwater.

Death caused by heart rhythm abnormalities is possible, and as strength and coordination diminish, the chance of drowning increases. What's more, as the brain cools, we think less clearly and may do foolish things, such as removing our personal flotation device (PFD) or swimming aimlessly.

The danger of cold water immersion is widely present in the wilderness environment. Water conducts heat 25 times faster than air. In North America, most water remains below 77°F year round. Lakes in the Rocky Mountains warm only to the mid-50s in summer. In Mexico, the Sea of Cortez averages 58°F in winter. We are unable to remain warm at any of these temperatures unless we wear protective clothing.

Immersion Hypothermia

Our common image of immersion hypothermia is that of a victim floating for hours in a cold ocean or lake. The body can also cool quickly in the cold moving water of a mountain stream.

While there may be subtle differences between hypothermia on land and in the water, these differences are not relevant to our field treatment. Treat immersion hypothermia by removing the victim from the water. Handle the patient gently, as rough handling may trigger lethal heart rhythm abnormalities. Treat the patient for hypothermia as discussed in Chapter 9 (Cold Injuries). Dry and insulate the patient, prevent further heat loss and ensure adequate airway, breathing and circulation, and place the patient in a sleeping bag, possibly with another person or using hot water bottles on the neck, chest and groin as heat sources.

Drowning

Drowning is the second most common cause of accidental death in children and the third leading cause of death in young adults. A majority of drowning victims are young males. Alcohol is involved in over half of drowning accidents. Freshwater drownings, especially in pools, are more common than saltwater drownings.

Risk Factors Related to Drowning

Age–toddlers and teenage males are at highest risk

Location–private swimming pools, small streams, ponds and irrigation ditches are common drowning sites

Gender–males dominate all age groups

Alcohol–a factor in one third to two thirds of drownings

Injury–cervical spine injury, as from diving or surfing

Seizure disorder–risk is greatest if poorly controlled; hyperventilation may cause predisposition to seizures

PFD–failure to wear personal flotation device

The Typical Drowning Includes:
Panic and Struggle: The victim frantically tries to keep his head above water, often using a vertical breast stroke, with the head held back and mouth open. The victim attempts to hold his breath when submerged, but eventually gasps for air.

Aspiration: Inhalation of water causes intense vomiting and further inhalation of water and vomit. Approximately 85 to 90

percent of victims experience a "wet" drowning in which they inhale water into their lungs. The other 10 to 15 percent experience a "dry" drowning: spasm of the larynx that obstructs the airway.

Unconsciousness: The victim becomes unconscious and stops breathing. Cardiac arrest and death may follow.

For first aid purposes, the type of water (salt, fresh, clean, dirty) or type of drowning (wet or dry) does not matter. Airway maintenance and, if necessary, rescue breathing and chest compressions are essential to the treatment of unconscious drowning victims. If you have any doubts about how long the victim was submerged, attempt resuscitation. There are rare case reports of people surviving submersion in ice water for more than fifteen minutes, with 69 minutes being the longest documented survival.

Treatment for Drowning

The goals of treatment are to remove the victim from the water, protect the cervical spine, prevent cardiac arrest and stabilize the patient's temperature.

Treatment for Drowning

Remove the victim from the water

Handle gently

Check the ABCs

Protect the cervical spine

Perform a secondary survey

Treat for hypothermia

Monitor vitals

Evacuate any person who required resuscitation, was unconscious in the water, exhibits shortness of breath or has a history of lung illness

---

Remove the Victim from Water

Remove the victim from water as quickly as possible. Rescuer safety is a priority. Remember the lifesaving adage "reach, throw, row and go." First try reaching for the victim, remaining in contact with the shore or boat. Second, throw a lifeline. Third, row or paddle to the victim. Attempt a swimming rescue only as a last resort.

Handle the Patient Gently
Handle the patient gently. A patient who was submerged in cold water may be hypothermic.

Check the ABCs
Assess and check the ABCs. Aggressive initiation of airway, breathing and circulation is the standard in drowning rescue. If available, administer oxygen.

Protect the Cervical Spine
Unless injury can be ruled out, assume the victim has a neck injury and use the jaw thrust technique to open the airway. Neck injuries can be caused from surfing, diving in shallow water, or from flipping a kayak or decked canoe in rapids.

Perform a Secondary Survey
A complete patient exam is warranted to assess for injury.

Treat For Hypothermia
Remove wet clothing, dry and insulate the patient to prevent further heat loss.

Evacuate the Patient
Outside the wilderness, any victim of involuntary submersion should be evaluated by a physician, as lung injury from inhaled water may not be immediately evident. In the wilderness, we don't evacuate every asymptomatic person who swims through a rapid or takes a dunking during a river crossing and comes up coughing. Evacuate the victim of a submersion incident if that person required any resuscitation, was unconscious in the water, exhibits shortness of breath or other symptoms of respiratory difficulty or has a history of lung disease.

The mode of transport and speed of the evacuation should be based on the seriousness of the patient's condition. For example, a patient who is unconscious following submersion should be quickly evacuated.

Final Thoughts

Safety around lakes, rivers and the ocean begins with respect for the power of moving water and the debilitating effects of cold water. Cold water, failure to wear a PFD and the inability to swim are, according to the Coast Guard, the most common factors in whitewater deaths.

In two out of three drownings, the victims are persons who could not swim, had no intention of entering deep water (and were thus ill prepared) and were effected by alcohol or drugs. Most drownings occur ten to thirty feet from safety, only one in ten drownings occurs in a guarded pool.

While awaiting rescue, assume the HELP position (Heat Escape Lessening Posture) by bringing your knees to your chest and crossing your arms over them. If you're with a group of people awaiting rescue, everyone in the group should face inward and huddle with arms interlocked. You must be wearing a PFD to assume either of these positions. If possible, get out of the water onto an overturned or partially submerged boat. It is always better to keep as much of yourself or the victim out of the water as possible, even when the wind is blowing.

Clothing selection for paddling or other activities around water requires finding a balance between overdressing–and overheating–and protecting the body against sudden immersion in cold water. Extra clothing should be easily accessible in the cockpit of your boat or in your pack and should be donned if developing conditions increase the likelihood of a cold dunking.

Well developed safety and rescue programs exist for swimming, sea kayaking, whitewater boating and sailing. If you're involved in any of these activities, seek out these programs for further training.

Summary: Treatment for Drowning
Remove the victim from the water
Handle gently
Check the ABCs
Protect the cervical spine
Perform a secondary survey
Treat for hypothermia
Monitor vitals
Evacuate any person who required resuscitation, was unconscious in the water, exhibits shortness of breath, or has a history of lung illness.

Chapter 14
ALTITUDE ILLNESS

Introduction

Each year approximately 6,000 people climb Mount Rainier–
elevation 14,408 feet. Another 6,000 trek to the base of Mount
Everest, reaching altitudes of 18,000 feet, and 800 people
attempt to climb Denali–elevation 20,320 feet. Skiers in the
Rocky Mountains often ski at altitudes of 11,000 to 12,000 feet;
many arrive at altitude and ski within 24 hours of leaving low
elevations. Thousands of people trek in Nepal, South America
and Africa every year at altitudes of over 13,000 feet.

All of these people are at risk for altitude illness. Recent studies
show that 66 percent of the climbers on Rainier, 47 percent of
the Everest trekkers, and 30 percent of the Denali climbers
develop symptoms of altitude illness.

NOLS expeditions have managed life-threatening cerebral
edema at 21,000 feet on Cerro Aconcagua in Argentina and
pulmonary edema at 9,000 feet in Wyoming's Wind River
Range. Prevention through acclimatization provides some
protection from altitude illness, but there is no immunity. If
you travel in mountains you need to know how to prevent,
recognize and treat altitude illness.

Altitudes are defined as:	
High altitude	8,000 – 14,000 feet
Very high altitude	14,000 – 18,000 feet
Extreme altitude	above 18,000 feet

Lack of oxygen is the number one cause of health problems at
altitude. Normally, oxygen diffuses from the alveoli into the
blood because the gas pressure is greater in the alveoli than in
blood. At altitude, diminished air pressure (barometric pressure) reduces the pressure in the alveoli and decreases the
amount of oxygen diffusing into the blood. For example, in a
healthy person at sea level, blood is 95 percent saturated with
oxygen. At 18,000 feet it is only 71 percent saturated; i.e., it is
carrying 29 percent less oxygen.

As altitude increases, barometric pressure falls logarithmically. Distance from the equator, seasons and weather also affect barometric pressure.

The greater the distance from the equator, the lower the barometric pressure, given the same elevation. For example, if Mt. Everest were located at the same latitude as Denali, the corresponding drop in barometric pressure would make an ascent without oxygen impossible.

As for seasons and weather, air pressure is lower in winter than in summer, and a low pressure trough will reduce pressure. While temperature does not directly affect barometric pressure, the combination of cold stress and lack of oxygen increases the risk of cold injuries and altitude problems.

Adaptation to Altitude

The body undergoes numerous changes at higher elevation in order to increase oxygen delivery to cells and improve efficiency of oxygen use. These adaptations usually begin almost immediately and continue to occur for several weeks. People vary in their ability to acclimatize. Some adjust quickly while others fail to acclimatize, even with gradual exposure over a period of weeks.

In general, the body becomes approximately 80 percent acclimatized after 10 days at altitude and approximately 95 percent acclimatized by six weeks. The respiratory rate peaks in about one week and then slowly decreases over the next few months, although it tends to remain higher than its normal rate at sea level. After 10 days, the heart rate starts to decrease.

When we descend, we begin losing our hard-won adaptations at approximately the same rate at which we gained them; 10 days after returning to sea level, we have lost 80 percent of our adaptations.

Adaptation to Altitude

Early Changes
Increased respiratory rate
Increased heart rate
Fluid shifts

Later Changes
Increased red blood cell production
Increased 2, 3 DPG production
Increased number of capillaries

Increased Respiratory Rate
During the first week of adaptation, a variety of changes takes place. Respiratory rate and depth increase in response to lower concentrations of oxygen in the blood, causing more carbon dioxide to be lost and more oxygen to be delivered to the alveoli. The increased respiratory rate begins within the first few hours of arriving at altitudes as low as 5,000 feet. The lost carbon dioxide causes the body to become more alkaline.

To compensate for the body's increasing alkalinity, the kidneys excrete bicarbonate—an alkaline substance—in the urine. This adaptation occurs within 24 to 48 hours after hyperventilation starts.

Increased Heart Rate
Cells require a constant supply of oxygen so the heart beats more quickly to meet the demand. Except at extreme altitudes, heart rate returns to near normal after acclimatization.

Fluid Shifts
Blood flow to the brain increases to provide the brain with its required volume of oxygen (equivalent to that available at sea level).

In the lungs, the pulmonary capillaries constrict, increasing resistance to flow through the lungs and raising pulmonary blood pressure. Dangerously high blood pressure in the pulmonary artery may cause fluid to escape from the capillaries and leak into the lungs (pulmonary edema).

Increased Red Blood Cell Production
As acclimatization continues, the bone marrow contributes by increasing red blood cell production. New red blood cells become available in the blood within four to five days, increasing the blood's oxygen-carrying capacity. An acclimatized person may have 30 to 50 percent more red blood cells than his counterpart at sea level.

Increased 2, 3 DPG Production
Within the blood cells 2, 3 Diphosphoglycerate (DPG) increases. This is an organic phosphate that helps oxygen to combine with red blood cells. Production of myoglobin, the intramuscular oxygen-carrying protein in red blood cells, also increases.

Increased Number of Capillaries
The body develops more capillaries in response to altitude. This improves the diffusion of oxygen by shortening the distance between the cell and capillary.

Altitude Illness
High altitude illness results from a lack of oxygen in the body. Anyone who ascends to altitude will become hypoxic (the condition of having insufficient oxygen in the blood). Why some people become ill and others don't is not known. It is known, however, that most people who become ill do so within the first few days of ascending to altitude. The only sure treatment is to descend.

Six Factors That Affect
The Incidence and Severity of Altitude Illness

1. Rate of ascent—the faster you climb the greater your risk.

2. Altitude attained (especially sleeping altitude)—the higher you sleep the greater the risk.

3. Length of exposure—the longer you stay high the greater the risk.

4. Level of exertion—hard exertion, without rest or hydration, increases the risk.

5. Hydration and diet—high fat, high protein diets and dehydration increase the risk.

6. Inherent physiological susceptibility—some people are more likely to become ill and we don't know why.

The three common types of altitude illness are acute mountain sickness (AMS), high altitude pulmonary edema (HAPE) and high altitude cerebral edema (HACE). AMS is the most common. It is not life-threatening, but if not treated it can progress into HAPE or HACE. HAPE is less common but more serious. HACE is rare but can be sudden and severe.

Acute Mountain Sickness

Acute mountain sickness is a term applied to a group of symptoms. It is more apt to occur in unacclimatized people who make rapid ascents to above 8,000 feet. It also occurs in people who partially acclimatize then make an abrupt ascent to a higher altitude.

Signs and Symptoms

Signs and symptoms tend to start six to 72 hours after arrival at high altitude. They usually disappear in two to six days. Symptoms are worse in the mornings, probably due to normal decrease in rate and depth of breathing during sleep, which lowers blood oxygen saturation. Symptoms include the following.

**Signs and Symptoms of
Acute Mountain Sickness**
Headache
Malaise
Loss of appetite
Nausea, vomiting
Peripheral edema
Disturbed sleep
Cyanosis

Headache
Increased cerebral blood flow helps the brain maintain its oxygen supply, but the expanded volume causes pain as the system adapts.

Malaise
Malaise (uneasy feeling), drowsiness and lassitude occur because of decreased oxygen in the blood.

Loss of Appetite, Nausea and Vomiting
When blood is shunted to the vital organs (heart, lungs, brain), perfusion of the gastrointestinal tract decreases, compromising its function. Anorexia, nausea and vomiting are the result.

Peripheral Edema
Persons with acute mountain sickness tend to retain fluid, resulting in edema, especially of the face and hands.

Disturbed Sleep
During sleep, a person's rate and depth of respiration may gradually increase until it reaches a climax. Breathing then ceases entirely for five to 50 seconds. This phenomenon is called Cheyne-Stokes respiration. Cheyne-Stokes breathing further decreases the level of oxygen in the blood.

Cyanosis
Cyanosis (a bluish appearance) in the fingernail beds, mucous

membranes and around the mouth occurs as a result of decreased oxygen saturation of the blood.

Treatment

Limit your activity during the first three days at altitudes greater than 8,000 feet; it may take three to four days to acclimatize. Drink copious amounts of fluids to help the kidneys excrete bicarbonate. Aspirin, acetaminophen or ibuprofen may ease the headache. If symptoms worsen, signs of ataxia or pulmonary edema become apparent or there is a change in the level of consciousness, descend to the altitude where symptoms began. Usually descending 2,000 to 3,000 feet is sufficient.

**Treatment for
Acute Mountain Sickness**

Hydrate
Rest

Descend if:
Symptoms worsen
Signs of HAPE or HACE develop

High Altitude Pulmonary Edema (HAPE)

HAPE is abnormal fluid accumulation in the lungs resulting from maladaptation to altitude. The cause is not clearly understood. HAPE rarely occurs below 8,000 feet and is more common in young males.

Assessment

The symptoms of HAPE result from the decreasing ability of the lungs to exchange oxygen and carbon dioxide. The symptoms usually begin 24 to 96 hours after ascent.

**Signs and Symptoms of
High Altitude Pulmonary Edema**

Signs of acute mountain sickness
Shortness of breath on exertion, progressing to
  shortness of breath in general
Fatigue
Dry cough progressing to a wet, productive cough
Increased heart rate and respiratory rate
Rales, sounds of fluid in the lungs
Ataxia

HAPE may initially appear with mild symptoms similar to AMS. The patient complains of a dry cough and shortness of breath and fatigue while climbing uphill. The heart and respiratory rate increase. Cyanosis of the fingernail beds may occur.

As HAPE worsens, the shortness of breath, weakness and fatigue occurs while walking on level ground. The patient complains of a harsh cough, headache and loss of appetite. The heart and respiratory rate remain elevated. The nail beds become cyanotic. Rales ("rattles") can be heard with a stethoscope. The patient may be ataxic. Signs and symptoms may be mistaken for the "flu," bronchitis or pneumonia.

As HAPE becomes severe, the patient complains of a productive cough, extreme weakness and shortness of breath while at rest. Heart rate is greater than 110/minute, and respiratory rate is greater than 30/minute. Facial and nail bed cyanosis may be apparent. Rales can be heard without a stethoscope. The patient coughs up frothy blood-tinged sputum. The patient becomes ataxic, lethargic or unconscious.

HAPE, like AMS, becomes worse at night due to Cheyne-Stokes respirations. HAPE is a life-threatening illness.

Treatment
Descend to a lower altitude as quickly as possible—at least 2,000 to 3,000 feet is mandatory. Give oxygen, if available. If the symptoms do not improve, descend until they do. Keep the patient warm, as cold stress can worsen the condition. The patient should avoid exercise for two to three days so the fluid in the lungs can be reabsorbed. People with mild HAPE may attempt to ascend again when the condition disappears. Watch for a relapse. A patient with moderate to severe HAPE must be evacuated from the mountain to a hospital.

Treatment

Descend at least 2,000–3,000 feet
until symptoms abate

If you are unable to descend and have oxygen available, give the patient 100 percent oxygen at a flow rate of four to six liters per minute. If the condition does not improve increase the flow of oxygen. Descend as soon as possible.

High Altitude Cerebral Edema (HACE)
HACE is swelling of the brain thought to be caused by hypoxia damage to brain tissue. HACE generally occurs above 12,000 feet but has been recorded at 10,000 feet in the Wind Rivers.

Signs and Symptoms
The classic signs of HACE are change in the level of consciousness, ataxia and severe lassitude. The patient may become confused, lose his memory or slip into unconsciousness. Ataxia is evident in the lower extremities first, then in the upper extremities. In severe cases the patient may be unable to hold a cup.

Other signs and symptoms may include headache, nausea, vomiting, cyanosis, seizures, hallucinations and transient blindness, partial paralysis and loss of sensation on one side of the body.

**Signs and Symptoms of
High Altitude Cerebral Edema**

Signs of acute mountain sickness
Changes in level of consciousness
Ataxia
Severe lassitude
Headache
Nausea and vomiting
Vision disturbances
Paralysis
Seizures
Hallucinations
Cyanosis

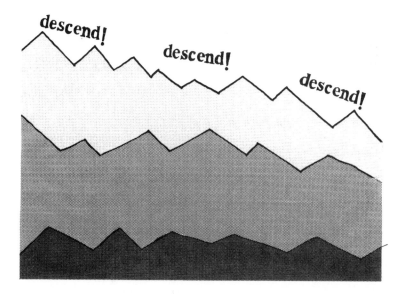

Treatment
DESCEND, DESCEND, DESCEND!! Do not hope the condition will get better if you wait. Waiting and hoping may be fatal. Descend to a lower elevation as soon as you notice any ataxia or change in the level of consciousness. Give oxygen if available.

Treatment
DESCEND, DESCEND, DESCEND!!

Thrombophlebitis
Studies have shown that there is an increased tendency for blood to thrombose (clot) in arteries and veins at high altitudes. Dehydration, increased red blood cells, cold constrictive clothing and immobility during bad weather have been cited as possible causes.

Signs and Symptoms
Clots most commonly occur in the deep veins of the calf. The calf is swollen and painful. The lower leg may be pale or cyanotic with decreased pulses in the foot. Flexing the foot upward or walking increases calf pain. If the clot breaks lose, it can travel to the lungs and cause a pulmonary embolism.

Treatment
Loosen constrictive clothing. Give aspirin (one or two) every four hours for pain and to decrease the blood's ability to clot. The patient should be carried down from altitude.

Prevention
Dehydration can predispose one to blood clots. Hydration is important for prevention. Exercise feet and legs a few minutes every hour if bad weather confines the group to tents. Be careful of constrictive clothing, such as tight gaiters.

Final Thoughts: Acclimatization

Start out sleeping at altitudes below 10,000 feet and spend two to three nights there before going higher. For every 2,000 to 3,000 feet gained, plan to spend an extra night acclimatizing to the new altitude.

Climb high and sleep low. It is best not to increase the sleeping altitude by more than 2,000 feet at a time. Set up camp at lower elevations and take day trips to high points. Ferry loads up to a high camp and then return to the low camp to sleep as you acclimatize.

Acclimatization

Ascend slowly

Climb high, sleep low

High carbohydrate diet

Hydrate

Eat a high carbohydrate diet. Carbohydrates require less oxygen for metabolism than fats and proteins. However, a diet of exclusively carbohydrates does not meet the body's overall nutritional needs. Eat protein and fat on rest days. Avoid eating fats and protein at night. The combination of decreased respiratory rate during sleep and increased requirement for oxygen to metabolize fats and proteins increases the risk of altitude illness.

Drink copious amounts of fluid. Urine should be clear not yellow. Avoid sleeping pills, which decrease respiratory rates, aggravating the lack of oxygen.

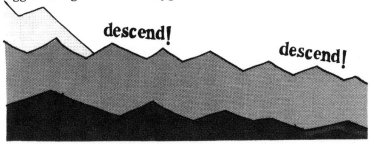

The Gamow Bag
A Recent Development In Treating Altitude Illness

The Gamow Bag is a portable hyperbaric (greater pressure than normal atmospheric pressure) chamber used to provide temporary first aid treatment to victims of altitude illness. The greater pressure inside the bag allows more oxygen to diffuse into the blood.

The bag is constructed of non-permeable nylon. The patient enters the bag, which is zipped closed and inflated with a foot pump. Depending upon the altitude, the increase in pressure inside can simulate an altitude decrease of up to 9,195 feet. The bag takes approximately two minutes to inflate and requires 10 to 20 pumps per minute to maintain pressure and flush out carbon dioxide. The bag, air pump and carrying pack weigh 15 pounds.

The Gamow Bag is a temporary treatment for emergencies; it is intended for use during evacuation to a lower altitude or if you are unable to descend immediately. Attempts to evacuate the victim to a lower altitude should be made as soon as possible.

For more information on the Gamow Bag, write:
Portable Hyperbaric Corporation
P.O. Box 510
Ilion, New York 13357.

Telephone: (315) 895-7485

Summary: Altitude Illnesses

The risks of altitude illness can be reduced by acclimatizing to altitude. Ascend slowly, climb high, sleep low, eat a high-carbohydrate diet and stay hydrated!

The only definitive treatment for altitude illness is to

DESCEND

    DESCEND

        DESCEND!!

descend!

CHAPTER 15
ATHLETIC INJURIES

Introduction

Living and traveling in the wilderness, carrying a pack, hiking long distances, climbing and paddling can be the sources of sprains and strains and tendinitis. Athletic injuries account for 40 percent of injuries on NOLS courses and are a frequent cause of evacuations.

When faced with an athletic injury, the first-aider in the wilderness has to choose between treating the injury in the field—possibly altering the expedition route and timetable to accommodate the patient's loss of mobility—or evacuation. If evacuation is indicated, the first-aider must decide between walking the patient out or carrying him out on a litter.

Athletic injuries can be difficult to diagnose if initial pain and swelling confuse the extent of the injury. The most common athletic injuries on NOLS courses are ankle and knee sprains, Achilles tendinitis and forearm tendinitis. Most of the athletic injuries we experience are minor, but even a moderate ankle sprain can take a week to heal. It is difficult for a NOLS student to rest for seven days without affecting a course traveling through the wilderness.

Common Causes of Athletic Injury on NOLS Courses

Playing games such as hug tag and hacky sack
Tripping while walking in camp
Stepping over logs
Crossing streams, including shallow rock-hops
Putting on a backpack
Lifting a kayak or raft
Falling or misstepping while hiking with a pack
  (on any terrain)
Falling while skiing with a pack
Shoveling snow
Bending over to pick up firewood

General Treatment (RICE)

Athletic injuries are generally treated with RICE: rest, ice, compression and elevation. Allowing these injuries to heal until they are free of pain, tenderness and swelling will prevent further aggravation of the condition. Gently rub the injured area with ice, wrapped in fabric to prevent frostbite, for periods of 20 to 40 minutes every two to four hours for the first 24 to 48 hours. Cooling decreases nerve conduction and pain, constricts blood vessels, limits the inflammatory process and reduces cellular demand for oxygen.

Compression with an elastic bandage will help reduce swelling. Care must be taken when applying the wrap not to exert pressure on an injury that swells dramatically or to cut off blood flow to the fingers or toes.

Elevating the injury above the level of the heart reduces swelling. Non-prescription pain medications such as acetaminophen and ibuprofen may help as well.

General Treatment for Athletic Injuries
(RICE)
Rest: allow time for healing
Ice: 20-40 minutes, every 2-4 hours for 24-28 hours
Compression: elastic bandage to reduce swelling
Elevation: reduces swelling

acetaminophen, ibuprofen for pain and inflammation

Sprains

Sprains are categorized as grades one, two and three. With a grade one injury, ligament fibers are stretched but not torn. A partly torn or badly stretched ligament is a grade two injury. Completely torn ligaments are grade three injuries. Grade one and two sprains can be treated in the field. Grade three injuries will require surgery to repair the severed ligament.

Assessment

A thorough assessment includes an evaluation of the mechanism of injury as well as of signs and symptoms. Knowing the mechanism helps you determine if the occurrence was sudden and traumatic, indicating a sprain, or whether it was progressive, suggesting an overuse injury.

Signs and symptoms of a sprain include swelling, pain and discoloration. Point tenderness and obvious deformity suggest a fracture. Ask the patient to try to move the joint through its full range of motion. Painless movement is a good sign. If the patient is able to use or bear weight on the affected limb and pain and swelling are not severe, he can be treated in the field.

Severe pain, the sound of a pop at the time of injury, immediate swelling and inability to use the joint are signs of a serious sprain, possibly a fracture. This injury should be immobilized and the patient evacuated from the field.

General Signs and Symptoms
Swelling and discoloration
Pain
Instability at joint
Loss of range of motion
Inability to bear weight

Ankle Sprains

Uneven ground, whether boulder fields in the backcountry or broken pavement in the city, contributes to the likelihood of sprains. Of all sprains, 85 percent are inversion injuries — those in which the foot turns in to the midline of the body and the ankle turns outward. Inversion injuries usually sprain one or more of the ligaments on the outside of the ankle.

Ankle Anatomy

The bones, ligaments and tendons of the ankle and foot absorb stress and pressure generated by both body weight and activity.

They also allow for flexibility and accommodate surface irregularities so that we don't lose our balance.

Bones
The lower leg bones are the tibia and the fibula. The large bumps on the outsides of the ankle are the lower end of these bones, the fibula on the outside and the tibia on the inside. Immediately under the tibia and fibula lies the talus bone, which sits atop the calcaneus (heel bone). The talus and calcaneus act as a rocker for front-to-back flexibility of the ankle. Without them we would walk stiff-legged.

In front of the calcaneus lie two smaller bones, the navicular (inside) and the cuboid (outside). They attach to three small bones called the cuneiforms. Anterior to the cuneiforms are five metatarsals, which in turn articulate with the phalanges (toe bones).

Ligaments
Due to the number of bones in the foot, ligaments are many and complex. For simplicity, think of a ligament on every exterior surface of every bone, attaching to the adjacent articulating bone.

There are four ligaments commonly associated with ankle sprains. On the inside of the ankle is the large, fan-shaped

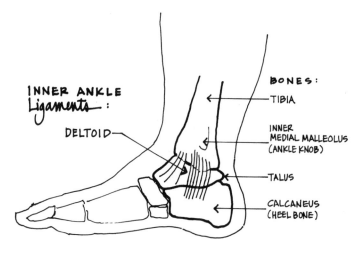

INNER ANKLE
Ligaments :
DELTOID

BONES:
TIBIA
INNER
MEDIAL MALLEOLUS
(ANKLE KNOB)
TALUS
CALCANEUS
(HEEL BONE)

deltoid ligament joining the talus, calcaneus and several of the smaller foot bones to the tibia. Rolling the ankle inward, an eversion sprain, stresses the deltoid ligament. Spraining the deltoid requires considerable force, and due to its size and strength it is seldom injured. In fact, this ligament is so strong that if a bad twist occurs, it will frequently pull fragments of bone off at its attachment points, causing an avulsion fracture.

On the outside, usually the weaker aspect, three ligaments attach from the fibula to the talus and the calcaneus. Together these three ligaments protect the ankle from turning to the outside.

Muscles and Tendons
Muscles on the lower leg use long tendons to act on the ankle and foot. The calf muscles, the gastrocnemius and soleus, shorten to point the toes. These muscles taper into the largest tendon, the Achilles, which attaches to the back of calcaneus. The peroneal muscles on the lower leg contract and pull the foot laterally and roll the ankle outward. Muscles on the front of the lower leg turn the foot inward and extend the toes.

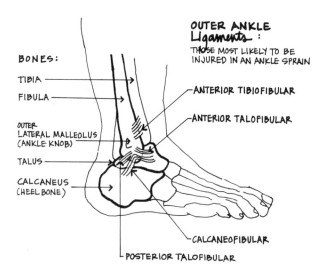

BONES:
TIBIA
FIBULA
OUTER LATERAL MALLEOLUS (ANKLE KNOB)
TALUS
CALCANEUS (HEEL BONE)

OUTER ANKLE Ligaments :
THOSE MOST LIKELY TO BE INJURED IN AN ANKLE SPRAIN
ANTERIOR TIBIOFIBULAR
ANTERIOR TALOFIBULAR
CALCANEOFIBULAR
POSTERIOR TALOFIBULAR

Treatment for Ankle Sprains

Sprains should have the standard treatment of rest, ice, compression, and elevation to limit swelling and allow healing. If a severe sprain or a fracture is suspected, immobilize the ankle. Aggressively treating a mild sprain with RICE for the first 24 to 48 hours and allowing it to rest for a few days has allowed patients to stay in the mountains rather than cut their trip short. A simple method for providing ankle support is to tape the ankle using the basket weave.

> **Treatment for Ankle Sprains**
> RICE
> Taping for support

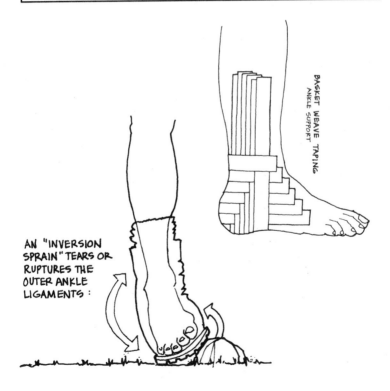

BASKET WEAVE TAPING
ANKLE SUPPORT

AN "INVERSION SPRAIN" TEARS OR RUPTURES THE OUTER ANKLE LIGAMENTS :

Knee Pain

Pain in the knee from overuse can be treated by ceasing the activity causing the discomfort and controlling pain and inflammation with RICE. In the event of a traumatic injury resulting in an unstable, swollen and painful knee, splint and evacuate. If the injury is stable and the patient can bear weight, use RICE to control pain and inflammation. If the patient can walk without undue pain, wrap the knee with foamlite for support.

Tendinitis

A tendon is the fibrous cord by which a muscle is attached to a bone. Its construction is similar to that of kernmantle rope, with an outer sheath of tissue enclosing a core of fibers. Some tendons, such as those that pull the finger, are long. The activating muscles are in the forearm but the tendons stretch from the forearm across the wrist to each finger. These tendons are surrounded by a lubricating sheath to assist their movement.

Tendinitis is inflammation of a tendon. When the sheath and the tendon become inflamed, the sheath becomes rough, movement is restricted and painful and the patient feels a grating of the tendon inside the sheath. Fibers can be torn or, more commonly, irritation from overuse or infection can inflame the sheath, causing pain when the tendon moves. There may be little pain when the tendon is at rest.

Tendons are poorly supplied with blood, so they heal slowly. Tendons are well supplied with nerves, however, which means an injury will be painful. Tendons can be injured by sudden overloading but are more frequently injured through overuse. Factors contributing to tendinitis include poor technique, poor equipment, unhealed prior injury and cool and unstretched muscles.

Assessment of Tendinitis

Tendinitis, in contrast to ankle sprains, is a progressive overuse injury, not a traumatic injury. Common sites for tendinitis are the Achilles tendon and the tendons of the forearm. The Achilles, the largest tendon in the body, may fatigue and become inflamed during or following lengthy hikes, especially with significant elevation gain. Boots that break down and place pressure on the tendon can provide enough irritation in one day to initiate inflammation.

Forearm tendinitis is common among canoeists and kayakers. Poor technique and inadequate strength and flexibility contribute to the injury. Similar tendinitis comes with repetitive use of ski poles, ice axes and ice climbing tools.

Tendinitis may also occur on the front of the foot, usually caused by tightly laced boots or stiff mountaineering boots. The tendons extending the toes become irritated and inflamed. Tendinitis causes swelling, redness, warmth, pain to the touch (or pinch), painful movement and sounds of friction or grinding (crepitus).

**Signs and Symptoms
of Tendinitis**
Redness
Warmth
Crepitus
Localized pain

Treatment for Tendinitis

Treat tendinitis with RICE: rest, ice, compression and elevation. It may be necessary to cease the aggravating activity until the inflammation subsides. Prevent or ease tendinitis of anterior muscles by varying boot lacing. Lace boots more loosely when hiking and more tightly when climbing.

Achilles Tendinitis

To relieve stretch on the Achilles tendon provide a heel lift. To relieve direct pressure from the boot, place a six-inch by one-inch strip of foamlite padding on either side of the Achilles tendon. The placement should take the pressure off without touching the Achilles.

**Treatment for
Achilles Tendinitis**
RICE
Heel lifts
Pads on ankle to protect the tendon

Forearm Tendinitis

Forearm tendinitis is primarily associated with the repetitive motion of paddling. Pay close attention to proper paddling technique! Keep a relaxed, open grip on the paddle. On the forward stroke keep the wrist in line with the forearm during the pull and push, and avoid crossing the upper arm over the midline of the body.

Other paddling techniques that may help prevent forearm tendinitis: keep the thumb on the same side of the paddle as the fingers, and switch a feathered paddle for an unfeathered paddle. The feathered paddle requires a wrist movement that can sometimes aggravate tendinitis.

Tendinitis of the forearm is treated with RICE. Also, the wrist can be taped to limit movement that aggravates the condition.

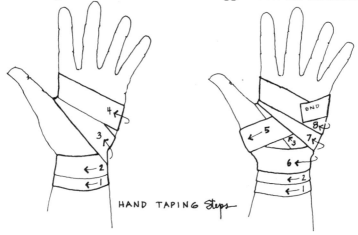

HAND TAPING Steps

> **Treatment for**
> **Forearm Tendinitis**
> RICE
> Taping wrist to limit range of motion

Muscle Strains

Muscles can be stretched and torn from overuse or overexertion. Initial treatment is RICE, followed by heat, massage and gentle stretching. Radiating muscle pain, strong pain at rest, pain secondary to an illness or pain from a severe trauma mechanism are reasons to evacuate for evaluation by a physician.

Final Thoughts: Prevention

Errors in technique and inadequate muscular conditioning or warm-up produce injury. Overuse of muscles and joints (when there is no single traumatic event as the cause of injury) generates many of the sprains and strains on NOLS courses.

Jerky movements, excessive force or an unnecessarily tight grip on the paddle while kayaking contribute to forearm tendinitis. Performing the athletic movements required for difficult rock climbs without warming up or paying attention to balance and form can cause injury. Even the seemingly simple actions of lifting a backpack or boat, stepping over logs and wading in cold mountain streams can be dangerous.

Steep terrain and wet conditions contribute to injuries. Slippery conditions make it harder to balance and can cause falls. Falls that occur in camp and while hiking are the cause of many athletic injuries. Surprisingly, injuries to backcountry travelers are as likely to occur when we are not wearing a pack as when we are. Possibly this is because we are more attentive to technique when hiking or skiing with a pack or because stiff boots protect the ankle.

We are more likely to be injured when we are tired, cold,

dehydrated, rushed or ill. We're not thinking as clearly, and our muscles are less flexible and responsive. Injuries happen more frequently in late morning and late afternoon when dehydration and fatigue reduce our awareness and increase our clumsiness. Shifting from a three-full-meals-a-day schedule to breakfast and dinner plus three or four light snacks during the day helps keep our food supply constant.

Haste, often the result of unrealistic timetables, is frequently implicated in accidents. Try to negotiate the more difficult terrain in the morning, when you are fresh. Take rest breaks before difficult sections of a hike or paddle. Stop at the base of the pass, the near side of the river, the beginning of the boulder field. Drink, eat, and stretch tight muscles. Check equipment: for loose gaiters that may trip you, for loose sprayskirts and unfastened life jackets and for poorly balanced backpacks.

The sustained activity of life in the wilderness and the need for sudden bursts of power when paddling, skiing or climbing necessitate physical conditioning prior to a wilderness expedition. A regimen of endurance, flexibility and muscle strength training will help prevent injuries and promote safety and enjoyment of the wilderness activity.

Summary: Athletic Injuries

General Signs and Symptoms
Swelling and discoloration
Pain
Instability at joint
Loss of range of motion
Inability to bear weight

General Treatment (RICE)
Rest: allow time for healing
Ice: 20-40 minutes, every 2-4 hours for 24-28 hours
Compression: elastic bandage to reduce swelling
Elevation: reduces swelling
Acetaminophen, ibuprofen for pain and inflammation

Treatment for Ankle Sprains
RICE
Taping for support

Signs and Symptoms of Tendinitis
Redness
Warmth
Crepitus
Localized pain

Treatment for Achilles Tendinitis
RICE
Heel lifts
Pads on ankle to protect the tendon

Treatment for Forearm Tendinitis
RICE
Taping wrist to limit range of motion

CHAPTER 16

GENDER-SPECIFIC MEDICAL CONCERNS

Introduction

Injuries of the genitalia can be embarrassing, frightening and life-threatening. A variety of illnesses can also affect the reproductive system. These range from epididymitis and urinary tract and vaginal infections to the more serious testicular torsion, pelvic inflammatory disease and ectopic pregnacy. It is our experience that these problems do occur on wilderness trips. The wilderness leader should be able to assess, treat and know when to evacuate a patient with injured or ill genitalia.

General Guidelines for Assessment

Provide a private place to talk. Maintain eye contact, be straightforward, respectful and non-judgmental. Use proper medical terminology or terms that you both understand–no jokes or slang. A member of the patient's sex should be present before and during any physical exam.

For female patients, gather information about the patient's menstrual and reproductive history. When was her last menstrual period? How long is her cycle? Does she use contraception? Has she had sexual intercourse in the past month, and what is normal for her? If she has had the problem before, how did she treat it?

Ask open-ended questions. For example: "Tell me about your normal menstrual cycle." This type of questioning will allow you to gather more information.

Male-Specific Medical Concerns

Male Anatomy

The male external genitalia consist of the penis and scrotum. The penis provides a route for urine to be expelled from the bladder and sperm expelled from the testes. The scrotum is a pouch-like structure located to the side of and beneath the penis. The testes lie within the scrotum and are the site of sperm and testosterone production.

Sperm travels out of the testes via the epididymis, a comma-shaped organ that lies behind the testes. The epididymis is composed of approximately 20 feet of ducts. From the epididymis, sperm travel through the ductus deferens, a tube approximately 18 inches long that loops into the pelvic cavity. Sperm can be stored here for many months.

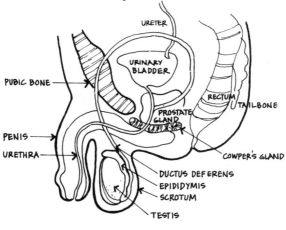

MALE REPRODUCTIVE System

Epididymitis

Epididymitis is an inflammation of the epididymis and can be caused by gonorrhea, syphilis, tuberculosis, mumps, prostatitis (inflammation of the prostate) or urethritis (inflammation of the urethra).

Signs and Symptoms

The patient suffers from pain in the scrotum, possibly accompanied by fever. The scrotum may be red and swollen. Epididymitis tends to come on slowly, unlike torsion of the testis, which comes on rapidly.

Treatment

The treatment is bed rest and support of the scrotum with a jock strap. Antibiotics are necessary, so the patient must be evacuated. Acetaminophen, aspirin or ibuprofen may decrease the fever and pain.

Torsion of the Testis

Torsion of the testis is a twisting of the testis within the scrotum. The ductus deferens and its accompanying blood vessels becomes twisted, decreasing the blood supply to the testis. If the blood supply is totally cut off, the testis dies. After 24 hours without blood supply the prognosis for saving the testis is poor.

Signs and Symptoms

The scrotum is red, swollen and painful, and the testis may appear slightly elevated on the affected side.

Treatment

Cool compresses and pain medication will provide some relief. The patient must be evacuated for treatment. A jock strap made from a triangular bandage will elevate the scrotum and may increase blood flow to the testis.

Female-Specific Medical Concerns

Female Anatomy

The female reproductive organs lie within the pelvic cavity. The vagina, or birth canal, is approximately three to four inches long. The vagina is continuously moistened by secretions that keep it clean and slightly acidic.

At the top of the vagina is the cervix, a circle of tissue pierced by a small hole that opens into the uterus. The cervix thins and opens during labor to allow the baby to be expelled.

The uterus is about the size of a fist and is located between the bladder and rectum. Pregnancy begins when a fertilized egg implants in the tissue of the uterus. The uterus is an elastic organ that expands with the growing fetus.

On either side of the uterus are the ovaries, which lie approximately four or five inches below the waist. The ovaries produce eggs and the female sex hormones estrogen and progesterone.

Each month an egg (ovum) is released from one of the the ovaries and travels down the fallopian tube to the uterus. The fallopian tubes are approximately four inches long and wrap around the ovaries but are not directly connected to them. When the egg is released from the ovary, the fimbria (finger-like structures at the end of the fallopian tube) make sweeping motions across the ovary sucking the egg into the fallopian tube.

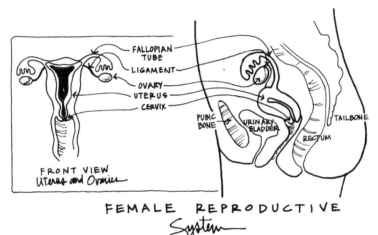

The Menstrual Cycle

At approximately 12 years of age, a woman starts her menstrual cycle, the monthly release of ova. Hormones regulate the cycle, which continues until menopause, or cessation of the menstrual cycle, at approximately 50 years of age.

The endometrial tissue that lines the uterus undergoes hormone-regulated changes each month during menstruation. The average menstrual cycle is 28 days long, with day one being the first day of the menstrual period. From days one through five the endometrial tissue sloughs off from the uterus and is expelled through the vagina. The usual discharge is four to six tablespoons of blood, tissue and mucus. During days six through 16 the endometrial tissue regrows in preparation for implantation of an ovum, becoming thick and full of small blood vessels.

Ovulation occurs on day 14; the egg takes approximately six and a half days to reach the uterus. Days 16 through 26 the endometrium secretes substances to nourish the embryo. If conception has not occurred, the hormones progesterone and estrogen decrease, causing the uterine blood supply to decrease and the lining of the uterus to be shed.

Mittelschmerz

Some women experience cramping in the lower abdomen on the right or left side or back when the ovary releases an egg. The pain is sometimes accompanied by bloody vaginal discharge. This is called Mittelschmerz (mittel = middle: schmerz = pain).

Signs and Symptoms

The pain may be severe enough to be confused with appendicitis or ectopic pregnancy, but a careful assessment should allow the first-aider to distinguish between the two. Ask the patient where she is in her menstrual cycle. Has she ever had this pain before? Typically, a woman will have had similar cramping in the past. Any light bleeding or pain should cease within 36 hours. The abdomen is soft. Women taking birth control pills do not ovulate, so they cannot have Mittelschmerz.

Dysmenorrhea

Dysmenorrhea is painful menstruation (cramps). Possible causes include prostaglandins, which cause the uterus to cramp, endometritis (inflammation of the endometrium), pelvic inflammatory disease or anatomic anomalies such as a displaced uterus.

Treatment

Antiprostaglandins such as ibuprofen reduce the pain as well as the volume of flow and the length of the period. Relaxation exercises such as yoga and massaging the lower back or abdomen help reduce pain. Applying heat to the abdomen or lower back may also help reduce pain.

A change in diet may help. Decreasing the amount of salt, caffeine, and alcohol in the diet while increasing the B vitamins — especially B6 (found in brewer's yeast, peanuts, rice, sunflower seeds and whole grains)–or raspberry leaf tea (1 tablespoon for each cup) can offer some relief during the acute phase of the cramps. Because exercise causes endorphins (natural opiates) to be released by the brain, many women find that cramps diminish when they participate in strenuous exercise.

Secondary Amenorrhea

Secondary amenorrhea is the absence of menstrual periods after a woman has had at least one period. Causes of secondary amenorrhea include pregnancy, ovarian tumors, intense athletic training, altitude and stress (physical and emotional). In the past it was thought that excessive weight loss in female athletes, resulting in low body fat, was the cause of amenorrhea. It is now believed that stress (physical and emotional) may cause hormonal changes resulting in amenorrhea. Changes in the menstrual cycle are common in the backcountry and may be normal adjustments to unfamiliar stresses.

Premenstrual Syndrome

Premenstrual syndrome (PMS) is a cluster of symptoms that occur prior to menstruation. Among ovulating women, 70 percent to 90 percent experience symptoms. PMS typically starts when a woman reaches her middle to late 20s and disappears in the late 30s to early 40s.

Signs and Symptoms

The most common symptoms are depression, anxiety, breast tenderness and food cravings. Other symptoms include anger, anxiety, irritability, bloating, edema, headache, fatigue and acne. Most researchers believe PMS is a physiological phenomenon but the exact cause is still unknown.

Treatment

Treatment includes decreasing stress, such as through yoga, meditation and deep-breathing exercises. A high carbohydrate diet low in caffeine and fat decreases breast tenderness. Reducing salt consumption helps control edema; reducing alcohol helps alleviate depression; reducing nicotine and caffeine lessens anxiety. A physician may prescribe diuretics to decrease edema.

Vitamin B6 supplements (25-50mg to start) may help to decrease the bloating, moodiness and depression that come with PMS. The dose should not exceed 200mg a day. B6 is better absorbed by the body when taken along with or as part of a B complex vitamin.

Oral progesterone has been prescribed by physicians to treat PMS, but studies of its effectiveness are inconclusive. Daily aerobic exercise such as running, hiking or exercise classes helps ease all symptoms.

Vaginal Infections

The normal pH of the vagina is slightly acidic. An alteration in the pH may cause a vaginal infection to develop. Infections usually result from lower body resistance due to stress (physical and emotional), a diet high in sugar or taking birth control pills and/or antibiotics. A diabetic or prediabetic condition also increases the risk of infection. Cuts and abrasions from intercourse or tampons, not cleaning the perineal area or changing underwear can lead to an infection.

There are three major types of vaginal infections: yeast (fungus), non-specific vaginitis (bacteria) and Trichomonas (a parasitic protozoan). For the purposes of field diagnosis, the symptoms are similar, and initial treatment is the same.

Symptoms

Symptoms of vaginal infection include excessive or malodorous discharge from the vagina with redness, soreness or itching in the vaginal area. There may also be a burning sensation during urination.

Signs and Symptoms of Vaginal Infection
Excessive, malodorous discharge
Redness, soreness, itching of vaginal area
Burning sensation upon urination

Treatment
Treatment should restore the acidity of the vagina. One approach is for the patient to douche with plain disinfected water (see Chapter 17, Hygiene and Water Disinfection) or a solution of one to two tablespoons of vinegar in a quart of warm disinfected water. Vaginal douches can also be made from povidone-iodine (two tablespoons of 10 percent povidone-iodine per liter of water) or zephiran chloride (1:1000 to 1:5000 strength). In the field, douching is accomplished by pouring the solution into the vagina while the patient lies on her back with hips elevated. This process may require two people. Ideally the patient should douche in the morning and evening at the onset of infection.

Women with a history of vaginal infections may want to take over-the-counter medication, such as Gyne-Lotrimin or Monistat 7, with them on extended expeditions. If these treatments don't provide relief within 48 hours, the patient should be evacuated. An untreated infection can develop into Pelvic Inflammatory Disease.

Treatment of Vaginal Infection
Douche with vinegar, povidone-iodine or
   zephiran solutions
Evacuate if symptoms persist for 48 hours

Prevention
The best prevention for vaginal infections is education. To help prevent vaginal infections, women should take care to clean the perineal area (the area between the vagina and anus) with plain water or a mild soap daily and to wear cotton underpants and loose outer pants. Unlike cotton, nylon doesn't allow air to circulate, thus giving bacteria a moist place to grow. Women should avoid coffee, alcohol and sugar, which can change the pH of the vagina.

Prevention of Vaginal Infection
Stay hydrated
Decrease sugar intake
Wear cotton underwear and loose-fitting clothes
Wash perineal area daily
Change tampons regularly
Decrease stress

Urinary Tract Infections

Urinary tract infections are common in women due to the relatively short length of the urethra. The infection can affect the urethra, ureters or bladder.

Signs and Symptoms

Urinary tract infections cause increased frequency or urgency of urination and/or a burning sensation during urination. The patient complains of pain above the pubic bone and a heavy urine odor with the morning urination. Blood and/or pus may be present in the urine. Urinary tract infections can progress to kidney infections. If the kidneys are infected, the patient complains of rebound tenderness in the small of the back and may have a fever.

Signs and Symptoms of Urinary Tract Infections
Increase in frequency of urination
Urgency and a burning sensation during urination

Treatment

The best treatment (also good for prevention) is to drink lots of water every day and empty the bladder often. A good way to tell if you are drinking enough is by the color of your urine. Unless you are taking vitamins, the urine should be clear, not yellow-colored. Persons taking vitamins tend to have yellow-colored urine.

The perineal area should be cleaned with water or mild soap daily. Taking 500 mg of Vitamin C daily and/or eating whole grains, nuts and fruits may make the urine more acidic, which prevents bacteria from growing. White flour, rice or pastas and refined sugars may predispose a person to bladder infections. Curry, cayenne pepper, chili powder, black pepper, caffeine, and alcohol should be avoided because these irritate the bladder. Vitamin B6 and magnesium or calcium supplements will help relieve spasms of the urethra.

On extended expeditions, consider carrying antibiotics to treat urinary tract infections. If an infection persists for more than 48 hours despite the use of antibiotics, the patient should be evacuated. Evacuate patients with symptoms of a kidney infection for further evaluation.

Treatment of Urinary Tract Infections
Increase fluid intake
Give vitamin B6, calcium and magnesium supplements
      to relieve bladder spasms
Change diet
      Avoid sugar and foods that irritate the bladder

Pelvic Inflammatory Disease (PID)
PID is an inflammation of the fallopian tubes, ovaries and/or uterus. It is primarily caused by gonorrhea, chlamydia or enteric bacteria.

Signs and Symptoms
Because PID affects the reproductive organs bilaterally, the patient complains of diffuse pain in the middle of the lower abdomen. The pain begins gradually and develops into a constant ache. She may also complain of pain in the right upper quadrant due to a bacterial irritation of the tissues surrounding the liver. Lower back or leg pain may also occur.

The patient may have a fever, nausea, vomiting, anorexia and swollen abdomen and lymph nodes. There may be a watery, foul-smelling discharge from the vagina. She may complain of irregular bleeding, an increase in menstrual cramps and pain or bleeding during or after intercourse. Some women develop acne-like rashes on the back, chest, neck or face. Usually these signs and symptoms start within a week following the menstrual period.

Signs and Symptoms of PID

Diffuse pain—middle of lower abdomen, possibly in upper right quadrant, lower back or leg

Swollen abdomen and lymph nodes

Watery, malodorous discharge

Acne-like rash on back, chest, neck, face

Fever, nausea, vomiting

Vaginal bleeding

Signs and symptoms of shock

Treatment

The treatment for PID is evacuation. Untreated PID can lead to peritonitis (inflammation of the lining of the abdomen), scarring of the fallopian tubes and sterility. PID is treated with antibiotics.

Ectopic Pregnancy

Ectopic pregnancies occur outside the uterus, most commonly in the fallopian tubes. Sperm usually fertilizes the egg in the upper two thirds of the tube. Due to congenital anomalies or scarring caused by infections, the egg starts growing in the tube.

Signs and Symptoms

At the time of the first menstrual period following conception, the patient experiences abdominal pain and bleeding. The onset of pain is rapid and unilateral. The fallopian tube ruptures in four to six weeks when the embryo becomes too large for the tube. The pain then becomes agonizing, and signs and symptoms of peritonitis develop. The patient may hemorrhage and die from shock, although slow bleeding is more common.

> **Signs and Symptoms**
> **of Ectopic Pregnancy**
> Rapid onset
> Lower abdominal pain
> Unilateral pain
> Vaginal bleeding
> Signs and symptoms of
>   peritonitis and shock

Treatment
Treat for shock and evacuate immediately.

Toxic Shock Syndrome (TSS)

Toxic shock syndrome (TSS) is an infection caused by the bacterium *Staphylococcus aureus*. Tampons have been suggested as one of the possible causes of TSS.

Super absorbent tampons that dry the vagina or cause backflow of blood into the peritoneal cavity may predispose a woman to TSS. Since 1980, TSS in menstruating women has declined, while the number of cases in men and non-menstruating women has increased. This may be due to better reporting. The highest incidence is still in 10- to 30-year-old menstruating white females.

Signs and Symptoms

The onset of toxic shock syndrome is abrupt. The patient has a high fever, chills, muscle aches, a sunburn-like rash, abdominal pain, sore throat, vomiting, diarrhea, fatigue, dizziness, and/or fainting. In some people the onset may be gradual and the characteristic rash does not appear for one or two days.

Mucous membranes are beet red. The sunburn-like rash appears on the palms or all over the body. It typically peels, just like a sunburn, one to two weeks later.

Treatment
Remove any tampon in use, treat for shock, and evacuate.

Prevention
To decrease the risk of TSS, women should change their tampons frequently and use pads at night and on light flow days. Pads and tampons should be carried out of the mountains or burned in a very hot fire. The staphylococcus organism is frequently found on the hands; good hand washing prior to inserting a tampon is a must. If the patient has had TSS previously, there is a 30 percent chance of recurrence.

Summary: Gender-Specific Medical Concerns

Testicular Torsion and Epididymitis
Signs and Symptoms
Pain in the scrotum
Red, swollen scrotum

Treatment
Give pain medication
Provide supportive care during evacuation

Vaginal Infection
Signs and Symptoms
Excessive, malodorous discharge
Redness, soreness, itching of vaginal area
Burning sensation upon urination

Treatment
Douche with vinegar, povidone-iodine or
zephiran solutions
Evacuate if symptoms persist for 48 hours

Prevention of Vaginal Infection
> Stay hydrated
> Decrease sugar intake in diet
> Wear cotton underwear and loose-fitting clothes
> Wash perineal area daily
> Change tampons regularly
> Decrease stress

Urinary Tract Infection
 Signs and Symptoms
> Increase in frequency of urination
> Urgency and a burning sensation during urination

 Treatment
> Increase fluid intake
> Change diet; avoid sugar and bladder-irritating foods
> Give vitamin B6, calcium and magnesium supplements to relieve bladder spasms

Signs and Symptoms of PID
> Diffuse pain—middle of lower abdomen, possibly in upper right quadrant, lower back or leg
> Swollen abdomen and lymph nodes
> Watery, malodorous discharge
> Acne-like rash on back, chest, neck, face
> Fever, nausea, vomiting
> Vaginal bleeding
> Signs and symptoms of shock

Signs and Symptoms of Ectopic Pregnancy
> Rapid onset
> Unilateral pain
> Vaginal bleeding
> Signs and symptoms of shock

Summary: Gender-Specific Medical Concerns, Cont.

Treatment for Ectopic Pregnancy and PID
    Provide supportive care during evacuation

Toxic Shock Syndrome (TSS)
  Signs and Symptoms
    Abdominal pain
    High fever, chills, muscle aches
    Sunburn-like rash
    Vomiting, diarrhea
    Fatigue, dizziness, fainting
    Beet red mucous membranes
    Signs and symptoms of shock

  Treatment
    Remove tampon
    Treat for shock and evacuate

Introduction

Assume all natural sources of water are contaminated. Americans may be surprised to learn that water in pristine wilderness areas may be contaminated, especially in light of our water treatment standards and the Clean Water Act, but the assessment is accurate. In other parts of the world, where human habitation and wild areas have coexisted for generations, water contamination continues to be a major health problem. Diarrheal illness is a leading cause of death in developing countries.

Wilderness expeditions require leaving behind modern sanitation and reliably disinfected tap water. Healthy people raised with Western medical standards may not understand the debilitating power of diarrheal illness. For them, maintaining strict hygiene practices in what appears to be pristine wilderness can be difficult.

Diarrheal illness afflicts 50 percent of travelers from industrialized countries who travel to developing countries. On NOLS courses, diarrhea and closely related flu symptoms are the most common illnesses. Contaminated water and food are the two main causes of these preventable illnesses.

Water-Borne Illnesses

In the U.S. wilderness, water-borne microorganisms account for most infectious diarrhea. Diseases that are spread through contaminated water include typhoid, cholera, camphylobacter, giardiasis and hepatitis A. The microorganisms causing diarrhea include bacteria, protozoa, viruses and parasitic worms.

While the most frequently diagnosed diarrhea-causing microorganism in the U.S. is Giardia, other bacteria and viruses are being identified with increasing frequency. In Wyoming's Teton Range the bacteria Camphylobacter causes more diarrhea than Giardia.

Giardia

Giardia is a microscopic protozoan. It has a two-stage life as cyst and trophozoite. The cyst, excreted in mammalian feces, is hardy and can survive two to three months in near-freezing water. If swallowed, the warmer internal environment causes the cyst to change into its active stage, the trophozoite. The trophozoite attaches itself to the wall of the small intestine and is the cause of the diarrhea associated with Giardia infections.

Humans are a major carrier of Giardia. Giardia has also been identified in both domestic and wild animals, specifically in beavers, cats, dogs, sheep, cattle, deer, elk and in reptiles, amphibians and fish. It is not clear whether contamination from Giardia is increasing or whether it is being diagnosed more frequently as a cause of diarrhea.

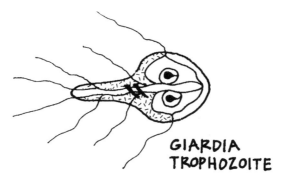

GIARDIA TROPHOZOITE

Giardia is difficult to diagnose due to the wide variation in symptoms. For a reliable diagnosis three stool samples should be examined. Most infections are without symptoms, and the unwitting patient becomes a carrier of Giardia, inadvertently spreading the illness.

The incubation period–from ingestion to the onset of infection–is one to three weeks. Symptoms include recurrent and persistent malodorous stools and flatus, abdominal cramping, bloating, "sulfur burps" and indigestion. Serious infections produce explosive watery diarrhea with cramps, foul flatus, fever and malaise.

Although drug therapy is available, prevention through hygienic habits and water disinfection is the best treatment. Giardia is sensitive to heat, easily filtered and can be killed with chemical disinfection.

Water Disinfection

Purifying water eliminates offensive odors, tastes and colors but does not kill microorganisms. Sterilization kills all life forms. Disinfection removes or destroys disease-causing microorganisms. What we commonly refer to as water purification is really disinfection. There are three main methods of water disinfection: heat, filtration and chemical treatment.

Heat

The common diarrhea-causing microorganisms are sensitive to heat. The protozoa Giardia and Amoeba, which cause amebiasis, die after two to three minutes at 140°F (60°C). Viruses and diarrhea-producing bacteria die within minutes at 150°F (65°C). Diarrhea-causing microorganisms are killed immediately by boiling water. By the time water boils, it is safe to drink. A five- to ten-minute boil sterilizes water.

Methods OF WATER DISINFECTION:

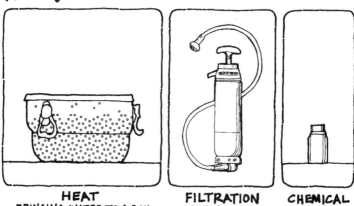

HEAT
BRINGING WATER TO A BOIL IS STILL THE MOST RELIABLE WAY TO MAKE SURE IT'S SAFE TO USE.

FILTRATION
REMOVES GIARDIA BUT NOT VIRUSES!

CHEMICAL
• IODINE
• CHLORINE

Remember, boiling point decreases with increasing elevation, but this does not affect disinfection. The boiling point at 19,000 feet is 178°F (81°C)—sufficient for disinfecting water.

Filtration

Filters remove particulate matter and large organisms. Several types of filters are available with pore sizes small enough to filter Giardia cysts, but viruses are too small to be eliminated by water filtration in the field.

Filters can be used on the trail more conveniently than boiling water, and filtration may reduce the amount of halogen necessary to chemically purify water. They are initially expensive, however, costing from $40 to $250. Also, they may clog. The inability of filters to remove viruses causes some experts not to recommend them for foreign travel, but since they do eliminate Giardia, they are recommended for use in North America.

Chemical Treatment

Chemical treatment is the addition of halogens—iodine and chlorine—to water. Halogens kill viruses, diarrhea-causing bacteria and protozoa cysts. The concentration of halogen and its contact time in water affect the degree of disinfection. Bacteria are highly sensitive to halogens. Viruses and Giardia require greater doses or longer contact time.

Factors that can affect halogen treatment include chemical binding, pH and temperature. Halogens bind with other organic and inorganic particles in water. If the halogen binds with debris in the water, less is available to destroy the diarrhea-causing microorganisms. Reduce debris before adding halogen; filter murky water with a manufactured filter or use an improvised strainer such as a coffee filter or a clean bandana. Drink mixes improve the taste but should be added after disinfection, as they bind with the halogen.

Halogens are affected by pH. The pH levels of natural water sources, however, are well within the range of halogen activity. Halogens are also affected by temperature. In cold water the effect of halogens decreases and contact time must be increased accordingly. In general, an iodine dose can be halved if the contact time for the recommended dosage is doubled.

Iodine

Iodine, the most commonly used halogen, is available as a tablet–tetraglycine hydroperiodide–known commercially as Globaline or Potable Aqua. Iodine crystals, 2 percent iodine, and 10 percent povidone-iodine solutions are also effective.

Iodine is affected less by pH than is chlorine and has less effect on the taste of the water. The low doses required for disinfection have proven safe for routine use in drinking water for adults. Iodine is not recommended for persons with thyroid disease or known iodine allergy. Iodine dosages are given in the table at the end of this chapter.

Chlorine

Halozone tablets and chlorine bleach are two common methods of water disinfection using chlorine. Chlorine, used as a disinfectant for over 200 years, is strongly affected by pH, organic debris and other pollutants. Chlorine dosages are given in the table at the end of this chapter.

Food-Borne Illnesses

When we leave the sanitation of flush toilets, reliably disinfected tap water, readily available hot water and proximity to advanced medical care, we need to adjust our habits to prevent illness. Proper human waste disposal, hand and utensil washing, food preparation and water disinfection, which are often taken for granted at home, are essential to health in the wilderness.

The major causes of food-borne illness are contaminated food and contaminated utensils. The optimum temperature for bacterial growth is between 45°F and 140°F. In only a short period bacteria can multiply to become the source of a diarrheal illness.

Heat destroys most bacteria. Cold keeps it from multiplying. Keep food hot or keep it cold, but don't keep it long. Storing cooked food invites disaster, so plan meals so all food is consumed when served. Besides promoting bacterial growth, keeping leftovers creates a waste disposal problem and attracts animals such as bears.

Large groups frequently use group cooking setups with chlorine rinses as an important step in keeping utensils clean. Other helpful techniques include setting up wash stations near latrines and at each camp.

An ill person or one with open cuts on his hands should not prepare food. It only takes one person to be the source for a group-wide illness.

Final Thoughts: Tips on Health and Hygiene

Disinfect your drinking water.

Wash hands with soap before preparing, serving or eating meals.

Wash hands with soap after relieving yourself, especially after a bowel movement.

Use toilet paper or be proficient with natural toilet paper.

Keep nails trimmed and clean.

For base camps, consider group cooking setups with chlorine dish rinses and handwashing stations.

Set up a handwashing station near a latrine or outhouse.

Set up a handwashing station in a central camp location.

Bathe regularly.

Do not share personal utensils or water bottles.

Do not use chipped or rough bowls. They promote bacterial growth.

Serve food with the serving utensil.

Boil cooking utensils daily.

Pour food from plastic bags instead of reaching into the bag.

Be sure you are healthy and clean before preparing food.

Plan meals to avoid storage of cooked food.

Rinse fresh fruit and vegetables before cooking or eating.

Note: Soap residues on dishes can be a source of diarrhea, but thorough rinsing will eliminate this problem. Remember to choose a phosphate-free soap and dispose of it away from water sources.

Summary: Hygiene and Water Disinfection

Contaminated water sources are thought to account for most infectious diarrhea in U.S. wilderness, although at NOLS we think person-to-person exchange from poor hygiene is a leading cause. Outside the wilderness, the most common route of infection is believed to be from person to person via hand-to-mouth contact or from contaminated utensils. Infection rates increase with close contact and poor hygiene. The habits of cleanliness and hygiene are essential to health and safety in the wilderness.

Strong motivation to practice proper hygiene is created when a long-anticipated trip is disrupted by:

a preventable illness,

weakness caused by illness

or an illness-precipitated safety incident.

Halogen Doses and Techniques Per Liter of Water

Formulation	*Water Temp*	*Clear Water*	*Cloudy Water*
Tetraglycine Hydroperiodide (Potable Aqua, Globaline)			
	Warm	1tab/15min	2tabs/15min
	Cold	1tab/45min	2tabs/45min
2% Iodine Solution (Tincture)			
	Warm	0.25ml/30min	0.5ml/30min
	Cold	0.5ml/60min	0.5ml/60min
10% Povidone-Iodine			
	Warm	0.4ml/30min	0.8ml/30min
	Cold	0.8ml/60min	0.8ml/60min
Iodine Crystals (aqueous)			
Polar Pure	Warm	15ml/30min	30ml/30min
	Cold	30ml/60min	30ml/60min
1% Chlorine Bleach			
	Warm	10drops/30min	20drops/30min
	Cold	10drops/60min	20drops/60min
4-6% Chlorine Bleach			
	Warm	2drops/30min	4drops/30min
	Cold	2drops/60min	4drops/60min
Halozone Tablets			
	Warm	5tabs/10 min	7tabs/10min
	Cold	5tabs/20 min	7tabs/20min

Warm water temperature >15°C (40F)   1 drop = 0.05ml

Source: Backer H. Field Water Disinfection. "Winter Wilderness Medicine," Syllabus, Wilderness Medical Society Meeting [Big Sky, MT] March 1992.

Chapter 18

SEIZURES, DIABETES AND UNCONSCIOUS STATES

Introduction

Seizures

Diabetes

Unconscious States

Final Thoughts: Prevention

Summary: Seizures, Diabetes and Unconscious States

Introduction

The topics typically discussed as medical emergencies in first aid texts include heart disease, heart attacks, congestive heart failure and respiratory illnesses such as asthma, emphysema and pneumonia, as well as diabetes, epilepsy, drug and alcohol abuse and anaphylaxis. While these are common emergency runs for ambulance crews, they are uncommon on wilderness expeditions. This discussion is limited to seizures and diabetes. These are two medical emergencies that may be encountered on educational wilderness trips, yet they rarely receive emphasis in wilderness first aid training texts.

Seizures

A seizure is a disruption of the brain's normal activity by a massive paroxysmal electrical discharge from brain cells. The seizure begins at a focus of brain cells, then spreads through the brain and to the rest of the body through peripheral nerves. This electrical disturbance may cause violent muscle contractions throughout the body or result in localized motor movement and possible loss of consciousness.

The causes of seizures include high fever, head injury, low blood sugar, stroke, poisoning and epilepsy. Low blood sugar is a cause of seizures in diabetics. Brain cells are sensitive to low oxygen and sugar levels, and if these fall below acceptable levels, a seizure may be triggered. The most common cause of seizures is epilepsy, a disease which manifests itself in recurring seizures.

The onset of epilepsy is not well understood. Often it begins in childhood or adolescence but can also be a consequence of a brain injury. Most persons with epilepsy control their seizures with medication. Interruption of the medication or inadequate doses is frequently the cause of seizures.

At one time seizures were attributed to mental illness. The source of these misperceptions may have been the dramatic visual impact of a writhing, moaning person having a seizure.

Educating bystanders and group members about epilepsy and seizures can help alleviate such misunderstandings.

Assessment
The typical generalized seizure begins with a short period, usually less than a minute, of muscle rigidity followed by several minutes of muscle contractions. The patient may feel the seizure approaching and warn bystanders or cry out at the onset of the episode. The patient suddenly falls to the floor twitching and jerking.

As muscular activity subsides, the patient remains unconscious but relaxed. He may drool, appear cyanotic and become incontinent of bowel and bladder. Pulse and respiratory rate may be rapid. The patient may initially be unconscious or difficult to arouse, but in time—usually within 10 to 15 minutes—the patient becomes awake and oriented.

When the seizure has subsided, open the airway, assess for injuries, and take vital signs. Place the patient on his side during the recovery phase to help maintain an open airway.

Treatment
Treatment for a seizure is supportive and protective. We cannot stop the seizure, but we can protect the patient from injury. The violent muscle contractions of a seizure may cause injury to the patient and to well-meaning bystanders who attempt to restrain the patient. Move objects that the patient may hit. Pad or cradle the head if it is bouncing on the ground.

A patient in seizure will not swallow his tongue; however, his airway may become obstructed by saliva or secretions, and he may bite his tongue. Most seizures happen without warning, with no opportunity to protect the airway. If you can, insert a padded object between the teeth to protect the tongue. This may be difficult because of the tightness of the jaw. Once the seizure starts, do not force the mouth open.

An accurate description of the seizure tells the physician much about the onset and extent of the problem. In most cases, a seizure runs its course in a few minutes. Repeated seizures, especially repeated seizures in which the patient does not regain consciousness and seizures associated with another medical problem such as diabetes or head injury, are serious medical conditions.

The epileptic patient with an isolated seizure requires evaluation by a physician but does not require a rapid evacuation. These occasional seizures are often due to changes in the patient's need for medication or failure to take the medication as prescribed. After recovering from the seizure, the patient should be well fed and hydrated and assessed for any injury that may have occurred during the seizure.

Diabetes

Diabetes is a disease of sugar metabolism, affecting, by conservative estimates, 10 million Americans. It is a complex disease characterized by a broad array of physiological disturbances. In the long term, diabetic complications include high blood pressure, heart and blood vessel disease and affects the vision, kidneys and healing of wounds. In the short term, the disturbance in sugar metabolism can manifest itself as too much or too little sugar in the blood.

Diabetes is thought to be caused by genetic defects, infection, or direct injury to the pancreas. The pancreas produces the hormones, most notably insulin, that help regulate sugar balance. Insulin facilitates the movement of sugar from the blood into the cells. An excess of insulin promotes the movement of sugar into the cells, lowers the blood sugar level and deprives the brain cells of a crucial nutrient. This disorder is known as hypoglycemia (low blood sugar) or insulin shock.

In contrast, a deficit of insulin results in cells starved for sugar and an excess of sugar in the blood, disturbing fluid and electrolyte balance. This disorder is known as hyperglycemia (high blood sugar) or diabetic coma.

A healthy pancreas constantly adjusts the insulin level to the blood sugar level. The pancreas of a person with diabetes produces defective insulin or no insulin. To compensate for this, a diabetic takes medication to stimulate his endogenous insulin or he takes artificial insulin.

Hypoglycemia (Insulin Shock)

Hypoglycemia results from the treatment of diabetes, not the diabetes itself. If a diabetic takes too much insulin or fails to eat sufficient sugar to match the insulin level, the blood sugar level will be insufficient to maintain normal brain function.

Hypoglycemia can occur if the diabetic skips a meal but takes the usual insulin dose, takes more than the normal insulin dose, exercises strenuously and fails to eat, or vomits a meal after taking insulin.

Assessment

Hypoglycemia occurs with a rapid onset. The most prominent symptoms are alterations in level of consciousness due to lack of sugar to the brain. The patient may be irritable, nervous, weak and uncoordinated, may appear intoxicated or in more serious cases may become unconscious or may even have seizures. Pulse will be rapid, the skin pale, cool and clammy.

Treatment

Brain cells need sugar and can suffer permanent damage from low blood sugar levels. The treatment of hypoglycemia is to administer sugar. If the patient is conscious, a sugar drink or candy bar can help increase blood sugar level. If unconscious, establish an airway, then place a small paste of sugar underneath the patient's tongue. Sugar is absorbed through the oral mucosa. Improvement is usually quick after administration of sugar.

Hyperglycemia (Diabetic Coma)

Diabetics who are untreated, who have defective or insufficient insulin or who become ill may develop a high level of sugar in their blood. Consequences of this may be: dehydration and electrolyte disturbances as the kidneys try to eliminate the excess sugar, and acid base disturbances as cells starved for sugar turn to alternative energy sources.

Assessment

In contrast to the rapid onset of hypoglycemia, hyperglycemia develops slowly. The first symptoms are loss of appetite, nausea, vomiting, thirst and increased volume of urine output. The patient's breath may have a fruity odor from the metabolism of fats as an energy source, also abdominal cramps or pain and signs of dehydration that include flushed, dry skin and intense thirst. Loss of consciousness is a late and very serious symptom.

Treatment

This patient has a complex physical disturbance and needs the care of a physician. Treatment is supportive: airway maintenance, vital signs and treatment for shock. Dehydration is a serious complication of hyperglycemia. If the patient is alert, give oral fluids.

Hypoglycemia or Hyperglycemia?

Hypoglycemia is usually rapid in onset, the patient is pale, cool and clammy and has obvious disturbances in behavior or level of consciousness. Hyperglycemia has a gradual onset. Often, the patient is in an unexplained coma, with flushed, dry skin. The fruity breath odor may be present. The patient in hypoglycemia will respond to sugar; the hyperglycemic will not, but the extra sugar will cause no harm.

Two questions to ask any diabetic patient are: "Have you eaten today?" and "Have you taken your insulin today?" If the patient has taken his insulin but has not eaten, you should suspect hypoglycemia. He will have too much insulin, not enough sugar and a blood sugar level too low to sustain normal brain function. If he has eaten but has not taken his insulin, hyperglycemia should be suspected. This person has more sugar in his blood than he can transport to the cells.

Most persons with diabetes are very knowledgeable about

their reactions and intuitively know if they are getting into trouble. Many diabetics measure their blood sugar levels daily; almost all diabetics test their urine for sugar daily.

It is important for persons with diabetes to eat at regular intervals. If there is a possibility that a diabetic's insulin could be lost or destroyed—for example, by a boat flipping on the river—make sure someone else in the group is carrying an extra supply. With control and care, diabetics can participate without problems in any activities they wish.

Unconscious States

A conscious patient can react to the environment and protect himself from sources of pain and injury. An unconscious patient is in danger. He is mute and defenseless, unable to rely even on the gag reflex to protect the airway. Many conditions cause unconsciousness: head injury, stroke, epilepsy, diabetes, alcohol intoxication, drug overdose and fever.

A patient who is unconscious for unexplained reasons poses a difficult diagnostic problem. The medical history may provide clues; use AEIOUTIPS as a guideline for a complete assessment of common conditions that may cause unconsciousness.

Often, all we can do is support the patient and transport him to a physician for further evaluation. Care for the unconscious patient includes airway maintenance and cervical spine precautions unless trauma can be ruled out entirely. All unconscious patients should receive sugar under the tongue. This will help the hypoglycemic patient and won't hurt the patient unconscious for any other reason.

Final Thoughts: Prevention

Persons with diabetes and epilepsy routinely participate in wilderness expeditions. The adverse consequences of these diseases—seizures and sugar imbalances—can be prevented through care and education. The physical and emotional stress, new physical and social environment, heavy packs, altitude, the sun and the battle against dehydration in the wilderness may be new challenges but ones that can be well managed.

Discuss the illness beforehand with the the diabetic or epileptic person undertaking the expedition. Make sure you both understand the disease, the timing and side effects of any medications, the appropriate emergency treatment and any other facets of the person's health needs. It is important to inform the rest of the group—especially the person's tentmates—about the condition and how to deal with it in an emergency.

Summary: Seizures, Diabetes and Unconscious States

Seizures are caused by epilepsy, high fever, head injury, low blood sugar, stroke and poisoning.

Treatment
Is supportive and protective
Move objects the patient may hit, protect the head
When the seizure subsides:
Open the airway
Assess for injuries

Hypoglycemia (low blood sugar) associated with diabetes is caused by missing a meal but taking insulin, taking an insulin overdose, exercising strenuously without eating, or eating and vomiting a meal. The low blood sugar affects the brain.

Hyperglycemia (high blood sugar) associated with diabetes is caused by lack of treatment, insufficient or ineffective insulin or the onset of illness. The high blood sugar causes dehydration and electrolyte disturbances.

Signs and Symptoms

Hypoglycemia	*Hyperglycemia*
rapid onset	gradual onset
pale, cool clammy skin	flushed, dry skin
disturbances in LOC	unconscious or coma
possible seizures	fruity breath odor
irritability, nervousness	abdominal cramps, nausea
weakness,	
lack of coordination	

Treatment

Hypoglycemia	*Hyperglycemia*
ABCs	ABCs
Sugar under tongue	fluids if conscious
	Treat for shock
	If unsure, give sugar

CHAPTER 19
HYDRATION

Introduction

NOLS Instructors constantly harp on hydration, urging their students to drink, drink, drink. They issue liter water bottles and large insulated mugs. They carry water in the desert and melt snow with a passion in winter environments. To the inexperienced outdoorsperson this appears to be an unnecessarily exaggerated process, when in fact it is based on need and experience. More than one NOLS student has been evacuated from the mountains with dehydration as the primary diagnosis. Most of our evacuations for illness are in part complicated by underlying dehydration. Addressing daily episodes of dehydration on the trail is a fact of life for wilderness travelers.

Dehydration is a contributing factor to hypothermia, heat exhaustion, heat stroke, altitude illness and frostbite. Dehydration worsens fatigue, decreases our ability to exercise efficiently and reduces our mental alertness. Often the fatigue, irritability, poor thinking, body aches and headache at the end of a day are the first signs of dehydration. Even by itself dehydration can be a life-threatening medical problem.

Physiology of Water Balance

Humans are bags of water. We hear through a medium of water, our brain is cushioned by fluid and our joints are lubricated by fluid. Blood is 90 percent water, and every biochemical reaction takes place in a medium of water.

Outside the wilderness we give little thought to hydration. Air conditioning, heating and lack of exercise enable us to avoid fluid stress most of the time. In the outdoors we exercise daily at high levels. Exercise causes water loss through sweating, breathing and metabolism. In the outdoors we adjust directly to the environment, whether hot or cold. In the desert we sweat to lose heat. In the cold we lose water to moisten the cold air we breathe.

In the outdoors hydration is not as simple as turning on the tap. In the desert we carry water, ration water and spend a lot of time searching for water. Our activity patterns may be altered to reduce heat loss. We rest during the hours of the hot, midday sun, work in the cool dawn and evening. In the winter we must melt the water we drink—a time-consuming process. There is always the difficulty of disinfecting potentially contaminated water sources.

It's harder to get water in the outdoors, we lose more of it responding to the environment and we need more of it to maintain health. Many people in the outdoors are dehydrated and more so at altitude and in winter.

Assessment

Dehydration is often overlooked as a cause of illness or injury in the outdoors. The signs and symptoms mimic altitude illness, hypothermia, fatigue, heat exhaustion and shock. Severe dehydration can cause significant mental deterioration, causing us to think the patient is having a serious brain problem. The key to assessment is suspicion. Dehydration is so common it must be considered in every patient treated in the outdoors.

General symptoms of a negative water balance are fatigue, heat oppression, thirst, irritability, dizziness, dark concentrated urine and headache. A seriously dehydrated patient appears to have signs of shock: rapid pulse, pale sweaty skin, weakness and nausea. Mental deterioration presents itself in loss of balance and changes in mental awareness. Tenting, when the skin forms a tent shape when pinched, is a sign of serious dehydration. Normal skin is sufficiently hydrated to collapse the tent. The tent stays in place in severe dehydration.

With a 2 percent fluid deficit we experience mental deterioration, decreased group cooperation, vague discomfort, lack of energy and appetite, flushed skin, impatience, sleepiness, nausea, an increased pulse rate and a 25 percent loss in efficiency.

A 12 percent fluid deficit results in an inability to swallow, a swollen tongue, sunken eyes and decreased neurological function.

Dizziness, tingling in the limbs, absence of salivation and slurred speech may also be present. A fluid deficit greater than 15 percent is potentially lethal. Signs include delirium, vision disturbances and shriveled skin.

Treatment

The mildly dehydrated patient—and all wilderness travelers—should drink clear water to replace fluids. It is the best fluid for hydration. Cold water is absorbed faster than warm water.

Electrolyte replacement drinks are acceptable but should be diluted to reduce their sugar content. Sugar increases the time it takes for fluid to be absorbed from the stomach. Coffee, tea and alcohol should be avoided. Coffee and tea contain caffeine, a diuretic that stimulates the kidneys to excrete fluid. Alcohol also increases urine production and fluid loss.

The severely dehydrated patient may have electrolyte imbalances as well as a fluid deficit. Such a patient cannot be rehydrated in the field and must be evacuated to a hospital for intravenous fluid therapy.

Final Thoughts: Prevention

There are several cornerstones to good health in the outdoors: staying warm and dry, eating well, resting, camping comfortably, climbing slowly at altitude and, most important, staying hydrated.

How much water should we drink to stay healthy? Probably more than we usually drink. Three to four liters a day is the minimum, with another liter added for cold or high altitude conditions. Thirst is a poor indicator, alerting us to the fluid deficit after we are already dehydrated and indicating we are satiated before we are fully rehydrated. Urine color and volume are helpful indicators; darker, more concentrated urine is an indicator of dehydration. Again, this is a later sign, appearing after our body has decided to conserve fluid.

Fluids must be forced to maintain hydration in the wilderness. Measure your daily fluid intake. Tank up to buffer your hydration margin. Drink early, anticipating fluid loss during the day. Drink often, preventing the subtle mental and physical deterioration of dehydration. Drink more than you think you need. Drink before you become dehydrated. DRINK, DRINK, DRINK (and drink some more)!

Summary: Hydration

Signs and Symptoms of Dehydration

Early Signs
    Fatigue
    Heat oppression
    Thirst
    Irritability
    Dizziness
    Dark, concentrated urine
    Headache
    Loss of group cooperation

Later Signs
    Rapid pulse, pale sweaty skin
    Weakness and nausea
    Loss of balance
    Changes in mental awareness
    Tenting

Serious Signs
    Inability to swallow, swollen tongue
    Sunken eyes
    Loss of consciousness
    Delirium

Treatment for Dehydration

DRINK, DRINK, DRINK
In severe cases, evacuation may be necessary

CHAPTER 20
DENTAL EMERGENCIES

Introduction

Toothaches

Broken Teeth or Fillings

Oral Irritations and Infections

Final Thoughts: Prevention

Introduction

Enduring a dental problem in the wilderness, several days from a dentist, can be an uncomfortable experience. There are simple field treatments for broken teeth or fillings, toothaches and gum irritations that can make life more comfortable during the evacuation. Although we do not experience many dental problems on NOLS courses, they account for 10 percent of problems seen among trekkers visiting the Himalayan Rescue Association clinics.

Toothaches

Exposure of the nerve, pulp, artery or vein of a tooth causes pain. In the backcountry, treatment is limited to pain medications, antibiotics and avoiding excessively hot, cold or spicy foods. Placing an aspirin on a toothache as treatment is an old wives' tale. Aspirin in direct contact with sensitive gum tissue can cause a serious acid burn.

Broken Teeth or Fillings

Various temporary filling materials are available for temporary treatment of broken teeth or fillings. Cavit is a pre-mixed compound available from your dentist. A non-prescription temporary filling available in many dental emergency kits is a combination of zinc oxide powder (not the ointment) and oil of cloves (eugenol). The oil of cloves is a topical anesthetic. NOLS staff have even had success using sugarless gum and ski wax to cover loose fillings and broken teeth.

Rinse the broken teeth or fillings thoroughly before covering with a temporary filling. Roll the temporary material into a small ball and gently press it into the hole in the tooth, sealing the exposed tissue.

A broken or avulsed tooth should be gently rinsed off slowly and gently placed back in the hole. If this is not possible, save the tooth for replacement. For a good prognosis, a tooth must be replaced within 30 minutes and receive the care of a dentist within a week.

If the socket is bleeding, it can be packed to place pressure on the tissue. A slightly moist tea bag makes an acceptable packing material. In fact, the tannic acid in non-herbal tea promotes clotting.

Oral Irritations and Infections

General mouth irritation is usually due to poor hygiene and can be treated with vigorous brushing and rinses with salt water (a teaspoon of salt per glass of water) three to four times a day.

Swelling around teeth or gums is an indicator of an infection. On remote expeditions, treatment with antibiotics and drainage of the infection may be considered. Evacuation to a dentist is the best treatment and the only choice on less remote trips in which there is no access to a physician or antibiotics.

Final Thoughts: Prevention

Preparation for a wilderness expedition includes a visit to your dentist to identify and treat any potential problems. In the field, brush and floss regularly. Anyone who has experienced the woes of a toothache, loose filling or dental infection in the wilderness knows that the need for dental hygiene does not cease when we venture into the woods.

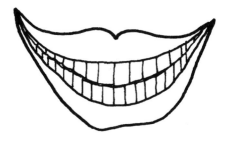

CHAPTER 21
STRESS AND THE RESCUER

Introduction

> Effects of Stress

Stress and the Rescuer

Assessment: Recognizing Stress Reactions

Treatment: Managing Stress in the Field

> The Field Debriefing

Final Thoughts

Summary: Acute Stress Reactions

Introduction

First aid training has traditionally concentrated on treatment and transport: the nuts and bolts of assessment, splinting and airway maintenance. The human elements of emergency medical care are equally important. We are beginning to recognize the impact of emergency stress on the rescuer as well as the victim.

Although there is little data on wilderness rescue, there is a growing body of literature on the effects of stress on emergency workers. Caring for the ill or injured, having responsibility for the life and safety of others is considered a significant stressor. Research is showing that high attrition rates, burnout and stress-related illness are common in emergency personnel.

Effects of Stress

A perceived threat or challenge or a change in the environment can cause stress–a state of physical or psychological arousal. Beneficial stress affects all living creatures and can be a positive factor in change, creativity, growth and productivity. Healthy exercise which increases our physical capabilities is a good stress. Continuous hard exercise without rest or adequate nutrition can become a destructive force with negative effects on our health, our families and our lives.

We may be stressed by noises, confined spaces, extremes in weather and other aspects of our environment. In our social environment, conflicts within a group, conflicts with our boss or our family are all stressors. We're also stressed by inactivity and boredom.

Stress produces intricate biochemical changes in the body. The brain becomes more active, chemicals secreted by the endocrine system cause muscles to tighten, pupils to dilate and heart rate, breathing rate and blood pressure to increase. Protein, glucose and antibody levels in the blood rise.

These physiological changes prepare us to meet challenge by making us more alert and ready for physical activity. In the short term they can be helpful. In the long term, or if the short-term stress is significant, the effects of stress can adversely affect our physical and psychological health by wearing us down and making us susceptible to a variety of physical and psychological problems. The Surgeon General estimates 80 percent of non-traumatic causes of death are actually stress-related disease such as coronary artery disease, high blood pressure, ulcers and cancer.

Stress and the Rescuer

Research on stress suggests that dedicated people who work hard and have high standards and deep personal interest in their work are vulnerable to stress.

The job demands of emergency personnel create an environment in which turnover and stress-related illness are common. Emergency situations may subject them to noise such as wind, rushing water, screams and sirens; to the confusion of the emergency scene; to having responsibility for the health and safety of patients and fellow rescuers in prolonged weather extremes; to difficult bystanders who may never be satisfied with the rescuer's performance; to equipment failures and inadequate equipment, which add to the difficulty of the situation; and to long hours of hard physical work. Lengthy rescues, rescues in which the patient dies, multiple casualty incidents and incidents in which emergency workers or friends are injured are particularly stressful.

Personality profiles of emergency personnel developed by Jeffrey Mitchell, Ph.D. show a tendency toward personality traits that make these individuals susceptible to stress. Emergency personnel are often perfectionists and risk-takers who are highly motivated and goal- and action-oriented; they feel the need to be in control. They are dedicated, take great personal satisfaction and interest in their work, and feel great need to be needed. These are traits that also apply to many outdoor leaders and educators.

Certainly, emergency stress will affect an outdoor leader or anyone thrown into the role of rescuer. Experience may help a person cope with these stresses, but it does not make him immune.

The leader of a notably difficult expedition experiences significant extra stress when weather, group dynamics, faulty equipment or complex logistics combine to create a high-pressure situation. In addition to caring for the ill or injured under these difficult conditions, the leader continues to be responsible for the safety and welfare of the group.

Assessment: Recognizing Stress Reactions

Stress in the short term may produce fatigue, nausea, anxiety, fear, irritability, lightheadedness, headache, memory lapses, sleep disturbances, changes in appetite, loss of attention span and indecision. These are normal reactions by normal people to abnormal events. A person experiencing an acute stress reaction may wander aimlessly on the scene, sit or stare blankly or engage in erratic or irrational behavior.

Long-term effects of stress include difficulty concentrating, intrusive images—recurring dreams or sensations of the traumatic event—sleep disturbance, fatigue and diseases such as ulcers, diabetes and coronary artery disease. Emotional signs include depression, feelings of grief and anger and a sense of isolation. Emergency workers suffering from cumulative stress may respond by avoiding emergency situations, taking excessive sick leave or being easily aroused or startled. It is beyond the scope of this book to discuss intervention for cumulative stress reactions.

Treatment: Managing Stress in the Field

Preparation for stress management includes anticipation of the difficulties of rescue and a realistic appraisal of your ability to cope. Of the emergency personnel on the scene of a serious rescue, 97 percent will experience at least some symptoms of stress. Rescuers need to remember that successful outcome of the emergency is not guaranteed, particularly if the patient is far from modern medical care. Rescue work, especially wilderness rescue, can be long and tedious. Recognition and thanks for the efforts of the rescuer are often sparse, while criticism from bystanders is common.

Short-term stress symptoms can be managed by attending to the physical needs for rest, food and hydration, by briefing the group on the sights, sounds and emotions they may experience during a long evacuation and by debriefing the group after the incident.

Acute stress reactions on scene can be managed by removing an overstressed person from the site. Give simple, clear directions to the stressed person, and assign productive tasks that can help shift his or her focus away from the immediate incident. Such tasks might include providing food and drink, building a litter and setting up tents.

If an emergency care giver is overly distressed, detached from reality or disruptive, someone may need to stay with him or her to lend a sympathetic ear. You can help such persons cope by talking with them and offering assurances that their feelings are valid and real. Provide emotional support with honesty and direct, factual answers to their questions.

The Field Debriefing

Following the rescue, attend to the physical needs of the rescuers by providing food, water, clean clothing and shelter. Light aerobic exercise, such as a hike or a game of hacky sack, may help relieve tension built up over the course of the rescue.

Debriefings are designed to provide a forum in which rescuers and/or group members can share their experiences, emotions and thoughts following a stressful situation. A debriefing seems to provide best results if it is conducted within 24 hours of the close of the rescue. The debriefing allows for ventilation and validation of feelings, encourages discussion and helps the facilitator gauge the well-being of the participants.

Debriefing should never include a critique of performance. A critique has a separate role in evaluating an emergency response, but it should be conducted at a separate time and place.

To debrief, gather the group in a quiet place. Set a tone of support and openness, and offer guidelines for discussion without critique. Your communication and group facilitation skills will come into play during the debriefing. If an individual does not want to talk, that's acceptable as long as he or she has been given the opportunity. It may help provide common ground for people who may have had different roles, if you begin by having each group member discuss an aspect of his or her experience. Asking for a person's first thoughts after he or she finished with the rescue and after the excitement abated may also be helpful. A debriefing should last long enough to give everyone a chance to talk.

Final Thoughts

Emotional reactions to accidents are perfectly normal and should be expected. We are beginning to train rescue personnel to recognize and manage incident stress. Trained teams of critical incident stress debriefers are set up throughout the country to help rescuers who have experienced a critical stress incident. The majority of reactions are short-term with no lasting consequences. For both patients and rescuers, the emotional first aid we provide is as important to their ultimate recovery as our physical care.

Summary: Acute Stress Reactions

Physical	*Emotional*	*Cognitive*
fatigue	anxiety	memory loss
muscle tremors	fear	indecision
nausea	grief	difficulty problem solving
profuse sweating	depression	confusion between
glassy eyes	hopelessness	trivial and major issues
chills	irritability	loss of attention span
difficulty	feeling over-	dizziness
breathing	whelmed	anger

Delayed Stress Reactions

Macabre humor

Excessive use of sick leave

Reluctance to enter stressful situations

Intrusive images

Obsession with the stressful incident

Withdrawal from others

Suicidal thoughts

Feelings of inadequacy

THE FIRST AID KIT

These are the contents of a standard first aid kit designed for a group of 12 on a month-long trip. Obviously, requirements will vary with group size, medical qualifications, trip length, location and remoteness.

Bandaging Material

2x2 sterile gauze pad	12 ea
4x4 sterile gauze pad	6 ea
3" gauze roller bandage	2 ea
Cravats	2 ea
Adhesive bandages (various sizes)	12 ea
Butterfly or Steri-strip	12 ea
35cc syringe	1 ea

Blisters and Athletic Injuries

1-1/2" athletic tape	4 rolls
3" elastic bandage	1 ea
Moleskin	1 ea 6"x12" sheet
Molefoam	1 ea 6"x12" sheet
Second Skin	1 package

Miscellaneous

Bandage scissors	1 ea
Zephiran/povidone-iodine	4 oz
Topical antibiotic cream	4 oz
Sub-normal thermometer	1 ea
Tweezers	1 pr
Cortizone cream	4 oz
Latex gloves	4 pr
Signal mirror	1 ea
Sawyer Extractor	1 ea
Non-prescription pain medications	

    Aspirin, ibuprofen or acetaminophen 50 tablets

SUGGESTIONS

Protect the sterile dressings from moisture by sealing them in groups of three or four in clear plastic.

If you have a planned resupply of food and fuel, consider including extra tape and blister material.

The kit should be accessible. Everyone should know its location.

Label all containers. Include instructions for all medications.

Thermometers break easily. A strong package is imperative; a spare thermometer a good idea.

The kit should be packaged in a distinctly colored and labeled bag that is durable, waterproof and not heavy or bulky.

If your first aid kit is too big, you will have a tendency to leave it behind. Many NOLS Instructors carry in their summit packs a small package of the most frequently needed items, including tape, moleskin, Second Skin and povidone-iodine. Others slide a small roll of tape, cravat and 4x4 into their helmet lining.

NOLS first aid kits do not include pre-made splints, such as airsplints or SAM splints. Pre-made splints may be carried in the first aid kit or suitable splints can be improvised from foamlite pads.

Keep a note pad, pencil, change for phone calls, evacuation report forms and emergency instructions with the first aid kit.

NOLS FIELD EVACUATION REPORT

The NOLS Field Evacuation Report is a legal document that provides the school with pertinent medical information and the evacuation logistics of an injury or illness. It is also used as a tool for collecting safety data. The following instructions are printed on the back of the final page of the report. These general guidelines are consistent throughout the school, although specific procedures may vary somewhat by branch school location.

Report Procedures

The Evacuation Report is printed in triplicate and is filled out completely for any evacuation. The course leader keeps the white copy for the course log. The evacuation leader brings out the pink and yellow copies; one becomes a part of the evacuee's file, the other a part of the school's safety record. Evacuation reports should be relinquished only to other authorized NOLS personnel, e.g. driver, horsepacker or the evacuation coordinator upon arrival at school headquarters in Lander.

Emergency Phone Instructions

1. Know location of nearest phone and take plenty of quarters.
2. Know which number to call first.
   a. Monday through Friday, 24 hours a day. [NOLS has a toll-free emergency phone number.]
   b. If no answer at above number after several tries, call scheduled coordinator at home (see list in course information packet).
   c. If unable to reach scheduled coordinator, call any coordinator at home (see coordinator schedule).
3. Identify your call as a "NOLS Emergency" and ask for an evacuation coordinator to help you.

4. Be prepared to give the person receiving the call your name, phone number and the exact location from which you are calling.

5. Check your phone's capacity to receive calls. If it can receive calls, stay by the phone until an evacuation coordinator returns your call. If not, get the evacuation coordinator's phone number and call him or her.

6. If a coordinator does not return your call within 20 minutes, phone again.

Information for the Evacuation Coordinator

Your name, location, and phone number

Name, sex and age of evacuee

Course/section with starting date

Course leader and instructors

Description of problem and condition of evacuee

Location of evacuee:

> Map name, latitude and longitude, number of students and number of instructors at location.

Location of others on course:

> Map name, latitude and longitude, number of students and number of instructors at location.

Driver requested?

Other support:

> Medical equipment or personnel
>
> Horse
>
> Motorized vehicles (boat, snow machine, helicopter)
>
> Is evacuation from a wilderness area?
>
> Pickup time
>
> Backup plans

NOLS FIELD EVACUATION REPORT

Name of Evacuee_____Evacuation Date_____
Course/Section_____Course Leader_____
Evac Team Leader_____
Location of Evacuee (latitude/longitude, common name, TRS)

_____
_____

Accident Location_____

Patient Report

Age_____ Sex_____
Chief Complaint (PQRST)_____

_____
_____

Date & Time of Incident_____
History of Present Illness/MOI_____

_____
_____
_____

Vital Signs (quantity and quality)

Time	LOC	Pulse	RR	BP	T°	CRT	SCTM	Pupils

Physical Findings/Appearance_____

_____
_____
_____

Past History_____

_____

Allergies_____
Medications_____
Emergency Care Rendered/Changes in Patient's Condition_____

_____
_____
_____
_____
_____
_____

Details of Evac Plan (timetable, backup, pickup point)_____

_____
_____
_____

Course Leader Signature_____
Date_____   Time_____

APPENDIX C
EMERGENCY PROCEDURES FOR OUTDOOR GROUPS

Introduction

Think

Preplan

Emergency Medical Care

Leadership

Organization

Decision Making

Communication

Reports

Introduction

This is an outline for organizing an emergency scene and a wilderness evacuation. It is not a checklist; it is a list of considerations we have found helpful in leading evacuations.

Think

1. A wilderness evacuation is a mental as well as physical challenge. Paul Petzoldt's wise advice to step aside and carefully review the situation is always pertinent.

2. Details are important; small omissions in planning can have great consequences. The evacuation team spending the night out because maps were forgotten is a liability, not an asset.

3. Errors in organization and technique have a tendency to multiply over time.

4. Time is an asset and a liability in the outdoors. Rapid transport is not possible. Use the time to think and plan.

Preplan

1. Research possible resources and evacuation options before the trip begins. Under what circumstances is self-rescue an option, and when must outside help be called upon. Know who is responsible for rescue in your wilderness area.

2. Be knowledgeable and proficient in first aid.

3. Prepare for the emergency by carrying water, shelter, matches and a first aid kit.

Emergency Medical Care

Address the physical and psychological needs of the patient. A thorough patient assessment is essential to making a wise decision regarding method and urgency of evacuation.

Leadership

In any evacuation, many things begin happening simultaneously. The following topics—organization, decision making, communication and reports—are presented as related elements rather than as a sequence of events.

Organization

As leader, you must assume the leadership role, delegate responsibilities, consider the circumstances, determine the type of evacuation and prepare for and execute the evacuation.

Assume Leadership

1. Review scene safety. Prevent situations that might create additional victims.

2. If the injury or illness is not serious, consider making an educational exercise of the rescue.

3. Organize the members of the group.

Delegate Responsibilities

Keeping everyone purposefully occupied reduces stress. In a complex evacuation there are always more tasks than people. Every task is important. Possible tasks include:

1. Feed the group. Cook food. Prepare hot drinks.

2. Prepare the evacuee's pack.

3. Build a litter.

4. Scout trail; break trail.

5. Find and mark landing site for helicopter evacuation; clear or pack soft ground if necessary.

6. Prepare evacuation and medical reports.

7. Gather and inventory all available gear: maps, first aid kits, food, water, stoves, shelters, technical climbing or boating gear.

8. Feed, shelter, hydrate the rescuers.

Decision Making

Consider the following when determining the type of evacuation:

Severity of Injury
How soon does this patient need to be in the hospital? Does the injury threaten life (ABC systems) or limb?

Distance to Roadhead
What is the distance to the phone or additional help? What are the distance and time of the evacuation considering a one to two miles per hour rate of travel?

Difficulty of Terrain
When will you reach the rough country? In the beginning when you are fresh or later when you're exhausted?

The Group's Physical Strength and Stamina

The Group's Technical Abilities and Experience, the Weather
Will you be able to deal with deteriorating weather or technical terrain?

Communication Possibilities
Can you communicate quickly with outside resources by telephone or radio, or must your message be carried by foot?

Outside Assistance
What are available rescue services–horsepackers, snowmobilers, etc.?

Transportation Schedule
Who will meet you at the roadhead?

Plan for Mechanical Failures

Suitability of Landing or Loading Site

Determine the Type of Evacuation
The following are common modes of evacuation:

Walking or Skiing
For the patient who is able, this is easiest and least complex.

Simple Carries
Whether or not you can carry the patient on your back depends on your strength and the nature of the patient's injuries. Can be faster and easier than litter carries.

Litter
Requires a larger group–at least 10 people–and is slow but safe and effective.

Request More Manpower
Consider starting for the roadhead and meeting support en route.

Horsepacking
Injury-dependent but fast. Commonly used in Western states.

Helicopter
Fast but expensive, risky in poor weather and mountains, requires special permission in wilderness areas.

Ski Sled Litter
Improvised sled litters using pulkas can be fast and effective.

Snowmobile
Limited by snow conditions.

Boat/Vehicle (4WD)

Execute the Evacuation
1. Arrange for the evacuation party:
Make sure you have enough manpower to carry out a safe and effective evacuation.

2. Be prepared with food, extra clothing, sleeping bags and marked maps.

Communication
Assuming that no radio or telephone communication is available, messages must be delivered on foot. They are generally one-way and must be accurate, concise and complete.

1. Determine whether messengers should be sent.

2. Designate messengers and leader.

3. Send sufficient number of messengers to ensure safety and effectiveness.

4. Consider: physical stamina, night travel, map, navigation and first aid skills, foul weather experience.

5. Send written instructions including medical and evacuation report form with a time control plan.

Reports

The full evacuation report should include both a medical report and the field evacuation report.

Medical Report

The medical report should include the following:

Age and gender

Chief complaint

Physical exam/vital signs

Present illness/injury

Past history

Treatment

Medications administered

Changes in patient's condition.

Evacuation Report

The evacuation report should include:

Type of evacuation (walk, helicopter, litter).

Marked maps showing:

1. Location of accident
2. Present location of group and victim
3. Anticipated route out of mountains
4. Roadhead destination.

Estimated date and time of arrival and return.

Any special requests (doctor, litter, etc.).

Plans for messengers returning to expedition and plans for the group remaining in the field.

IMPORTANT! Always include an alternate plan in your report!

The
PACKFRAME LITTER:

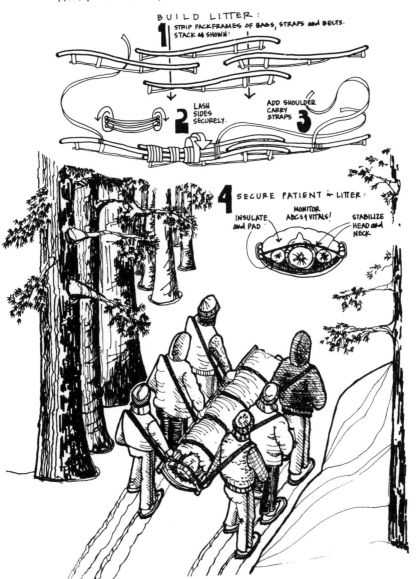

BUILD LITTER:

1 STRIP PACKFRAMES OF BAGS, STRAPS and BELTS.
STACK as SHOWN:

2 LASH SIDES SECURELY.

3 ADD SHOULDER CARRY STRAPS

4 SECURE PATIENT in LITTER:

INSULATE and PAD·

MONITOR ABCS & VITALS!

STABILIZE HEAD and NECK

GLOSSARY OF FIRST AID TERMS

Anaphylaxis. A hypersensitive reaction of the body to a foreign protein or drug.

Anorexia. A lack of appetite.

Appendicular. Refers to the limbs, the legs and arms.

Ataxia. Incoordination of muscles. Usually seen when voluntary movement is attempted; e.g., walking.

Axial. Referring to the midline through the skeleton, the skull, vertebrae and pelvis.

Axillary. Referring to the armpit.

Avulsion. A forcible tearing away of a body part. It can be a piece of skin, a finger, toe or entire limb.

Bacteria. Unicellular organisms lacking chlorophyll.

Basal metabolic rate. The metabolic rate of a person at rest. Usually expressed in kilocalories per square meter of body surface per hour.

Basal metabolism. The amount of energy needed to maintain life when the body is at rest.

Brachial. Refers to the arm, usually the brachial artery or nerve.

Brain stem. The portion of the brain located below the cerebrum, which controls automatic functions such as breathing and body temperature.

Camphylobacter. A genus of bacteria implicated in diarrheal illness.

Capillary. The smallest of the blood vessels, the site of oxygen, nutrient and waste product exchange between the blood and the cells.

Cerebellum. The portion of brain behind and below the cerebrum, which controls balance, muscle tone and coordination of skilled movements.

Cerebrum. The largest and upper region of the brain. Responsible for higher mental functions such as reasoning, memory and cognition.

Comminuted. A fracture in which several small cracks radiate from the point of impact.

Congenital. A condition present at birth.

Conjunctiva. The mucous membrane that lines the eyelid and the front of the eyeball.

Convection. Heat transferred by currents in liquids or gases.

Cornea. The clear transparent covering of the eye.

CRT. Capillary refill time. An abbreviation commonly used by EMTs. For example, "Capillary refill time is three seconds."

Crepitus. A grating sound produced by bone ends rubbing together.

Cyanosis. Bluish discoloration of the skin, mucous membranes and nail beds indicating inadequate oxygen levels in the blood.

Diabetes. A disease resulting from inadequate production or utilization of insulin.

Distal. Farther from the heart.

Electrolyte. A substance which, in solution, conducts electricity. Common electrolytes in our body are sodium, potassium, chloride, calcium, phosphorus, and magnesium.

Embolism. An undissolved mass in a blood vessel. May be solid, liquid or gas.

Epilepsy. Recurrent attacks of disturbed brain function. Classic signs are altered level of consciousness, loss of consciousness and/or seizures.

Eversion. A turning outward (as with an ankle).

Giardia. A protozoan, a simple unicellular organism.

Globule. Any small rounded body.

Hematoma. A pool of blood confined to an organ or tissue.

Hyperglycemia. High blood sugar.

Hypoglycemia. Low blood sugar.

Intercostal. The area between the ribs.

Irrigate. To flush with a liquid.

Kilocalories. A unit of heat. The amount of heat needed to change the temperature of one gram of water one degree centigrade.

LOC. Level of Consciousness. An abbreviation commonly used by EMTs.

Meninges. The three membranes that enclose and help protect the brain.

MOI. An abbreviation commonly used by EMTs to refer to the mechanism of injury for an accident.

Morbidity. The state of being diseased.

Palpate. To examine by touching.

Paraplegia. Paralysis affecting the lower portion of the body and both legs.

Paroxysmal. A sudden, periodic attack, spasm or recurrence of symptoms.

PFD. Personal Flotation Device (life jacket).

Plasma. The liquid part of blood.

Prodromal. The initial stage of a disease.

Quadriplegia. Paralysis affecting all four limbs.

Rales. Crackly breath sounds due to fluid in the lungs or airways.

RR. Respiratory rate. An abbreviation commonly used by EMTs. For example, "RR is 18 and unlabored" or "RR is 22 and shallow and regular."

SCTM. Skin Color Temperature and Moisture. An abbreviation commonly used by EMTs. For example, "Skin is pale, cool and moist" or "skin is red, hot and dry".

Seizure. A sudden attack of a disease as in epilepsy.

Signs. An indication of illness or injury that the examiner observes.

Sprain. Trauma to a joint causing injury to the ligaments.

Strain. A stretched or torn muscle.

Symptoms. Pain, discomfort or other abnormality that the patient feels.

Tendinitis. Inflammation of a tendon.

TRS. Township, Range and Section. A grid system used as a legal description of location. The coordinates are available on many topographic maps.

Varicose veins. Distended, swollen, knotted veins.

Vasoconstriction. Narrowing of blood vessels.

Ventricular. Referring to the two lower pumping chambers of the heart, the ventricles.

Vertigo. The sensation of objects moving about the person or the person moving around in space.

Virus. A microscopic and parasitic organism dependent on the nutrients inside cells for its reproductive and metabolic needs.

Wheezes. Whistling or sighing breath sounds resulting from narrowed airways.

BIBLIOGRAPHY

General

Auerbach, Paul, and Edward Geehr. *Management of Wilderness and Environmental Emergencies.* 2nd ed. St. Louis: Mosby, 1988.

Bowman, Warren D. *Outdoor Emergency Care.* Denver: National Ski Patrol System, Inc., 1988.

Caroline, Nancy L. *Emergency Medical Treatment.* 2nd Ed. Boston: Little, 1987.

Gentile, Douglas A., John A. Morris, and Tod Schimelpfenig. *Epidemiology of Wilderness Injuries and Illness.* Lander, WY: National Outdoor Leadership School, unpublished manuscript, 1991.

Iserson, K. V., ed. *Position Statements of the Wilderness Medical Society.* Point Reyes Station: The Wilderness Medical Society, 1989.

Karren, K. J., and B. Q. Hafen. *First Responder: A Skills Approach.* Englewood, CO: Morton, 1990.

Stewart, C. E. *Environmental Emergencies.* Baltimore: Williams, 1990.

Tilton, B., and F. Hubbell. *Medicine for the Backcountry.* Merrillville, IL: ICS, 1990.

Wilkerson, J. *Medicine for Mountaineering.* Seattle: The Mountaineers, 1986.

Chapter 1— Patient Assessment

Brown, B. E. "Patient Interviewing." *The EMT Journal,* 5, No. 4 (1984), 35-37.

Dernocoeur, K. *Streetsense.* Bowie: Brady, 1985.

Floren, T. M. "Impact of Death and Dying on Emergency Care Personnel." *The EMT Journal,* 4, No. 3 (1980), 6-8.

Judd, R. L. "Death and the Dying, Trauma, Critical Illness." *The EMT Journal,* 8, No. 3 (1984), 20-26.

Neely, K. "Staying in Control." *Journal of Emergency Medical Services*, 9, No. 12 (1985), 30-34.

Chapter 2 — Shock

Bennet, B. R. "Shock: An Approach to Teaching EMT's Normal Physiology Before Pathophysiology." *The EMT Journal*, 2, No. 1 (1978), 26-31.

Geeloheod, G. W. "Shock and Its Management." *Emergency Medical Services*, 5, No. 6 (1976), 41-50.

Gorgen, T. "Shock: The Lay-up, The Sinker, The Bounce." *Journal of Emergency Medical Services*, 13, No. 12 (1988), 31.

———. "Compensated Shock." *Journal of Emergency Medical Services*, 13, No. 12 (1989), 26-30.

O'Brien, J. "Vasogenic Shock." *Journal of Emergency Medical Services*, 14, No. 3 (1989), 32-40.

Chapter 3 — Soft Tissue Injuries

O'Hara, M. M. "Emergency Care of the Patient with a Traumatic Amputation." *Journal of Emergency Nursing*, 273-277.

Sinkinson, C. A. "Maximizing A Wound's Potential for Healing." *Emergency Medicine Reports*, 10, No. 11 (1989), 83-90.

Chapter 4 — Burns and Lightning Injuries

Bourn, M. K. "Thermal Burns: A Comprehensive Approach for Prehospital Care Providers." *Journal of Emergency Medical Services*, 12, No. 5 (1987), 42-47.

Fontanarosa, P. B. "Boom! Lightning and Related Injuries." *Journal of Emergency Medical Services*, 13, No. 7 (1988), 37-43.

Thygerson, A. L. "Hot Water Scalds." *Emergency*, 8, No. 4 (1984), 50-54.

Chapter 5 — Fractures and Dislocations

Bowman, W. D. "Common Sense in Wilderness Accident Management." Proceedings, NOLS Wilderness Medical Conference [Lander, WY], June 1986.

Burtzloff, H. E. "Splinting Closed Fractures of the Extremities." *Journal of Emergency Medical Services*, 10, No. 3 (1981), 7.

Gustafson, J. E. "Contraindications to the Repositioning of Fractured or Dislocated Limbs in the Field." *JACEP*, 16, No. 5 (1976), 184.

Schussman, L. C., and L. J. Lutz. "Mountaineering and Rock-Climbing Accidents." *The Physician and SportsMedicine*, 10, No. 6 (1982), 53-61.

Serra, J. "Management of Fractures and Dislocations in the Wilderness Environment." Syllabus, Wilderness Medical Society Annual Meeting [Jackson, WY], Sept. 1988.

Shlim, D. R., and R. Houston. "Helicopter Rescues and Deaths Among Trekkers in Nepal." *JAMA*, 261, No. 7 (1989), 1017-1019.

Williamson, J. *Accidents in North American Mountaineering*. New York: The American Alpine Club, 1989.

Chapter 6 — Head and Spinal Cord Injuries

Barrer, A. E. *Understanding the Etiology of Head Injury*. Southboro: The National Head Injury Foundation, 1984.

Dick, T. "Horse Sense: Immobilizing Necks that Don't Fit Cervical Collars." *Journal of Emergency Medical Services*, 7, No. 12 (1982), 23-25.

Roberts, S. "Spinal Injuries in Deep Water." *Journal of Emergency Quarterly*, 1, No. 1 (1985).

Simon, R. H. "Management of Critical Head Injuries." *Emergency Care Medical Services*, 13, No. 5 (1988), 34-36.

Smith, M. "Ties that Bind: Spinal Immobilization." *Journal of Emergency Medical Services*, 14, No. 4 (1989), 28-35.

Wolf, A. L. "Initial Management of Brain and Spinal Cord Injured Patients." *Journal of Emergency Medical Services*, 18, No. 6 (1989), 40-42.

Chapter 7 — Chest Injuries

Houston, C. S. "Diseases of the Respiratory System." In *Medicine for Mountaineering.* Ed. J. A. Wilkerson. Seattle: The Mountaineers, 1985, pp. 256-273.

Smith, M. G. "Penetrating the Complexities of Chest Trauma." *Journal of Emergency Medical Services,* 14, No. 8 (1989), 50-58.

Chapter 8 — Abdominal Injuries

Darvill, F. T. "Gastrointestinal Diseases." In *Medicine for Mountaineering.* Ed. J. A. Wilkerson. 3rd ed. Seattle: The Mountaineers, 1987, pp. 288-313.

Edwards, F. J. "Liver Trauma." *Emergency Medical Services,* 19, No. 3 (1990), 31-39.

Price, S. A., and L. M. Wilson. *Pathophysiology: Clinical Concepts of Disease Processes,* 2nd ed. New York: McGraw Hill, 1982, pp. 257, 265-272.

Smith, C. E. "Abdominal Assessment." *Nursing 81,* 11, No. 2 (1981), 42-48.

Chapter 9 — Cold Injuries

"Effects of Restricted Water Intake on Performance in a Cold Environment." Technical Report No. T2-84. Natick: U.S.A. Research Institute of Environmental Medicine, March 1984.

Forgey, W. W. *Hypothermia, Death from Exposure.* Merrillville, IL: Indiana Camp Supply Books, 1985.

McCarroll, J. E., and R. E. Jackson. "Morbidity Associated with Cold Weather Training." *Military Medicine,* 10 (1979), 14-44.

"Medical After Action Conference, Mount Hood, 1986 Bypass Rewarming." Technical Report No. T10-88. Natick: U.S.A. Research Institute of Environmental Medicine, Feb. 1988.

Mills, W. F. "Summary of Treatment of the Cold Injured Patient." *Alaska Magazine,* 145, No. 5 (1980), 56-57.

Paton, B. C. "Accidental Hypothermia." *Pharmac. Therapy*, 122, No. 22 (1982), 331-377.

Pozos, R. S., and D. O. Born. *Hypothermia, Causes, Effects, Prevention.* Piscataway: New Century, 1982.

Vaughn, P. B. "Local Cold Injury—Menace to Military Operations." *Military Medicine*, 145, No. 5 (1980), 305-310.

Wilkerson, J. A., C. C. Bangs, and J. S. Hayward. *Hypothermia, Frostbite and Other Cold Injuries.* Seattle: The Mountaineers, 1986.

Chapter 10 — Heat Illness

Weiss, E. A. "Environmental Heat Illness." Syllabus Annual Meeting of the Wilderness Medical Society [Snowbird, UT], July 1990.

Yarbrough, B. E., and R. W. Hubbard. "Heat Related Illness." In *Management of Wilderness and Environmental Emergencies.* Ed. Paul Auerbach and Edward Geehr. 2nd ed. St. Louis: Mosby, 1988, pp. 119-143.

Chapter 11— Poisons, Stings and Bites

Callahan, M. "Prehospital Management of Envenomation by North American Fauna." Syllabus of the Annual Meeting of the Wilderness Medical Society [Straton, VT], Sept. 1989.

Cason, D. "Anaphylactic Shock." *Journal of Emergency Medical Services*, 14, No. 2 (1989), 42-51.

Daniels, T. "The Lyme Disease Invasion." *Natural History*, July 1989, pp. 4-10.

Davidson, T. M., and S. F. Schafer. "First Aid and Management of Rattlesnake Bites." *The Physician and SportsMedicine*, 17, No. 4 (1989), 148-167.

———. "Rattlesnakes: The Animal and the Venom." *The Physician and SportsMedicine*, 17, No. 4 (1989), 148-167.

Gentile, D. "Tick-Borne Disease." Syllabus of the Annual Meeting of the Wilderness Medical Society [Straton, VT], Sept. 1989.

Habermehl, G. *Venomous Animals and Their Toxins.* Berlin: Springer-Lahl, 1977.

Klauber, L. *Rattlesnakes.* Berkeley: University of California Press, 1982.

Valentine, M. D. "Insect Venom Allergy: Diagnosis and Treatment." *Journal of Allergy Clinical Immunology,* 73, No. 6 (1984), 299-307.

Chapter 12 — Marine Envenomations

Halstead, B.W. *Poisonous and Venomous Marine Animals of the World.* Volume 2. Washington, D.C.: U.S. Government Printing Office, 1967.

Chapter 13 — Cold Water Immersion and Drowning

Avery, M. "Cold Shock." *Sea Kayaker.* Spring 1991.

Bolte, R. "Submersion Injury in Children." Syllabus of the First Winter Meeting of the Wilderness Medical Society. Feb. 1991.

Pozos, R. S. and L. Wittmers, Jr. *The Nature and Treatment of Hypothermia.* Minneapolis: University of Minnesota Press, 1983.

Smith D. S. *Water Wise.* Smith Aquatic Safety Service. St. Charles, MO. 1984

Steinman, A. M. and Hayward, J. S. "Cold-Water Immersion." In *Management of Wilderness and Environmental Emergencies.* Ed. Paul Auerbach and Edward Geehr. 2nd ed. St. Louis: Mosby, 1988.

Chapter 14 — Altitude Illness

Houston, C. S. "Going Higher: The Story of Man and Altitude." Burlington, VT: Free Press, 1983.

———. "Altitude Illness in 1989." Proceedings, National Outdoor Leadership School Wilderness Education Conference [Lander,

WY], Sept. 1989.

Levine, B. D., et al. "Dexamethasone in the Treatment of Acute Mountain Sickness." *JAMA*, 321, No.25 (1989), 1707-1719.

Tortora, G. J., R. L. Evans, and N. P. Anagnostakos. *Principles of Human Physiology.* New York: Harper and Row, 1982.

Chapter 15 — Athletic Injuries

Brody, D. M. "Running Injuries." *Clinical Symposia*, 32, No. 4 (1980).

Chisholm, J. A. "Backcountry Guide to Lower Extremity Athletic Injuries." Lander, WY: National Outdoor Leadership School, unpublished manuscript, 1986.

Hoyt, C. "Treating Inflammation." *Sea Kayaker*, Fall 1985, pp. 52-53.

Knight, K. L. "ICE for Immediate Care of Injuries." *The Physician and SportsMedicine*, 10, No. 2 (1982), 137-138.

Moseley, M. A. "Traumatic Disorders of the Ankle and Foot." *Clinical Symposia*, 17, No. 1 (1965).

Roy, S. P. "Evaluation and Treatment of the Stable Ankle Sprain." *The Physician and SportsMedicine*, 92, No. 8 (1977), 34-42.

Smith, R. L. "Tendinitis." *Sea Kayaker*, Spring 1984, pp. 40-46.

Chapter 16 — Gender-Specific Medical Concerns

Ayvazian, A. "Women on Wilderness Expeditions: Special Concerns." Amherst, MA: Hampshire College, School of Natural Science, unpublished manuscript, 1981.

Devalon, M. L., and J. W. Bachman. "Premenstrual Syndrome." New York: *Postgraduate Medicine*, 86, No. 7 (1989), 51-59.

Dickinson, E. T. "Gynecological Emergencies." *Journal of Emergency Medical Services*, 15, No. 3 (1990), 20-31.

Hughey, H., and M. Weber. *The American Medical Association's Book of Women Care*. New York: Random House, 1982.

Maughan, J. J., and K. Collins. *The Women's Guide to Sports, Fitness Nutrition*. Harrisburg: Stackpole Books, 1983.

McGregor, J. A. "Toxic Shock Syndrome." *Clinical Gynecology*, 43, No. 1 (1987), 1-7.

Olds, S. B., M. L. London, and P. A. Ladewig. *Maternal Newborn Nursing*. 2nd ed. California: Addison-Wesley, 1984.

Russell, J. B., et al. "The Relationship of Exercise to Anovulatory Cycles in Female Athletes: Hormonal and Physical Characteristics." *Obstetrics and Gynecology*, 63, No. 4 (1984), 452-455.

The New Our Bodies Ourselves. Boston Womens Health Book Collective. New York: Simon and Schuster, 1984.

Wroblewski, S. S. "Toxic Shock Syndrome." *American Journal of Nursing*, 81 (1981), 82-85.

Chapter 17 — Hygiene and Water Disinfection

Backer, H. "Traveler's Diarrhea and Clinical Approach to Diarrheal Illness." Syllabus, Wilderness Medical Society Annual Meeting [Straton, VT], Sept. 1989.

Hampton, B., and D. Cole. *Soft Paths: How to Enjoy the Wilderness Without Harming It*. Harrisburg: Stackpole Books, 1988.

Morgan P., and R. J. Karper. "Test of Chlorine Toxicity of Iodine as Related to the Purification of Water." *U.S. Armed Forces Medical Journal*, 4 No. 5 (1953), 725.

Sanitary Food Service Instructor Manual. Cincinnati: U.S. Dept. of Health Education and Welfare, 1969.

Chapter 18 — Seizures, Diabetes and Unconscious States

Bourn, S. "Diabetic Ketoacidosis." *Journal of Emergency Medical Services*, 13 No. 5 (1988), 60-65.

Chisholm, C. D., and R. Chisholm. "Hypoglycemia: A Metabolic Disorder of Many Faces." *Journal of Emergency Medical Services*, 14, No. 6 (1989), 29-38.

Davis, B. "Wilderness Adventure and Diabetes." *Off Belay*, 46 (1979), 27.

Dumont-Herskowitz, R. "Outward Bound, Diabetes and Motivation: Experiential Education in a Wilderness Setting." *Diabetic Medicine*, 7, No. 10 (1990), 1-6.

Gavin, J. "Diabetes and Exercise." *American Journal of Nursing*, 14, No. 2, 153-155.

Jornsay, D., and D. Lorber. "Traveling with Diabetes." *Practical Diabetology*, 2, 1 (1987).

Chapter 19 — Hydration

Askew, E. W. "Nutrition for a Cold Environment." *The Physician and SportsMedicine*, 17, No. 12 (1989), 76-89.

Levensky, N. G. "Fluids and Electrolytes." *Harrison's Principles of Internal Medicine*. Philadelphia: McGraw-Hill, 1977.

Strauss, R. H. *Sports Medicine*. Philadelphia: Saunders, 1984.

Chapter 20 — Dental Emergencies

Forgey, W. *Forgey's Wilderness Medicine*. Merrillville, IL: Indiana Camp Supply Books, 1979.

Herrmann, H. "Wilderness Dental Emergencies." Syllabus, Annual Meeting of the Wilderness Medical Society [Snowbird, UT], July 1990.

Webber, R. "Treating Dental Emergencies." *Wilderness Medicine Newsletter*, 4, No. 12 (1989), 1-3.

Chapter 21 — Stress and the Rescuer

Bangs, C. "Complete Care of the Accident Victim." Proceedings, Yosemite Institute Mountain Medicine Symposium [Yosemite,

CA] March 1975.

Conover, K. C. "Wilderness EMT Curriculum: Stress Management and Critical Incident Stress Debriefing." Syllabus, Appalachian Search and Rescue Conference [Pittsburgh, PA], 1990.

Graham, N. K. "Done in, Fed Up, Burned Out: Too Much Attrition in EMS." *Journal of Emergency Medical Services*, 6, No. 1 (1981), 24.

Kennedy-Ewing, L. "Delaware County Critical Incident Stress Management Program." Media, PA: Delaware County Department of Human Resources, 1988.

Mitchell, J. "Development and Functions of a Critical Incident Stress Debriefing Team." *Journal of Emergency Medical Services*, 12, No. 12 (1988), 42-46.

Mitchell, J., and G. Bray. *Emergency Services Stress*. Englewood: Brady, 1990.

Seyle, H. *The Stress of Life*. New York: Free Press, 1956.

INDEX